CAMBRIDGE SOUTH ASIAN STUDIES

PRIVATE INDUSTRIAL INVESTMENT IN PAKISTAN
1960–1970

CAMBRIDGE SOUTH ASIAN STUDIES

These monographs are published by the Syndics of Cambridge University Press in association with the Cambridge University Centre for South Asian Studies. The following books have been published in this series:

PRIVATE
INDUSTRIAL INVESTMENT
IN PAKISTAN 1960–1970

RASHID AMJAD

CAMBRIDGE UNIVERSITY PRESS

Cambridge
London   New York   New Rochelle
Melbourne   Sydney

Published by the Press Syndicate of the University of Cambridge
The Pitt Building, Trumpington Street, Cambridge CB2 1RP
32 East 57th Street, New York, NY 10022, USA
296 Beaconsfield Parade, Middle Park, Melbourne 3206, Australia

First published 1982

Photoset and printed in Malta by Interprint Limited

Library of Congress catalogue card number: 81-17996

British Library Cataloguing in Publication Data
Amjad, Rashid
Private industrial investment in Pakistan, 1960
–1970. (Cambridge South Asian studies; 26)
1. Pakistan–Industries
I. Title
338′.09549′09   HC440.5
ISBN 0 521 23261 9

CONTENTS

TABLES

ix

APPENDICES

FIGURES

PREFACE

When I started my research in the early seventies, the existing work on Pakistan's industrial growth had passed through two distinct stages. The first covered the period till the mid sixties when Pakistan was built up as a success story of private enterprise. The second followed the collapse of the Ayub government in the late sixties and the focus of attention shifted towards the broader questions of the inequalities which the growth strategy had generated and, specifically in the industrial sector, the concentration of industrial power – the so-called 'twenty-two families' – received great prominence. I felt that there was considerable need to study the behaviour of private industrial investment for the entire period of the sixties and to produce an analysis of investment behaviour which took into account the institutional features of the economy. The study was completed in Spring 1977 and only minor alterations have been made to the original text.

In carrying out this study, I have received generous help from a large number of people. First and foremost I owe a special debt to Professor R. R. Neild, for his untiring and constructive criticisms throughout the research and especially his assistance in exposition and presentation. I would like to thank him for both the keen interest he has taken and the patience and understanding he has shown throughout the period of this study. I am especially grateful to Dr R. P. Smith, M. A. King and Dr. B. McCormick for reading the drafts of the chapters on investment behaviour (Chapter 5, 6 and 7) and suggesting specific improvements concerning estimation techniques. The work as it stands, however, including any errors, omissions or inconsistencies is entirely my own responsibility.

During my stay at Cambridge, I was very lucky in having as contemporaries a number of research students from South Asia. I would like to especially mention Ashwani Saith and Abhijit Sen for their suggestions and acute and lucid criticisms on almost all the sections of the study. I would also like to mention M. Hossain, W. Mahmud, A. Ghose and other participants of the

South Asian Workship and the Singh/Paine Seminar. Many of the results of this research were first presented in these forums and received constructive comments at a formative stage of work.

This applied study would certainly not have been possible if it had not been for the considerable help I received in getting access to unpublished data and government reports. I would like to especially thank Dr Mubashir Hassan for making available the 'Report on the Anti-Cartel Law Study Group' (1965) which had not been released by the previous government despite considerable public pressure. I am also grateful to Chemical Consultants (Pakistan) Limited for making available the report on the nationalised industries.

When I was nearing completion of my research on the monopoly houses and the concentration of industrial power in Pakistan, I learnt that L. J. White of Princeton University had also been working on this field and his study was subsequently published in the summer of 1974. I am grateful to L. J. White who read my own preliminary results (published in a monograph form in April 1974) for his encouragement and suggestions both in my correspondence with him and when I met him at Princeton in the spring of 1976.

My acknowledgements would certainly be incomplete if I were not to record my special thanks and gratitude to my wife, Maliha, who has been a source of strength to me throughout the period of our stay in Cambridge. I must especially thank her for looking after Sehr, our daughter, who was born when this study was nearing completion and I was completely immersed in it.

I would also like to thank the Economics Department, Punjab University, Lahore, for granting me leave for the period of my research and to the Pakistan government for providing me the Central Overseas Training Scholarship to finance my stay in Cambridge.

Finally, I would like to thank Shahid Amjad Chaudhry and Omar Asghar Khan for their considerable help in the editing of the final manuscript.

ABBREVIATIONS

C.M.I.	Census of Manufacturing Industries
C.S.O.	Central Statistical Office, Karachi, Government of Pakistan
I.B.R.D.	International Bank for Reconstruction and Development, Washington
I.C.P.	Investment Corporation of Pakistan
I.D.B.P.	Industrial Development Bank of Pakistan
I.P. and S.	Investment Promotion and Supplies Department, Karachi, Government of Pakistan
N.I.T	National Investment (Unit) Trust
P.I.C.I.C.	Pakistan Industrial Credit and Investment Corporation

Equivalents: Rs 1 lac = Rs 100,000 (one hundred thousand)

INTRODUCTION

A REVIEW OF DEVELOPMENT POLICIES
1947–70

The first twenty years of Pakistan's existence saw an underdeveloped predominantly agricultural economy, trying to achieve rapid industrialisation through active support to the private sector. Although by the end of the sixties Pakistan's political edifice had collapsed leading amongst other things to the dismemberment of the country, its experience, especially during the sixties, is one from which other developing countries can learn in analysing and evaluating the performance of the private sector as the means of achieving industrial growth.

For the knowledge of the level and pattern of private investment and of the factors which influence it is essential to an understanding of how economic development is proceeding in any country and to the formulation of economic policy. Yet investment is not easy to measure and its determinants in a market economy – or the market sector of a mixed economy – are complex. Indeed, the level and pattern of investment in a country is a set of responses to virtually the sum total of economic events in that country. It is true that these events can be said to generate signals through the medium of profitability, actual and expected, but especially in manufacturing industry in a developing country, where competition is imperfect and market conditions are greatly influenced by government policies, the assessment of future profitability involves assessment of market prospects, of rivals actions and of government policies – as well as an assessment of how far one can influence these policies.

In an applied study one can hope only to assess the proximate causes of investment behaviour. That is what is examined here with reference to the large-scale manufacturing sector[1] in Pa-

---

1 The large scale manufacturing sector, as defined by the Central Statistical Office (C.S.O.), Government of Pakistan consists of all firms which employ 20 or more workers on any day during the year and use power in their manufacturing operations. Lack of reliable statistics make it impossible to trace either the exact share of small-scale industries in gross domestic product or their growth rate. In the national income accounting statistics compiled by the Government of Pakistan an indirect estimation technique is used for

kistan in the sixties, in the first half of which private industrial investment rose at an unprecedented rate, to be followed by a sharp decline in 1965 and then stagnation for the rest of the decade. The approach adopted is institutional and empirical. The developments studied appeared to be very much the product of the institutional setting of Pakistan, which is different from that of most advanced countries but may not be so different from that in many other developing countries.

In order to see the sixties in perspective, we review, albeit briefly, Pakistan's economic performance since independence in 1947 and look at the broad policy measures adopted by different governments during the period and then go on to discuss some of the major interpretations of Pakistan's development experience in general and of the growth of the industrial sector in particular.

A review of government policies

Pakistan gained independence in August 1947, after a struggle resulting from the muslims of the sub-continent's aspirations for a separate homeland. The country was geographically divided into two wings, separated by 1000 miles of Indian territory. The West covered a much larger physical area, 310,000 square miles, as compared to the East with only 55,000 square miles, whereas the population of the West was smaller, being 33.8 million, as compared to the East with a population of 42 million in 1951.

Political conditions in the fifties were extremely unstable and led to frequent changes in governments. The task of framing the country's constitution which was entrusted to the Constituent Assembly in 1947 was not completed till 9 years later in 1956. Unfortunately, the new constitution had been in operation for only a brief period when, in October 1958, a coup d'état established a military dictatorship. For the period of the fifties the government had been mainly run by the civil services – a legacy of the colonial period. With the military take over their control over the government became complete, with little interference from political forces.

small-scale manufacturing. An estimate of a bench mark year, 1959-60, was computed and subsequently a growth rate equal to the growth rate of population was assumed. (For details of the calculation of the bench mark estimate see C.S.O., 1972, p. 541).

At the time of independence, the areas which became Pakistan were predominantly agricultural with almost no industry. In the initial years, two economic events had important consequences.[2] The first was the devaluation of the Indian currency in 1949, and when Pakistan did not follow suit (principally to achieve better terms of trade with India on the sale of raw jute) it led to a suspension of trade between the two countries and hence blocked the major source of manufactured imports into the country. The government at the same time adopted an import tariff which gave considerable advantage to producers of import substitute consumer goods and quantitative controls of a rather loose sort were used on imports and exports. The second event followed the Korean boom. During the boom, which lasted from mid 1950 to late 1952, the increase in foreign exchange earnings permitted the government to dismantle the system of controls. But with the collapse of the Korean boom, the government, fearing a foreign exchange crisis as export prices fell, re-imposed import controls. Detailed physical controls on imports and exports were then maintained throughout the fifties. The result of these import controls was an increase in manufactured consumer good prices which changed the terms of trade in favour of industry and against the agricultural sector,[3] leading to a sharp increase in profitability in the industrial sector. Traders who had made extremely high profits during the boom now invested in industry where the rate of return was so high that they were able to

---

2 For a detailed account of government policies in the fifties, see Papanek (1967), Andrus and Mohammad (1958), Mason (1966) and First Five Year Plan, 1955-60 (Planning Board, 1957).

3 *Agriculture's domestic terms of trade relative to world price standards*[a]
3 Year Average

1951/52 − 1953/54	39.8	1957/58 − 1959/60	54.1
1952/53 − 1954/55	36.7	1958/59 − 1960/61	57.6
1953/54 − 1955/56	36.2	1959/60 − 1961/62	59.1
1954/55 − 1956/57	43.0	1960/61 − 1962/63	62.0
1955/56 − 1957/58	48.8	1961/62 − 1963/64	61.9
1956/57 − 1958/59	53.9		

[a] This is the ratio of the implicit exchange rate of agricultural goods (weighted by marketings) to manufactured goods (weighted by agricultural purchases). The implicit exchange rate being the ratio between the domestic wholesale price of a commodity in local currency and the foreign price of the same item. For terms of trade faced by the agricultural sector at domestic prices, see Lewis and Hussain (1966) and Lewis (1970b).
Source: Lewis (1970a), p. 65

recover their initial investments in a period of one of two years.[4] The incentive to re-invest profits was, therefore, considerable and an extremely high rate of growth was achieved in the industrial sector. The government, too, played an important role in early industrialisation by setting up industries where the private sector was initially shy (e.g. the jute and paper industries in East Pakistan) and then selling them to the private sector at nominal prices.[5]

By 1958, however, when the military government took over, the economy had run into certain serious difficulties. The adverse policies followed by the government towards the agricultural sector[6] – a combination of import controls and consequently higher prices of industrial products, export taxes and price controls on agricultural produce – resulted in its stagnation throughout the fifties, and, with increasing population, especially in the urban areas, supplies available for towns became increasingly inadequate. The industrial sector, after an initial spurt of very rapid growth, had also begun to slow down. This was the result of two factors. The first was a gradual exhaustion of import substitution opportunities in manufactured consumer goods, as well as a lack of growth of the domestic market – a result of the stagnant agricultural sector. The second was the operation of a foreign exchange constraint (made worse by the need to import foodgrains) which was now being increasingly felt as the Korean boom surpluses had run out. This meant a considerable reduction in industrial investment since almost all capital goods had to be imported. Finally, the situation was further worsened by increasing labour unrest in the country; real wages were stagnant, if not declining, throughout the fifties.[7]

On taking over, the new military government adopted a series of policy measures, principally to boost up the confidence of the private sector. It reaffirmed the faith of the government in the

4 To quote Papanek, 'With high prices for consumer goods and low prices for the capital goods needed to produce them, annual profits of 50-100 per cent were possible' (Papanek, 1967, p.33).
5 For details of disinvestments of projects by the government sponsored corporation, Pakistan Industrial Development Corporation, see Amjad (1974, p.19).
6 For details of these policies see Falcon & Gotsch (1968) and I.B.R.D. (1968).
7 For the behaviour of wages in Pakistan see Khan (1967), Hamid, N. (1974) and Lewis (1970a, p. 43).

role of the private sector in the economic development of the country.[8] It came down harshly on industrial labour by banning all Trade Union activity and imposed sentences of up to two years of imprisonment for labour strikes. It began to dismantle[9] the direct controls for regulating foreign exchange which had become an important feature of the economy in the fifties. This was made possible by a considerable increase in the rate of capital inflow including aid into the country which increased from about 2.5 per cent of G.N.P. in the mid fifties to about 7 per cent in the mid sixties. The government also adopted more favourable policies towards the agricultural sector, notably the subsidy on fertiliser and plant protection and lower export duties on raw jute and cotton and also subsequently an increased volume of government investment in the agricultural sector. Finally, the government made economic planning a central part of its development strategy. The Planning Board was reorganised – renamed the Planning Commission – and was made part of the President's Secretariat with with far greater power and influence in the running of the economy.[10]

It was against a background of these policies that there occurred the investment boom in the early sixties with high rates of growth in both the industrial and agricultural sectors.

After 1965, however, the government's strategy suffered set backs. In the early part of the year, at the request of the U.S.A., the Aid-to-Pakistan Consortium meeting was postponed,[11] and following the September war with India, all foreign aid was

8 To quote from the Second Plan, 'The Plan places greater reliance on market mechanism and fiscal and monetary policies, instead of a direct price, profit and allocation controls', and 'It is a basic assumption of the Plan that for the implementation of the industrial development programme reliance will be placed primarily on private enterprise' (Planning Commission, 1960, pp. 8 and 225).

9 Initially on taking over, the new government had increased controls. All consumer goods were subject to price controls, profit margins were regulated and distributive margins were fixed. These measures were, however, soon abandoned before the Second Plan was launched in June 1960.

10 See Waterston (1963) for a detailed description of the planning machinery in Pakistan.

11 The slowing down of foreign economic assistance during the late 1960s was partly due to the outbreak of the Indo-Pakistan hostilities in 1965, which led to the cessation of foreign aid during 1965/66. But it was also due to the fact that Pakistan slowly shifted away from the close military alliance with the U.S.A. in terms of her active association in CENTO and SEATO and closer relationship with China (See Islam, 1972, p. 504).

temporarily stopped. Aid was subsequently resumed in 1966 but at a much lower level than had been planned for during the Third Plan period. The effect of the curtailment of aid was further worsened by large claims made by the defence forces on Pakistan's exchange resources during and after the war with India and the cessation of military grant assistance from abroad. Also, during 1965/66 and 1966/67 the agricultural sector faced a severe drought, with the volume of production of major crops remaining roughly stagnant at the 1964/65 level and with food crops, as a group, showing a decline in production. This meant that foodgrains had to be imported at a time when P.L. 480 assistance was less available, so that the country's own foreign exchange resources had to be used to finance food imports.

The major effect of these factors was a sharp slowing down in the rate of growth of the industrial sector. The import liberalisation policies which had been introduced by the government suffered a severe set-back and the industrial strategy outlined in the Third Plan, with greater emphasis on capital goods, had to be abandoned in favour of export-oriented consumer goods industries. The agricultural sector, however, recovered in the last three years of the sixties, principally in response to the introduction of new high yielding varieties of seeds which led to very large increases in agricultural production. [12]

In the winter of 1968, large-scale political unrest broke out throughout the country. It was concentrated in the urban areas and led by students, the industrial labour class and other professional groups. It was triggered off by a large increase in the price level – after a period of considerable price stability in the first half of the sixties. [13] Also there was considerable resentment against the increasing inequalities, not only amongst income groups but also between East and West Pakistan, [14] which the

12 For studies on the 'green revolution' in Pakistan, see Nulty, L. (1972), Hamid, J. (1970), Amjad (1972) and Falcon & Gotsch (1968, pp. 269-315).

13 The general price index in the sixties moved as follows:

1959/60	100.0	1965/66	117.5
1960/61	103.0	1966/67	133.9
1961/62	105.9	1967/68	128.6
1962/63	104.8	1968/69	136.1
1963/64	104.6	1969/70	140.0
1964/65	112.4		

Source: C.S.O. (1972).

14 For a comprehensive study on the question of inter-regional disparity, see Planning Commission (1970a, Vol. I, pp. 21–177). Also, see Griffin and Khan (eds.) (1972) for a study of growth and inequality in Pakistan.

growth strategy had generated. Ayub had to resign in March, 1969. Martial law was once again declared and certain reforms were introduced. Minimum wages for industrial labour were fixed, labour unions were permitted to be organised and strikes were legalised. The political unrest had considerably shaken up business confidence but the re-imposition of martial law appeared to do much to improve it. The military remained in power until 1971, although its last year was spent completely engaged in the Civil War in East Pakistan. With the rise of the Pakistan People's Party to power in December 1971, and the division of the country, economic policies embarked in new directions.

Overall growth strategy – the doctrine of 'functional inequality'[15]

Pakistan's industrial strategy must be viewed within the framework of the overall growth strategy which was pursued, without any basic change, during the fifties, as well as the sixties. This strategy, which is outlined in the various Five-Year Plans and in Haq (1966) and Papanek (1967), rests on the proposition that in the early stages of capitalist development a high degree of inequality is necessary in order to promote savings and create entrepreneurial dynamism.

To quote from the introduction of the First Five-Year Plan – 'The inequalities of income and wealth in the commercial and industrial sector present a different problem. The businessman and industrialist is playing a useful part in the economic development of the country, and the functioning of its economy, though he extorts an unduly high price for his services. His high incomes nevertheless serve a social purpose, and since the building and strengthening of our productive mechanism must have a high priority we cannot contemplate any forcible means to deprive him of his gain ... we regard private enterprise as an agency for performing the tasks which it can completely discharge. Private enterprise is a desirable agency in this sense' (Planning Board, 1957, p. 4).

This official view is reiterated in the Second Plan. 'It will be necessary to tolerate some initial growth in income inequalities to

15 Maddison (1971, p.136) uses this term to describe Pakistan's growth strategy in this period.

reach high levels of saving and investment' (Planning
Commission, 1960, p. 49). In the Third Plan it is said, 'What is
basic to Islamic Socialism is the creation of equal opportunities
for all rather than the equal distribution of wealth' (Planning
Commission, 1965, p. v) and this sentiment is repeated in the
Socio-Economic Objectives of the Fourth Five-Year Plan, 'We
cannot distribute poverty. Growth is vital before income
distribution can improve' (Planning Commission, 1968, p. 17).
The most complete economic formulation of this growth strategy
is by Haq (1966) who after describing economic development as a
'brutal and sordid process' (Ibid., p. 1) goes on to state that the
'road to eventual equalities may inevitably lie through initial
inequalities' (Ibid., p. 3). Papanek (1967) spells out the growth
strategy in such candid terms as 'squeezing the peasant',
'Robber Baron industrialisation', and the 'Social Utility of
Greed'.[16]

As described by Griffin (1965), according to this strategy
resources are to be channelled to those groups in the community
whose average and marginal savings rates are thought to be
relatively high. In practice this has meant that incomes have been
redistributed away from the massive agricultural population in
favour of the small class of wealthy urban industrial
entrepreneurs.

The manner in which this income distribution takes place is
through an indirect method, that of changing the terms of trade
between the industrial and agricultural sectors, i.e. the prices of
industrial goods are raised relative to those of agricultural goods
which leads to large profits being generated in the industrial sector
which are channelled into savings. The reason why it is done in this
particular manner is spelt out by Chowdhury (1969):

Mobilisation of domestic savings for economic development may be
attempted by several alternative methods; namely, through taxation and
public revenue surplus, through high incentives to savers and financial
intermediaries and through income distribution in favour of sectors with
incentives to save and invest. In view of the lack of an active financial

16 Both Haq and Papanek were closely associated with the formulation of
    economic policy in Pakistan. Papanek was adviser to Pakistan's Planning
    Board from 1954 to 1957 and acting Project Field Supervisor to the Planning
    Commission 1957-58. Haq was chief economist of the Planning Commission
    in the sixties. For critical assessment of the role of foreign advisors in the
    formulation of economic policy in Pakistan, see Minsky (1970), Nulty,
    T. and Nulty, L. (1971) and MacEwan (1971).

sector, fiscal weaknesses and other market imperfections, Pakistan primarily depended on the last strategy to mobilise domestic savings (op.cit., p. 95).

Previous interpretations of Pakistan's industrial growth[17]

Earlier writers on Pakistan's industrial experience can be divided into three broad categories. First are those who tried to portray Pakistan's industrial experience from the fifties to the mid sixties as a success story of private enterprise and how the correct mixtures of private enterprise and government's support policies could bring about rapid industrialisation. The second were those who mainly emphasised the 'efficiency' aspects of Pakistan's industrial structure which had emerged by the mid sixties and how government policy had distorted the price structure and resulted in 'inefficiencies' in terms of 'world prices'. Finally, there were those who, after witnessing the collapse of Ayub's government in the late sixties, questioned the basic assumptions of the growth and the industrial strategy which had been followed during that period.

Prominent among those who played a major part in popularising Pakistan's industrial experience were Papanek (1967) who after reviewing the period of partition (i.e. 1947) to the end of the Second Plan (i.e. 1965) wrote that, 'it is possible to state with considerable confidence that entrepreneurs respond to economic incentives in deciding what investments to make, what to produce and how to produce. In Pakistan, as in developed countries, there are at least some individuals who act largely as economic men in their business dealings' (Papanek, 1967, p. 73). Papanek was also optimistic about the possibilities of future growth and pointed out, 'that there is no obvious reason why Pakistan's growth should not continue to expand and import substitution for some complex manufacturing can continue' (Ibid., p. 239).

Of those who concerned themselves with the 'efficiency' aspects of the industrial structure which emerged, Lewis's (1970a) is the most exhaustive work and covers the period from 1950 to 1965. His earlier work (Lewis, 1969) concerned itself more with

---

17 For a detailed discussion and criticism of the works of the authors mentioned see Amjad (1977).

the overall rate of growth and the pattern of industrial investment.

Lewis's hypothesis is that Pakistan came into existence with a 'disequilibrium' in her domestic productive structure and that a substantial part of the growth that occurred after partition was a process of adjustment to a normally balanced economy as a result of severance of trade with India and import protection vis-à-vis other countries.[18] He further goes on to argue that the industrial structure which emerged was 'inefficient' in terms of world prices. In 1963/64, for example, one half to two thirds of actual value added was the result of distortions in the price structure (Lewis, 1969, p. 167).

Leaving aside the questions relating to the 'efficiency' aspects of Pakistan's industrial structure – on which there can also be considerable dispute if one is not prepared to accept the underlying assumptions regarding the concept of 'world prices'[19] – there are two major problems with Lewis's explanation of Pakistan's industrial growth.

The first is that, as regards the overall rate of growth, he ignores 'supply constraints'. He assumes that the necessary capital (both savings and the ability to obtain machines which in fact had to be imported), entrepreneurship and technical skills somehow become available. It is not surprising, therefore, that the role of foreign aid in Pakistan's industrial growth in the sixties is not given any prominence at all.

The second point concerns his explanation of the pattern of industrial investment which emerged in the fifties and in the sixties. Lewis himself admits that the import licensing system (i.e. direct quantitative controls) were dominant in setting prices and incentives (Lewis, 1969, p. 111). However, when it comes to establishing any relationship between these incentives and the rate of growth in various industries, he finds that none exists. In a market economy in which the private sector was supposed to have moved in response to price incentives, the reasons why this did

18 See Lewis (1969), pp. 50-9 for detailed discussion.
19 For a criticism of this neo-classical approach adopted in Lewis (1970a) and other studies conducted by the O.E.C.D. as part of its project on industrialisation and trade policy see Bagchi (1971). The other studies in the series besides Lewis (1970a) for Pakistan were King (1970) for Mexico, Bhagwati and Desai (1970) for India, Bergsman (1970) for Brazil, Power and Sicat (1971) for the Philippines and Hsing (1971) for Taiwan. There is also a comparative study by Little, Scitovsky and Scott (1970).

not happen at the industry level leaves a major gap in his explanation.

Of those who questioned the basis of the growth strategy which was pursued during the sixties the most prominent were Griffin (1965) and Nulty, T. (1972).

Griffin (1965) was amongst the first to evaluate critically the growth strategy being pursued and he did so at a time when the general atmosphere was one of considerable 'optimism' after the success of the Second Plan in generating high growth rates. Griffin argued that despite government policy measures to redistribute income in favour of the industrial classes this had not led to any significant increases in domestic savings during the first half of the sixties as envisaged in the strategy. He also pointed out that to a large extent the entire social and economic system that had been built up by the mid-sixties was heavily supported by and sustained through foreign assistance and that the burden of foreign debt was increasing rapidly.

Nulty, T. (1972) like Griffin also questioned the basis of the growth strategy which was followed during this period – i.e. that increasing inequalities lead to an increase in the domestic savings rate – but carried out his analysis for the entire period of the fifties and sixties. Nulty argued that, until the fifties, the new class of industrialists was isolated and insecure and the high rates of return on investment led to high rates of investment and savings. But, after this period, their political and social isolation began to break down as lines of communications and common interests were established with other branches of elite groups, especially the civil servants and through them the government. Also, their financial isolation was declining rapidly with their control over the banking system and financial institutions. They were, therefore, able to substitute savings from other sectors (principally the agricultural sector where incomes had been rising in the sixties) and foreign aid for their own savings. Most of their own incomes, therefore, were available for consumption.

Nulty concluded that,

The prototype for the behaviour of the capitalist entrepreneurs comes to approximate more closely to that archetypal aristocratic landlord who consumed most of his income and spent considerable energy on political, legal and economic suppression of potential rivals rather than the abstinent, accumulating, maximising entrepreneurs of western mythology which Dr. Haq and Dr. Papanek and many others so enthusiastically extol (Nulty, T., 1972, p. 150).

In terms of the behaviour of private industrial investment one implication of Nulty's hypothesis is that the domestic savings rate especially of the capitalist entrepreneurs could have acted as a constraint during the latter half of the sixties. The existing evidence on the savings rate of the corporate sector would contradict this view.[20] Our analysis suggests that in the industrial sector where investment opportunities existed and that foreign exchange resources were available to realise these investments, domestic savings were not the constraint. Joan Robinson's dictum, 'where prospects of profits are high, finance is easy to come by', (1970, p. 140) appears to have been true for the relationship between private industrial investment and domestic savings in the sixties.

Apart from the criticisms on the existing work on industrial growth that we have indicated, none of the authors explore the role of foreign aid and the influence it has on private industrial investment in the framework of the institutions of Pakistan. Our aim, therefore, is to re-examine the behaviour of private industrial investment. We shall cover the entire period of the sixties whereas the other authors mostly covered only the first half of the period; and we shall, in particular, explore the role of foreign aid, a factor largely ignored by the others.

Our broad hypothesis, which was sharpened as we pursued alternative explanations on a rather pragmatic basis, is that the explanation for the boom in private industrial investment in the first half of the sixties and its subsequent slowing down lies principally in the change in foreign aid inflows to the industrial sector in the sixties. In putting forward this hypothesis, we do not belittle either the role of the government in creating conditions which were conducive to the working of the private sector and guaranteed a high rate of return on industrial investment, nor the response of the private sector to the incentives created. Both play an important part in our explanation. What we suggest is that foreign aid played a crucial role in the creation of those favourable conditions and had a direct impact on the private sector.

20 If we examine the savings rate of the corporate sector during the period 1959–69, gross savings (i.e. retention plus depreciation) were over 50 per cent of gross profits and if we include tax provisions the figure increases to over 80 per cent. Also gross savings were higher in the period 1964/69 as compared to the earlier period (see Amjad, 1973, for details). Also new shares offered at the Karachi Stock Exchange were heavily oversubscribed for the period of the sixties (see Amjad, 1977, for details).

PART I

THE INSTITUTIONAL SETTING

1

MACRO AND THEORETICAL
FRAMEWORK

Our first task was to establish the behaviour of the overall economy and the level and pattern of fixed investment in the sixties by critically examining the official series available, by seeking new data and by making independent estimates against which to check them. Given the important differences between West and East Pakistan we constructed a national expenditure series separately for the two provinces to trace the behaviour of key national accounting variables.[1]

After having established the level and movements of private industrial investment in the sixties as accurately as possible from alternative data sources we then present a broad framework in terms of a range of factors which can influence industrial investment and which provides us with the basis for our subsequent analysis and explanation.

1.1 Overall behaviour of the economy 1950–70

The growth rates of the important sectors between 1950 to 1970, divided amongst the Plan periods, are given in table 1.1. During the fifties, there is the sharp contrast between the achievements of the agricultural and large-scale manufacturing sectors. Whereas the former stagnated, the latter, albeit so small that any substantial absolute step forward would represent a high growth rate, grew at the rate of almost 25 per cent until 1954/55, after which it began to slow down. Given the domination of the economy by the agricultural sector and the small initial contribution of industry (table 1.2), and the rapid rate of growth of population, G.N.P. per capita failed to increase in the fifties.

The period of the sixties witnessed a very impressive growth rate in the agricultural sector as well as a significant rate of growth of per capita income. The large-scale manufacturing sector in the first half of the sixties again achieved a very high

---

1 This was necessitated by the fact that the official C.S.O. series was un-satisfactory and there were no separate series for the two provinces.

The institutional setting

Table 1.1 *Annual compound growth rates by sector (at 1959/60 factor cost)*

Sectors	1949/50 to 1954/55 Pre-plan Period	1954/55 to 1959/60 First Plan	1959/60 to 1964/65 Second Plan	1964/65 to 1969/70 Third Plan
Agriculture	1.3	1.4	3.5	4.1
Large-Scale Mfg	23.6	9.3	16.2	7.7
All others	2.5	2.7	5.5	7.2
G.N.P.	2.6	2.4	5.3	5.8
Population	2.5	2.5	2.6	2.6
G.N.P. (per capita)	0.2	0.0	2.7	2.9

Sources:

  (i) All figures except for Third Plan period and large-scale manufacturing for Second Plan are based on Lewis (1970a, p. 8).
 (ii) For Third Plan (excluding large-scale mfg), Planning Commission (1971, p. 7).
(iii) Figures for large-scale mfg for Second and Third Plan are based on Kemal (1976), Alamgir and Berlage (1974) and C.S.O., *Census of Manufacturing Industries* (various issues).

growth rate, this time from a more significant base. The figure of over 16 per cent was amongst the highest in the world; in the second half of the decade, the rate slowed down to less than half this level, though at 7.7 per cent it was still respectable by international standards.

Table 1.2 *Composition of G.N.P. in Pakistan (at 1959/60 factor cost) (percentages)*

Sectors	1949/50	1954/55	1959/60	1964/65	1969/70
Agriculture	60.0	56.0	53.3	49.1	44.4
Manufacturing	5.9	8.0	9.3	11.0	12.2
(i) Large-scale	1.4	3.6	5.0	7.1	9.0
(ii) Small-scale	4.4	4.4	4.3	3.8	3.2
Other Activities	34.1	36.0	37.4	40.0	43.4
Total	100.0	100.0	100.0	100.0	100.0

Sources:

 (i) Planning Commission, (1965, p. 2).
(ii) Planning Commission, (1971, p. 8).

The large increase in the growth of the manufacturing sector in the fifties and sixties led to a rapid change in the composition of G.N.P. with the large-scale manufacturing sector now contributing almost 10 per cent as compared to 1.4 per cent in 1949/50.

1.1.1 Investment, foreign aid, government expenditure and domestic savings in the sixties[2]

Given the fact that there were major differences in the performance of the two wings of the country, we have given estimates of these key variables not only for All Pakistan but also separately for West and East Pakistan (see figure 1.1 and table 1.3).

Total investment as represented by gross domestic fixed capital formation[3] (G.D.F.C.F.) as a proportion of G.N.P. increased from 9.3 per cent in 1959/60 to 16.9 per cent 1964/65, in the boom years of the Second Plan. This was followed by a decline in the period of the Third Plan by the end of which it had come down to 13.3 per cent. The fall in investment was, in fact, greater if we take into account the increase in depreciation and replacement requirements. Both private and public investment followed closely the behaviour of total investment, with private investment almost doubling and public investment increasing by 70 per cent during the Second Five Year Plan. The slowing down, however, was more pronounced in the private sector where investment fell from 8.5 in 1964/65 to 5.9 per cent of G.N.P. in 1969/70, as compared to the public sector where it declined from 8.4 to 7.5 per cent.

2 Estimates are based on our series of national expenditure accounts for this period, details of which are given in Appendix A, tables A.1 to A.3.

3 These estimates are based on government surveys and foreign trade statistics. Estimates of the public sector are based on analysis of the budgets and for autonomous bodies through detailed questionnaire. For the private sector, with the exception of the large-scale manufacturing sector, where it is based on a sample survey, a commodity flow method is used. According to this method, input–output type coefficients are derived relating the availability or sales of key inputs to gross investment and the actual availability is then multiplied by coefficients to get investment estimates (For details see C.S.O., 1972, p. 546).

Our series includes non-monetised investment. We have confined total investment to *fixed* investment by excluding changes in stocks, mainly because the available data on stocks is extremely poor. Stocks, however, represented only a small proportion of total investment in the sixties, less than 10 per cent for all years, except in 1959/60 and 1966/67.

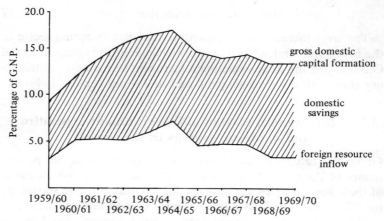

Figure 1.1. All Pakistan

There is a strong association between the behaviour of investment and the inflow of foreign real resources[4] during this period. As a percentage of G.N.P. the inflow increased from 3.1 per cent

Table 1.3 *Share of investment, foreign resource inflows, savings and government expenditure in gross provincial expenditure*

	West Pakistan			East Pakistan		
	1959/60	*1964/65*	*1969/70*	*1959/60*	*1964/65*	*1969/70*
1 Gross domestic fixed capital formation	11.4	21.1	15.6	6.8	11.2	10.5
(i) Private	4.4	11.3	8.1	3.6	4.7	3.5
(ii) Public	7.0	9.8	7.5	3.2	6.5	7.0
2 Foreign resource inflow[a]	5.4	8.9	3.1	0.3	4.6	3.2
3 Government consumption expenditure	9.2	7.9	10.0	4.4	5.5	5.5
4 Domestic savings (1–2)	6.0	12.2	12.5	6.5	6.6	7.3

[a] Includes balances with East (or West) Pakistan.
Source: See Appendix A, tables A.1 to A.3.

4 The inflow of foreign resources has been measured as the difference between the total imports and exports of goods and services in this period. This is a measure of physical resources made possible by foreign aid and other financial transactions including use of reserves and net income from abroad. The latter was, however, not important in the period covered.

in 1959/60 to 7.1 per cent in 1964/65, but then subsequently declined to 3.0 per cent by 1969/70. The importance of foreign financing can be seen from the fact that it represented almost 50 per cent of total imports and about 40 per cent of all investment in the boom period of the Second Plan but during the Third Plan these figures had come down to 35.1 per cent and 22.6 per cent respectively.[5]

The importance of foreign resource inflows and their slowing down in the second half of the sixties brings us to the behaviour of Pakistan's own foreign exchange earnings. As a percentage of G.N.P. exports remained around 6 per cent in the 1960s.[6] However, compared with no growth in export earnings from 1954/55 to 1959/60, exports increased by over 7 per cent in value during both the Second and Third Plan periods. In the Second Plan, this was mainly the result of the increase in exports of primary commodities and the performance of the major manufactured exports, cotton textiles and jute manufactures, was far below the Plan targets.[7] During the Third Plan, the reverse was true. Primary commodity exports declined and were lower in 1969/70 by about 25 per cent than the actual receipts in 1964/65. This decline was, however, compensated for by a rapid increase in the export of manufactures which achieved a rate of growth of over 20 per cent during the Third Plan period.[8]

A major factor in Pakistan's export performance in the sixties was the subsidy given to exports through the export bonus scheme,[9] together with the diversification of trade into new markets (especially developing countries and the socialist block) and a major shift in the commodity composition of exports.[10] Despite the creditable export performance, the country was still heavily dependent on foreign resources, especially for the import of capital goods for the industrial sector. The growth of export earnings in line with G.N.P., however, must have served to help

5 Based on Appendix A, table A.1.
6 Ibid.
7 See Planning Commission (1966, pp. 21–2).
8 See Planning Commission (1971, pp. 33–5).
9 Essentially this scheme provided a subsidy for exports and a limited free market for imports. For details of the working of this scheme see Bruton and Bose (1963), Islam (1969), Ikram (1970) and Gerakis (1974.)
10 Exports of raw jute fell from 60% of total export earnings in 1957/58 to about 20% in 1968/69. Similarly, exports of cotton textiles and jute manufactures increased from 8.3 to 35% and other manufactures from less than 2% to about 20% in the same period (see Stern & Falcon, 1970, p. 26).

that growth to some degree and to cushion the effects of the loss of foreign aid in the second half of the 1960s.

Domestic savings (private-cum-public) measured as the difference between gross domestic capital formation and foreign resource inflow, both as a proportion of G.N.P., showed a large increase in the first three years of the Second Plan but then remained relatively stagnant from 1962/63 onwards. Government consumption expenditure as a proportion of G.N.P. was higher in the Third Plan (average 8.2 per cent) as compared to the Second Plan period (average 6.8 per cent). This was mainly the result of the increase in military expenditure following the war with India in September 1965.

If we look separately at the performance of the two provinces, West Pakistan dominates the behaviour of the overall economy in the movements of the key variables. There are, however, certain important differences for East Pakistan which can be listed as follows:

(a) Total investment, foreign resource inflows and government expenditure are much lower in East Pakistan than in West Pakistan. In the peak year of the boom, i.e. 1964/65, total investment in East Pakistan was only 38.6 per cent of that in West Pakistan and foreign resource inflows and government expenditure were 37.6 and 50.7 per cent respectively.

(b) The behaviour of investment is also different in the East. It increased at the beginning of the Second Plan, but reaches a peak in 1963/64, a year earlier than in the West. Investment falls in the beginning of the Third Plan but unlike the West, there is a recovery in the last three years. This increase was mainly the result of a deliberate policy on the part of the government to increase investment in the province. Private investment had failed to show any major increase in the Second Plan and when it slowed down in the Third Plan the government stepped in by increasing public investment.

(c) The foreign resource inflow[11] in the East never reached as

---

11 This is measured as the balance of trade on goods and services of East Pakistan with West Pakistan and the rest of the world. (Inter-wing trade was recorded by the C.S.O.). It has, however, been argued that figures for inter-provincial trade are not comparable with world trade because of differences in prices. Radhu (1973) has adjusted figures for inter-provincial trade in terms of 'world prices' and Naseem (1975) has given inflows of foreign resources based on these figures. The basic trends, however, remain very similar as do the actual magnitudes.

large a proportion of the G.N.P. as in the West, though in both regions it rose in the Second Plan and declined in the Third Plan.

1.2 Estimates of private industrial investment, foreign investment and investment in other sectors

The estimates of private industrial investment[12] together with the provincial break down are given in table 1.4 at constant prices. The following movements in the behaviour of private industrial investment clearly emerge:

(i) There was a sharp increase during the Second Plan period which reaches a peak in 1964/65.[13] It then declined in 1965/66 and showed no recovery until 1969/70 when it increased slightly but was still below the level it had been in 1964/65.

12 Estimates of gross fixed capital formation in the large-scale manufacturing sector for the period 1963/64 to 1969/70 are based on C.S.O. figures and for the earlier years we have had to rely on sanctions of private industrial investment as given in the plan documents.

The C.S.O. estimates cover all expenditures on fixed assets of over Rs 2 million in the large-scale manufacturing sector. For those firms already in production, estimates are based on an annual sample survey with a reasonably wide coverage. For new firms, estimates are based on the amount of sanctioned investment, figures for which are obtained from the Department of Investment Promotion and Supplies. (It is assumed that 70 per cent of the sanctioned investment is actually invested and this is then spread over three years.)

Since the series came from two sources and for the early years were based on 'sanctions' by the I.P. & S. Department, we decided to cross-check them by constructing alternative figures based on quoted companies on the Karachi Stock Exchange (K.S.E.). The estimates so derived agree broadly with the official series and show the same trend although there are differences for individual years.

Estimates of private industrial investment based on mfg co's.
on the K.S.E. All Pakistan (constant prices)

1960/61	1961/62	1962/63	1963/64	1964/65	1965/66	1966/67	1967/68	1968/69	1969/70
943.9	1008.6	733.5	1178.4	1480.8	1317.8	1368.7	1233.5	1268.0	1408.8

Source: See Appendix A, table A.4

13 Both the 'official' and our alternative estimates of private industrial investment show a break in this trend with a decline in 1962/63. The reason for this appears to be the fact that the original investment schedule which was supposed to cover the entire Second Plan period was exhausted in only 18 months after the start of the plan and the revised schedule to cover the rest of the plan period was not published until the beginning of 1963. During the interim period, therefore, there could have been a hold-up in the sanctioning of industrial investment. (For details see Section 2.1).

Table 1.4 Estimates of private industrial investment (constant prices) [a] (Rs million)

	1960/61	1961/62	1962/63	1963/64	1964/65	1965/66	1966/67	1967/68	1968/69	1969/70
All Pakistan	966.8	1204.9	873.5	1309.4	1447.8	1266.7	1239.2	1271.9	1229.3	1302.9
West Pakistan	805.1	810.0	640.5	1025.6	1106.2	974.8	880.1	895.8	836.8	922.2
East Pakistan	161.7	394.9	233.0	283.8	341.6	291.9	359.1	376.1	392.5	380.7

Note: Figures in current prices are given in Appendix A, table A.6.
Sources: (i) For 1960/61 to 1962/63 (at current prices) Planning Commission (1966, p. 189).
(ii) For 1963/64 to 1969/70 (at current prices) figures obtained from the Central Statistical Office, Karachi (unpublished).
[a] Based on a price index of industrial investment (1959/60 = 100) constructed by the author separately for West and East Pakistan (See Appendix A, table A.5)

(ii) For West Pakistan, the overall movements of private industrial investment dominate the movements of the economy as a whole. In the case of East Pakistan, where the level of investment was much lower, we neither witness the sharp increase during the Second Five Year Plan, as in the case of West Pakistan, nor the fall in investment during the period of the Third Plan. However, even during the Third Plan there was no substantial increase in investment.

Foreign investment accounted for a very small proportion of total private investment.[14] Only during the last three years of the Third Plan was there some increase in foreign investment but even at its peak in 1968/69 it accounted for only 6.2 per cent of total private industrial investment.

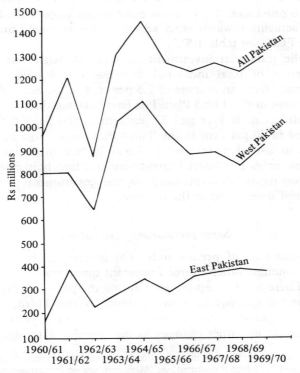

Figure 1.2 Behaviour of private industrial investment in Pakistan (constant prices)

14 See Appendix A, table A.7 for estimates of foreign private investment in the manufacturing sector.

Given the fact that throughout the sixties government policy had always been very favourable towards foreign investment, with no restrictions on the remittances of current profits and with assurances that foreign capital might be repatriated at any time (to the extent of the original investment) and an undertaking against any nationalisation, the amount of foreign investment is certainly very low. One reason for this might well have been the complicated exchange rate system which existed during this period.[15]

The decline in private investment in the manufacturing sector during the Third Plan was also not the result of any major shift in total private investment towards other sectors. Figures for the breakdown of private investment for different sectors are available from 1963/64 onwards for Pakistan as well as separately for the two provinces. They do not point to any major shift from the manufacturing towards other sectors of the economy during the Third Plan (see table 1.5).

Public industrial investment in West Pakistan was a small proportion of total industrial investment and only increased marginally from an average of 7.5 per cent in the Second Plan to 11 per cent in the Third Plan. For East Pakistan the situation was quite different. It averaged 23 per cent in the Second Plan and doubled to 40 per cent in the Third Plan. This large increase in public industrial investment was mainly to compensate for the very low private industrial investment and largely in response to the growing political pressure on the government to increase industrial investment in the province.

Some preliminary observations

The behaviour of private industrial investment in the sixties raises, amongst others, three important questions.

(i) There was a sharp increase during the period of the Second Plan and a subsequent slowing down in the Third. The behaviour of private industrial investment was not influenced to any large extent by either changes in the amount of foreign private

15 For the view of foreign investors on the effects of government policy and practices in foreign investment, see 'Memorandum on Industrialisation Policy for the Fourth Plan together with a Note on Foreign Investment' (Overseas Investors Chambers of Commerce & Industry, 1969).

Table 1.5 *Private investment in large-scale manufacturing as percentage of total private investment (i.e. all sectors) (percentages)*

	1963/64	1964/65	1965/66	1966/67	1967/68	1968/69	1969/70
All Pakistan	36.3	37.0	34.8	33.9	34.7	35.1	36.4
W. Pakistan	35.6	35.9	34.5	31.4	33.0	33.2	35.1
E. Pakistan	40.6	42.4	37.6	42.7	40.8	42.8	43.0

Source: Appendix A, table A.8

investment, nor by any shift in domestic private investment between industry and other sectors, nor in the West was it associated with any shift in emphasis to public industrial investment. What then were the factors which were responsible for the boom in the Second Plan and the subsequent slowing down in the Third?

(ii) There is a strong association between the behaviour of *total* private investment (i.e. in all sectors) and the inflow of foreign resources. To what extent was the behaviour of private industrial investment influenced by the inflow of these resources and, if it was, what was the mechanism through which this relationship worked?

(iii) Private industrial investment was mainly concentrated in the West and its behaviour dominates the movements for the economy as a whole. East Pakistan raises a different question. Why was there such a low level of investment in that province?

In this book we will mainly concentrate on the first two questions. The third has already been the subject of considerable controversy and research by economists;[16] also, since the break up of the country itself, the comparative significance of this issue obviously has declined. However, to the extent that data availability permits when we look into the factors which influenced private industrial investment, we shall study them for the country as a whole and then separately for the two provinces.

16 Besides the Reports of the Advisory Panels for the Fourth Five Year Plan (Planning Commission, 1970a, Vol. 1) which gives the views of both the East Pakistani and West Pakistani economists (they wrote separate reports), also see Rahman (1968), Sengupta (1971) and Nations (1975, pp. 266–72).

1.3 Factors which influence private industrial investment

Industrial investment is a function of a vast range of factors. The codification of these causes is difficult, not only because there is a considerable degree of interaction between factors but also because their actual influence is specific to a particular time and place. We have, therefore, presented a broad schema, which seems appropriate to Pakistan in the period considered.

Growth of private industrial investment $= f$(business confidence; expected rate of return; availability of finance – domestic and foreign; existence of a market; entrepreneurs).

Each of these factors themselves are influenced by a combination of factors which in some cases overlap. These can be listed as follows:

(1) *Business confidence:* By this we mean the expectation that the political and economic environment will be favourable to private investment.

Business confidence $= f$(stability of the government; strong policies against labour; support of the western capitalist economies; minimum government interference in the form of 'direct' controls on investment and other inputs).

(2) *Expected rate of return (Overall):* Here we are concerned with the factors which influence the overall profitability of the industrial sector.

Expected overall rate of return $= f$(1 General government policy measures: (a) exchange rate policy (b) import controls (c) rate of interest (d) export subsidies in general; (e) fiscal concessions; 2 level of real wages).

(3) *Expected rate of return in a particular industry:* We distinguish between the overall rate of return and that specific to a particular industry.

Expected rate of return (particular industry) $= f$(1 Government policies specific to that industry i.e. protection, export subsidy etc.; 2 existence of a market – internal or external; 3 market structure; 4 capacity utilisation).

(4) *Market:* By the market is meant the capacity to absorb the output of the manufacturing sector. It can be separated into the internal and external market.

(a) Internal $= f$(import substitution possibilities; rate of growth of the economy – principally the agricultural sector).

(b) External $= f$(competitiveness in relation to other countries – through lower costs or subsidies, growth of world trade, restrictions by importers).

(5) *Availability of finance:* In an economy dependent on imported machinery it is crucial to differentiate between the foreign exchange and domestic components of finance.

(a) Foreign exchange $= f$(export earnings; foreign aid).

(b) Domestic savings $= f$(rate of return; income distribution; structure of banking system and other intermediaries; consumption habits; government controls on conspicuous consumption; growth rate of the economy.)

(6) *Entrepreneurs:* If the industrialisation process is going to be carried out by the private sector, then you require people who are prepared to invest in industry – whether they come from the trading community, the agricultural sector or the military and the bureaucracy.

Supply of entrepreneurs $= f$(rate of return; degree of risk; barriers to entry; links with government in power; social factors.)

Factors listed under (2), (3) and (4) can be seen as influencing the growth of industrial investment from the demand side, while (5) and (6) can be seen as constraints from the supply side.

In analysing the behaviour of private industrial investment in the sixties we have taken into consideration most of the factors outlined above. The approach adopted, however, was not to investigate separately the movements of each of the variables but to concentrate on those particular factors which we felt were of crucial importance in interpreting the behaviour of industrial investment in the period. We then supplemented the major findings of our study with evidence from existing literature on the other variables so as to build up a complete picture.

The factors which are emphasised by us are first and foremost the peculiar institutional arrangements in which private industrial investment took place, then on the demand side the level of profitability and expansion of the market and on the supply side foreign aid disbursed as loans by the financial institutions. It is these which we first individually highlight and then combine together in a simple model of investment behaviour so as to econometrically test the nature of the relationship between investment and these key variables. Because the data are weak the econometrics used are perforce somewhat rugged. Generally speaking, we regard the econometric results as suggestive rather than anything more, and we have brought qualitative evidence to bear too whenever possible.

The study starts in Part I by analysing the institutional setting termed as the 'corporate environment' in which private industrial investment took place in this period so as to bring out its dramatis personae – the monopoly houses, the government and the financial institutions, which were dependent on foreign aid for the foreign exchange loans which they granted. It is the corporate environment which both determines and has a direct bearing on the existing investment climate, business confidence, the overall rate of return and the flow of financial resources to the manufacturing sector.

Part II empirically investigates the factors which influenced profitability in this environment. Our aim here is two-fold. The first is to see how profitability behaved over the period, and in particular to see whether there occurred any appreciable decline in the second half of the period which could help to explain the slowing down in private industrial investment. The second is to show that profitability is not influenced only by measures taken by the government, such as import controls and protection, but that factors such as market structure and links between the industrial and trading interests are also extremely important in influencing profitability at the industry level.

Part III then explores the relationship of investment to profitability and other factors, especially foreign aid, in the peculiar corporate environment which existed in Pakistan in the sixties. The study is first carried out at the level of the firm and starts by setting up a simple model of investment behaviour based on the conventional profit and accelerator hypotheses. The model is then modified to take into account the dependence of firms on foreign exchange loans from the financial institutions, a characteristic of the institutional framework in which they operated.

Our model of investment behaviour of firms is then extended to monopoly houses. This is done because, as we show, it is the monopoly house and not the firm which is the unit of decision making in the corporate sector. We then test the model of investment behaviour set out at the firm level and see to what extent the results have to be modified when we carry out the study at the monopoly house level.

From our study at the micro level, we move to investment

behaviour at the industry level. Here we try to see to what extent the existence of direct government controls on industrial investment together with the profit and accelerator theories of investment behaviour help explain the pattern of industrial investment which emerged in the sixties.

Finally, we use the results of our analysis and existing evidence from other sources to present our interpretation of the behaviour of private industrial investment in the sixties.

2

THE CORPORATE ENVIRONMENT

Private industrial investment in Pakistan in the sixties took place in a peculiar institutional framework which made conditions quite different from those of a market economy of the advanced industrial countries. In this chapter, this institutional setting, termed the 'corporate environment', is studied so as to show how the interaction of three sets of institutions influenced the behaviour of private industrial investment. The first was the government, which laid out the main aims and objectives of the industrial strategy to be followed and which, through a combination of different policy measures, tried to achieve the objectives laid out. The second were the monopoly houses, family-controlled conglomerates, which were the principal agents that undertook most of the industrial investment in this period. Finally, there were the financial institutions, which played a mixed role, acting both as intermediaries for the flow of foreign aid, providing loans as well as foreign exchange to the private sector, and also acting as agents of the government in influencing the pattern of investment. These institutions had representatives of foreign shareholders,[1] the monopoly houses and the Pakistan government directly associated in their management and thus can be expected to give expression in their policies to the interests of these parties.

The financial institutions had the power to exert a strong influence on industrial investment for two reasons. In the first place, the lack of a domestic capital goods industry in the country meant that in almost all cases the decision to invest entailed importing machinery from abroad. Secondly, firms could apply for cheap foreign exchange loans from the financial institutions at

---

1 Among these shareholders were David Rockefeller, Bank of America, I.C.I., Mitsubishi Bank and International Finance Corporation (I.F.C). (See, P.I.C.I.C., 1970, pp. 65–6.)

On the Board of Directors sat representatives of British, Japanese, German and American shareholders, as well as representatives of the I.F.C. (P.I.C.I.C., 1970, p. 5).

the official exchange rate, which was between two to two and a half times cheaper than the market rate. The alternative was to import the machinery at the market rate – or to buy it from those who had done so – but given the wide divergence between the market and the official rate this would only be done in special circumstances. The extent to which this influence was used in order to make investment conform to government plans varied, as we shall see, between the two plan periods.

This chapter is divided into three sections, dealing with the roles of the government, the monopoly houses and the financial institutions.

2.1 The government's role

2.1.1 Government 'direct' controls over private industrial investment

In Pakistan in the sixties, the government influenced the level and pattern of private industrial investment by two methods. First, by a mixture of fiscal, monetary and commercial measures (discussed in the next section, i.e. Section 2.1.2) which we can call 'indirect' and which would be reflected in most cases in increased profitability in the industrial sector as a whole or in the favoured industries. Secondly, by a policy of 'direct' controls, whose main purpose was to influence the pattern of private industrial investment; these we discuss in this section.

The government's blueprint for the pattern of industrial investment which it wanted over a plan period was published in the form of an industrial investment schedule. These schedules were based on production targets outlined in the plan documents, which were themselves based on the planners' assessment of the total amount of resources, both domestic and foreign, which would be available to the industrial sector. These schedules contained a detailed and comprehensive list of projects on a province-wise basis together with the foreign exchange and rupee component of each investment.[2] The government's resolve, however, to implement these schedules changed considerably over the two Plan periods, and we shall look at the periods separately.

2 The criteria by which the government decided on its targets for industrial investment are discussed in Section 7.1.

During the beginning of the Second Plan, it was not very clear to what extent the government wished to implement the investment schedule published in November 1960. In the outline of the plan, it had stated that 'the government intends to let the industrial pattern respond to market prices, not to trammel it by prescribing a rigid plan for industrial development' (Planning Commission, 1960, p. 222). It went on to add, however, 'that it is important to establish what industries can best be developed and to indicate where the national interest appears to lie' (Ibid., p. 222).

In the first few years of the Second Plan, the actual implementation of the schedule went almost by default. The department in charge of the implementation of the schedule, the Investment Promotion and Supplies Department (I.P. and S.), did not know, except with a long delay, the extent of the loans sanctioned in the different industrial groups by the Pakistan Industrial Credit and Investment Corporation (P.I.C.I.C.) and the Industrial Development Bank of Pakistan (I.D.B.P.) and the provincial governments. This situation was further complicated by the fact that imports of machinery against bonus vouchers were not known.

When at the end of 1961, the I.P. and S. Department reviewed the implementation of the schedule for the period July 1960 to December 1961 it came up with some spectacular findings.[3] In West Pakistan, the total amount of sanctions during these eighteen months exceeded the schedule allocations which were meant for the entire plan of five years by about 140 per cent. In East Pakistan, sanctions exceeded allocations in the case of nineteen industries, although total sanctions were 88.5 per cent of total allocations.

The exhaustion of the investment schedule in only eighteen months following the start of the Plan necessitated the publication of a Revised Industrial Investment Schedule (R.I.I.S.) to cover the rest of the period from March 1963 to June 1965. There was, however, one major difference between the old and revised schedules. In the case of a few industries[4] the amount of

---

3 See Durrani (1966) for details.
4 These were industries in which government thought strict supervision was essential. The important industries were oil refineries, fertilisers, petrochemicals, radios, wires and cable and machine tools. (For details see I.P. & S., 1963).

investment which could take place was not specified and these industries were captioned as 'specific'.

During the period of the Third Plan in contrast to the Second Plan the government had to exercise much greater restraints on industrial investment. This was necessitated by changes in the resources available to the industrial sector which meant changes in both the rate of growth and the pattern of industrial investment envisaged by the government over the plan period. As many as three investment schedules were published in the period of five years.

The Comprehensive Industrial Investment Schedule (C.I.I.S.) which was to cover the entire period of the Third Plan had been drafted before the plan period started. However, the government decided not to implement it because of 'the uncertain conditions created by the war with India in September 1965, the freezing of the Consortium Aid to Pakistan and the increase in defence expenditure' (see I.P. & S., 1966c, p. ii). Instead, it published what it called the 'Hard Core Schedule', which was to be the first phase of the C.I.I.S., listed 63 items and envisaged an investment of about one third of the C.I.I.S.

With the resumption of foreign aid in April 1966, the government felt that it could now go ahead with the original schedule. Also the evidence showed that there was considerably greater demand than had been provided for in the Hard Core Schedule, and provisions in a number of industries had already been exhausted. Also, a number of investors were interested in investing in industries which were not covered by the Hard Core Schedule.

The original schedule was in operation from April 1966 to the middle of 1968 when the government had to abandon it because of 'the balance of payments situation and the import liabilities of the industries already set up and those approved under the C.I.I.S.' (I.P. & S., 1968, p. ii). It was replaced by the 'Priority List of Industries' (P.L.I.) Schedule for the rest of the Plan period. Industries which were not included in the P.L.I. were subject to considerably greater government control and it was difficult to get permission to invest in them.

Forms of 'direct' controls

The direct controls used by the government during the sixties and the way they affected the investors' decisions to invest in a particular industry were as follows:

(1) Getting official permission to undertake an investment posed the least problem in two cases:

(a) If it was based on domestic machinery or was to be imported on bonus vouchers. However, given the fact that domestic industry was extremely small, the first was rarely possible; and the greater extra cost of importing machinery on bonus vouchers meant that the latter method would be used only in special circumstances.

(b) If the industry was listed on the investment schedule in operation at the time and the total provisions made on the schedule had not been exhausted (or the government was not aware that they had run out, as in the first few years of the Second Plan). In such cases, the investor could go directly to P.I.C.I.C. or I.D.B.P. which gave loans as well as foreign exchange to import the machinery.

(2) If the industry was not on the schedule, then the procedure was more complicated. The investor had to go through different government departments for permission depending upon the industry in which he wished to invest and the policy in operation at the time. This could entail applying for permission from the I.P. and S. Department, or the Central Permissions Committee (comprising members of the Planning Commission, P.I.C.I.C., I.D.B.P. and the State Bank) or the Economic Committee of the Cabinet (which comprised Ministers of Finance, Industries and Commerce and the Deputy Chairman of the Planning Commission).

Difference in degree of 'direct' control during the two plan periods

The implications of all this for the *degree* of 'direct' controls in the different periods over private industrial investment were these:

(a) During the period of the Second Plan, the private sector was reasonably free to invest in those industries where it wished to do so. Actual targets specified in the schedule were ignored. Only in the last two years of the Second Plan in the case of certain industries was permission required from the Central Permissions Committee.

(b) In the Third Plan, both in the earlier years as well as in the last two years, investors faced far greater controls over industrial investment. In the period from June 1965 to May 1966, they could only invest in those industries which were listed on the Hard Core Schedule and only for the amount of provisions made on it. In the end of the period, June 1968 to June 1970, that of the Priority List of Industries, they could only invest in the few industries specified, and if they wished to invest in any other industry they had to get permission from either the Central Permissions Committee or the Economic Committee of the Cabinet. Only in the two intervening years, i.e. May, 1966 to 1968, when the Comprehensive Schedule was in operation, did the private sector have considerable freedom to invest, as the schedule covered almost all industries.

2.1.2 Incentives, exchange control policy and import liberalisation measures in the sixties

The government's fiscal and commercial policies had a direct impact on profitability in the manufacturing sector in the sixties. The main features were these:

(a) Tax system

The government tried to encourage private industrial investment by giving generous fiscal incentives in the form of exemptions and rebates of tax on industrial profits. This meant that in most cases companies did not have to pay the full statutory rates of corporation tax, which remained at about 60 per cent throughout this period.

By far the most important of these incentives was the 'tax holiday' on income from new industrial ventures and expansion of existing units. The tax holiday had a duration of two years in the case of industries set up in developed areas (like Karachi, Lahore and Dacca), four years for semi-developed areas and six years for undeveloped areas. Although initially it was meant only for those industries which were based on indigenous raw materials, in 1964/65 conditions were so relaxed that it covered almost all industries.

Besides the tax holiday, depreciation allowances were also granted on an accelerated basis. Although not exactly a remission on tax, they had nearly the same effect by making a quick write off of investment possible. Besides the normal depreciation at the rate of 10 per cent on machinery, there was an initial depreciation of 25 per cent in the first year and extra depreciation at the rate of 50 and 100 per cent of the normal annual depreciation allowance for double and triple shifts respectively. This enabled a company to recover 57 to 78 per cent of plant costs of new investments in the first five year period.

(b) Exchange control and import licensing system[5]

The exchange control system, which was originally designed in the early fifties to protect the balance of payments, evolved into a powerful device for raising the profitability of the industrial sector in the fifties as well as in the sixties. Its main features were:

(1) Low prices of industrial inputs paid by the manufacturers. This had been achieved by allowing the exports of major domestically produced raw materials at the official exchange rate (Rs 4.76 per U.S. $) which meant that they were sold to the domestic processing industry essentially at world market prices. Similarly, as we have seen, capital equipment through foreign loans was imported at the official exchange rate. Also imported raw materials were allowed to authorised users[6] at the official exchange rate until 1968, after which, although the system was changed by raising the cost of foreign exchange, it was still less than the market price.

(2) In contrast, prices of manufactures had been raised substantially above the world market level. This had been achieved through high tariff protection and import prohibitions of selected goods (which had, to a large extent, insulated the domestic market from world prices) and, on the export side, by a system of export subsidies at varying rates for different products.

The import control system was regulated through a very

---

5 For a more detailed account of the working of the import licensing system, see Thomas (1966), Naqvi (1964, 1966), Child (1968a and b), Glassburner (1968) and Lewis (1969).

6 These were those who had their investment properly sanctioned by following the procedures laid out by the government and described in the previous section.

complicated licensing procedure. Since one of the important reforms introduced during this period by the government was the reduction in the reliance on direct controls, we look briefly at the system which existed when the military government took over in October 1958, the changes which it introduced and the effect these had on the manufacturing sector.

There were basically three systems of foreign exchange control in Pakistan: (a) government imports[7] (which have averaged around 30 per cent); (b) private capital good imports which were subject to control by the investment sanctioning procedure (which we have discussed earlier and which averaged around 20 per cent); and (c) private consumer goods, raw materials for industries, spare parts for industries and commercially imported capital goods which were covered by the import licensing system, administered by the office of the Chief Controller of Imports and Exports (C.C.I.E.).

Licences for the third category of imports were given in the fifties to certain privileged commercial and industrial importers. The former were generally expected to re-sell the commodities imported, the latter to import items for their own use. The commercial importers were primarily those firms which had imported during the 1950–52 period and the amount they could now import was determined by the amount they had imported during that period. These established importers were called 'category-holders' and this policy was referred to as the 'category system'. The industrial importers had their amounts of imports fixed on the basis of an industrial survey carried out in 1955 and a firm could become a registered industrial importer if it had its investment sanctioned 'properly', i.e. followed the official procedure for sanctioning investment described in the earlier section.

In 1959/60, the government took a number of measures to 'liberalise' the import policy and to reduce the impact of direct control on imports and to rely more on market forces.

The first measure was the *export-bonus scheme* which was introduced in January 1959. Essentially it provided a subsidy for

7 These are those made by Ministries and Departments of the Central and Provincial Government and autonomous/semi-autonomous bodies like the Pakistan Industrial Development Corporation and Water and Power Development Authority.

exports and a limited free market for imports. Exporters whose commodities were covered by the scheme received a voucher equal to a certain proportion of the value of their exports, the proportion being determined by the government. This voucher could be freely sold and entitled the holder to purchase an equivalent amount of foreign exchange to be used for imports of items on the bonus list.[8] Given the scarcity of foreign exchange, such vouchers usually sold at a premium of 150 to 180 per cent of their face value. (The effective exchange rate for items imported on bonus in the mid sixties was approximately Rs 12/$ and for exporters at 20 per cent bonus about Rs 6.30/$).[9]

In 1961, there were two further moves towards liberalisation. The first was the adoption of the Open General Licensing system whereby newcomers to the import trade (i.e. those who had not imported during the 1950/52 period) were allowed to apply for import licences to import goods commercially for legal resale in the country. Secondly, there was the introduction of the 'Repeat and Automatic Licensing Scheme' for certain commodities which could be imported under either commercial or industrial licences and which provided for the automatic granting of licences upon proof of the exhaustion of the initial licence.

In January 1964, the government took its biggest step towards import liberalisation with the introduction of the 'free list' for imports. Items placed on the free list could be imported by anyone without a licence. Initially the list covered only four iron and steel items and the cost of the scheme was borne by the U.S.

8 These items included iron and steel, chemicals, machinery, sugar, rubber manufactures, motorcars and commercial vehicles.
9 The effective exchange rate for imports and exports on bonus can be worked out as follows:

$$R_x = R_o (1 + vr)$$
$$R_m = R_o (1 + r)$$

Where

R_o = official exchange rate

R_x = effective exchange rate for bonus exporters

R_m = effective exchange rate for bonus importers

v = percentage allowed as a voucher on rupee equivalent of foreign exchange earned.

r = premium on the voucher expressed as a percentage of the amount of foreign exchange that the voucher entitles one to purchase.

Aid Commodity Loan. In July 1964, the goods on the free list were extended to more than fifty items.

As a result of these government policy measures to dismantle import controls and liberalise the import policy, the items imported on licence declined from 90.3 per cent of total imports (regulated by the Chief Controller Imports and Exports) in 1960/61 to about 39.5 per cent by 1964/65 and those on the free list increased to 48.9 per cent while those on bonus increased to 11.6 per cent (see table 2.1).

These attempts to dismantle the import control machinery, especially the experiment with the free list, suffered a serious set-back after June 1965, when, because of the foreign exchange constraint, the government felt it necessary to re-introduce an increasing degree of import control. The free list was not completely abandoned, but the items placed on it were subject to considerable administrative controls. The government also introduced the *cash-cum-bonus* scheme according to which half the foreign exchange needed to import certain goods had to be covered by bonus vouchers purchased by the importer, which had the effect of raising prices by about 75 per cent (the premium on bonus vouchers was about 150 per cent). This scheme mostly covered raw materials for manufacturing which had originally been imported at the official rate.

To conclude, the impact of the import liberalisation policies on the industrial sector were the following:

(i) It decreased the amount of administrative controls on imports and made it possible to avoid bureaucratic delays.

(ii) The easier availability of imported raw materials led to an increase in capacity utilisation.[10]

(iii) It led to a slight decline in the prices of imported raw materials, especially those placed on the free list.[11]

However, attempts towards import liberalisation were closely linked with the increased supply of foreign aid in the first half of the sixties. Once the foreign exchange squeeze became operative in the second half, the government had to abandon a number of its import liberalisation policies. Because of the increase in these controls, the mark-up on imported goods increased quite

10 See Brecher and Abbas (1972, p. 138).
11 See Pal (1964 and 1965).

Table 2.1 *Import liberalisation in the sixties (percentage of imports regulated by C.C.I.E.[a])*

Year	Licensed	Free list[b]	Bonus
1960/61	90.3	—	9.7
1961/62	89.6	—	9.4
1962/63	86.3	2.8	10.9
1963/64	75.3	14.9	9.8
1964/65	39.5	48.9	11.6
1965/66	32.6	40.0	27.4
1966/67	26.2	49.9	23.9
July/Dec 1967	42.9	32.4	24.7

[a] Chief Controller of Imports and Exports.
[b] After June 1965, the free list in fact was subject to varying and increasing degrees of administrative restrictions.
Source: Government of Pakistan, 'Report of the Working Group on Import Policy' (1967, pp. 15–16).

substantially.[12] Similarly, by placing items on the cash-cum-bonus scheme, the government increased the cost of raw materials to the manufacturers and this also led to a decline in capacity utilisation.[13]

2.2   The monopoly houses

In this section we examine the peculiar characteristics of the 'monopoly house' and how it differs from the modern corporation of the advanced industrial countries; we assess their importance and see the extent of their control over the industrial, banking and trading sectors of the economy.

2.2.1   Some basic characteristics

R. K. Hazari (1966) in his study of the structure of the corporate sector in India defined a monopoly house as 'consisting of units

12 Alamgir (1968) in a follow up study to Pal (op. cit.) found that the mark-up on imported goods on the free list increased quite substantially during the period after 1965 and he blamed this on the increasing number of controls which had been introduced on the free list (op. cit., p. 49).
13 See Planning Commission (1971, p. 24).

which are subject to the decision-making power of a common authority' (Ibid., p. 5). It is characterised in almost all cases by family ownership, has a centralised decision-making authority and consists of several legally separate companies engaged in highly diversified activities ranging from industry to trade, finance and insurance.

To illustrate, Adamjee was the third largest monopoly house in Pakistan in 1970. It controlled over twenty legally separate companies. In the industrial sector it was engaged in the production of cotton textiles, jute manufacturing, sugar, paper and board, chemicals, assembly of motor engines and production of vanaspati ghee. It had its own shipping corporation and had three trading companies dealing in a large number of products ranging from raw and blended tea to cotton and jute textiles. It owned the third largest commercial bank and the fourth largest insurance company in the country. Finally, it had a managing agency for its companies engaged in industrial production.

Although the monopoly house with its wide ranging diversity of interests might be likened to a giant corporation[14] of the western industrial countries there exist certain major differences between the two.[15] These can be outlined as follows:

(1) The large corporations are characterised by a separation of ownership and control but in the case of monopoly houses the control of the owning family over the group is absolute and all important decisions are taken by members of the family.[16]

(2) The monopoly house is broken up into several legally separate companies whilst the large corporation is usually one indivisible financial unit. In most cases the expansion of a monopoly house takes place by setting up new companies.

(3) The monopoly houses in almost all cases have continued

---

14 For a study of the characteristics and working of the modern corporation, see Galbraith (1967), Marris (1964), Marris & Wood (1971), Penrose (1959) and Singh & Whittington (1968).

15 Some of these differences in relation to monopoly houses in India are discussed in Ghose (1972) and Patnaik (1973, pp. 84–8).

16 In many cases, in fact, there seemed to be a single member of the family who had acquired a special status and prestige and who took all the major decisions and could over-rule other members of the family. This, for example, was the case of the Dawood Group (A. Dawood), Fancy Group (Amirali H. Fancy), Nishat Group (Mian Yahya) and the Saigol Group (Saeed Saigol). (Information collected by author on the basis of interviews with members of these groups.)

their strong links with the trading sector.[17] This was the result of the historical development of these groups starting basically as traders and then moving into industry after the collapse of the Korean boom. The modern corporation in the industrial sector rarely has such links with the trading sector.

(4) The monopoly houses have links with banks, insurance companies and other financial intermediaries. The modern corporation is dependent mostly on internal finance for its growth and does not display such links between financial and industrial capital.

(5) Even within the industrial sector, the monopoly houses are engaged in a greater range of activities (from say textiles to chemicals to engineering) than the typical multi-product corporation (though possibly some conglomerates have as wide a range of products).

(6) There is a wide range in the size of companies controlled by the monopoly groups. This is especially pronounced in the case of the Isphani and Habib groups who, besides controlling amongst the largest companies in the country, also had a large number of very small companies engaged in manufacturing and run by family members of the group.[18]

In order further to illustrate the difference between the monopoly house and the modern corporation and to bring out the nature of family control by the group over its companies, we can take as an example two firms in the chemical industry belonging to the Valika and Zafar-ul-Ahsan groups.[19] The former was amongst the older and most solidly established monopoly houses. The Ahsan group, on the other hand, was a medium-sized group and was set up in the sixties, being amongst those which were started by entrepreneurs with strong military or bureaucratic backgrounds.[20]

17 See Papanek (1967, pp. 40–50) and Amjad (1974, pp. 16–19) for the growth of the monopoly houses in the fifties.
18 It was pointed out to the author by a member of the Habib group that they had bought a number of small oil crushing mills (in the late sixties) to be run by younger members of the family who could not be given important positions at that time in the larger companies.
19 Information on these firms was made available to the author after the nationalisation of the chemical industry by the government in 1972. (See 'Survey of the First Group of Industrial Establishments controlled by the Government under the Economic Reforms Order 1972' – Report by Chemical Consultants (Pakistan) Ltd. and Associated Organisations, Lahore, January 1972.)
20 A list of those monopoly houses which emerged in the sixties with similar backgrounds is given in Section 6.4.

In the case of Valika Chemicals, all control in the running of the company was shared between two members of the Valika family. One of them was exclusively responsible for the administrative control of the factory and had absolute powers over technical and administrative matters. The other member (who was in the head office) was largely responsible for policy decisions, liaison with the government and negotiations with the suppliers of the machinery and the consultants. In addition to those two family members, there was also a technical director (who was the son of one of the two members mentioned before) who was principally concerned with production, maintenance and sales. The managing agents of the company were Messrs Kamruddin Valibhai, a company completely controlled by the Valika group (and having on its Board of Directors the two members of the family mentioned earlier). Although, due to the rather poor performance of the company, the managing agents did not receive any payment, the rate of payment had been fixed at 5 per cent of profits. The sole agents for the sale of products were Messrs Chemdeals who were close relatives of the Valika family. They received a commission of between 2.5 and 3.0 per cent on sales of products, although they did not handle the goods which were directly dispatched from the factory to the customers.

In the case of Indus Chemicals and Alkalis (belonging to the Zafar-ul-Ahsan group) the Managing Director was Mr Ahsan himself who was responsible for the running of the plant. All sales, finance, purchases and secretarial functions were supposedly performed by the Managing Agency (Silver Agencies) which belonged to the group and was run by the son of Mr Ahsan. All sales were arranged through this managing agency which was paid a commission of 7.5 per cent of total profits although they seemed to be performing no function and did not have any separate establishment.

The management structures of these two firms were by no means exceptional in having companies and agency arrangements designed as much to spread post-tax income and jobs amongst the members of the family as to do anything else. In fact, the report of the Chemical Consultants (1972) showed this to be the case for almost all firms run by the monopoly houses which were later nationalised by the government. The other interesting point which emerged from this report was that the role of the Managing Agency

was very different from that in pre-partition India.[21] Then the
agency system was used actively to manage different companies
under the control of a group. In Pakistan in the fifties and the
sixties, agencies seem to have taken little part in the actual running
of the companies. In fact, in many cases they seem to have been used
only as a convenient way of siphoning profits from the companies
controlled by the group in order to gain tax advantages on profits
earned. This was done, as illustrated earlier, by charging a certain
percentage of profits earned as Managing Agency fees or acting as
sole agents and selling the company's output at a commission on
sales. In certain cases the managing agents also acted as sole agents
for providing raw materials for the company – again charging a
certain rate of commission.

2.2.2   Extent of concentration of industrial economic power

The domination of the industrial sector by a small number of
monopoly houses had clearly emerged by the end of the fifties.
Papanek (1967) had shown that in 1959, sixty industrial groups
(out of a total of 3000 firms) controlled 60.6 per cent of all private
industrial assets and 43.5 per cent of all private industrial sales.
Out of these sixty, only seven controlled 24.4 per cent of total
private industrial assets and 15.6 per cent of total private sales of
the industrial sector (Papanek, 1967, p. 67).

Throughout the sixties, the concentration of ownership of the
industrial wealth in the country was an important political issue
and its existence was widely accepted even by the government.[22]

---

21 See King, B. (1966) for the working of the Managing Agency system in India
before independence.

22 Haq (1973) gives the rather misleading impression that he was the first to draw
attention to the existence of concentration of industrial economic power in the
country. To quote, 'it was little surprise to me that the mention of the 22
families in that atmosphere was treated as a bombshell both by a stunned
government and by the private sector in Pakistan'.

   In fact in the sixties, the newspapers abound with reports of the existence of
concentration of wealth. For example, *Pakistan Times* (20 Nov. 1961): 'A
protected market provided opportunities for industries to grow and expand
rapidly. But this has also made possible the concentration of wealth in a very
short period. This concentration is the result of ... official patronage, import
permits, industrial licenses and above all excessive price charging' (Islam G.,
'Industry's need for public goodwill').

   M. Shoaib (then Finance Minister), 'most industries in Pakistan had been
held by a small number of family groups' (*Pakistan Times*, 12 January 1963).

Haq's claim that 22 families controlled 66 per cent of the total industrial effort in the country, 70 per cent of the total insurance and 80 per cent of the total banking assets was, however, never substantiated (*Dawn*, 25 April 1968).[23]

More recently, however, certain attempts have been made to estimate the actual extent of concentration of economic power as it existed by the end of the sixties (see Economist (1969), *Alfatah* (1971), Shibli (1972) and White (1974a)).[24] The present author published an analysis in 1974 (Amjad (1974)) but since then the unpublished report of the study group set up by the government in 1963 has been made available to him containing detailed information on companies controlled by the monopoly houses in 1964.[25]

By reference to company accounts, studies of individual industries and direct enquiries in Pakistan, we have updated these estimates to 1970 to allow for new acquisitions as well as increasing the coverage from 21 to 44 monopoly groups. The results are presented in table 2.2 and details of the methods used are given in Appendix B. The extent of concentration was measured in terms of control over gross fixed assets by the monopoly houses. The extent of concentration was first measured in terms of all non-financial companies listed on the Karachi Stock Exchange (K.S.E.), then in terms of only manufacturing companies listed on the K.S.E. and finally in terms of the entire large-scale manufacturing sector. Each of these sectors was further sub-divided into private companies (i.e. excluding

President Ayub Khan, 'some groups of persons were running industries, banks and insurance companies or they were the managing agents of some industry and at the same time wholesalers and retailers for the product of the industry (*Pakistan Times*, 27 April 1965).

23 By strange coincidence, the earliest mention of the 22 families was made in the National Assembly by an opposition member also named Mul Haq: 'P.I.C.I.C. has created cartels under the patronage of the government. It has been extending loans to a very few families. Out of the total credit of Rs. 244 crores advanced an amount of Rs. 138 crores was distributed amongst 21 families. And the number will soon go up to 22' (*Pakistan Times*, 1 August 1963).

24 For earlier studies, see Iqbal (1964). Sobhan (1965, p. 109) also gave some rough estimates of concentration in the ownership of industrial assets.

25 The Anti-Cartel Law Study Group (Government of Pakistan, 1965) set up in 1963 to investigate 'business malpractices, the higher prices charged and exploitation of consumers', submitted its report in 1965. Despite considerable pressure by the opposition members in parliament and the press, it was not then made public.

Table 2.2 Control of Assets^a by Monopoly Houses in 1970

Size^c (Rs million)	Non-financial companies listed on the K.S.E.^b				Manufacturing companies listed on the K.S.E.			Large-scale manufacturing sector		
	Number	All	Private^d	Private Domestic^e	All	Private	Private domestic	All	Private	Private domestic
All Pakistan										
Over Rs 100	18	40.0	55.2	62.4	53.9	55.8	62.7	25.4	31.8	34.8
Rs 50–Rs 100	13	7.3	10.1	11.4	10.6	11.0	12.4	6.0	7.5	8.2
Less than Rs 50	13	3.6	5.0	5.6	5.3	5.4	6.1	2.4	3.0	3.2
Total	44	50.9	70.3	79.4	69.8	72.2	81.2	33.8	42.3	46.2
West Pakistan										
Over Rs 100	12	31.1	46.5	54.3	44.7	46.7	54.6	23.7	26.3	28.7
Rs 50–Rs 100	13	9.5	14.2	16.6	15.0	15.7	18.4	8.9	9.9	10.8
Less than Rs 50	17	6.4	9.5	11.1	8.6	9.0	10.5	4.6	5.1	5.6
Total	42	47.0	70.2	82.0	68.3	71.4	83.5	37.2	41.3	45.1
East Pakistan										
Over Rs 100	6	53.8	53.8	55.1	57.6	57.6	57.6	19.9	33.9	37.0
Rs 50–Rs 100	4	11.7	11.7	11.9	12.6	12.6	12.6	4.4	7.5	8.2
Less than Rs 50	6	4.5	4.5	4.6	4.8	4.8	4.8	2.6	4.4	4.8
Total	16	70.0	70.0	71.6	75.0	75.0	75.0	26.9	45.8	50.0

Notes: ^a Gross fixed assets at cost;
^b Karachi Stock Exchange;
^c All manufacturing companies;
^d Excluding government controlled companies;
^e Excluding foreign owned and government controlled companies.

government controlled companies) and private domestic companies (i.e. excluding the government controlled and foreign controlled companies).

Our study shows that, in 1970, 44 monopoly houses controlled about 77 per cent of gross fixed assets of all manufacturing companies listed on the K.S.E. and about 35 per cent of all assets for the entire large-scale manufacturing sector. In terms of only private domestic companies these 44 monopoly houses controlled 80 per cent of assets for companies listed on the K.S.E. and about 48 per cent of the assets of the total large-scale manufacturing sector.

Out of these 44 monopoly groups, 18, with assets of more than Rs 100 million, controlled over 60 per cent of assets of private domestic companies quoted on the K.S.E. and about 35 per cent of the domestic assets of the entire large-scale manufacturing sector.

The control of the monopoly houses over industrial assets is also shown separately for the two provinces. In East Pakistan, 16 monopoly houses controlled 50 per cent of private domestic assets of the province's large-scale manufacturing sector as compared to 45 per cent of assets controlled by 42 monopoly houses in West Pakistan. In terms of the number of monopoly houses controlling a given share of industrial assets, there was much greater concentration in East Pakistan. This reflected the fact that a number of monopoly houses did not invest in East Pakistan and the industrial sector there was dominated by the few monopoly houses that did.

Our estimates confirm a high degree of concentration in the manufacturing sector even though the figure is not as high as claimed by Haq. The control of the monopoly houses, however, was not limited to the manufacturing sector and it is to the financial sector that we now turn.

2.2.3   Control of financial intermediaries by monopoly houses

The close linkage between industrial and finance capital was another important aspect of the corporate environment which existed in Pakistan in the sixties. The monopoly houses controlled both banks and insurance companies and were influential in the running of the main aid disbursing agency, P.I.C.I.C.

The control over banks by the monopoly houses is shown in table 2.3, in terms of the proportion of total deposits and total loans and advances made by their banks in 1970. Of the 17 banks incorporated in Pakistan, seven were under the direct control of the monopoly houses.[26] These banks accounted for about 60 per cent of total deposits and 50 per cent of loans and advances made by all banks operating in Pakistan, i.e. including 19 foreign owned banks.

If we exclude the banks incorporated outside Pakistan and one state-controlled bank (the National Bank of Pakistan) the figure for the control by the monopoly houses comes to over 86 per cent of deposits and over 84 per cent of all loans and advances made by private domestic banks in 1970.

The monopoly houses also controlled a large share of the assets of the insurance companies (table 2.4). There were 47 Pakistani insurance companies and 30 foreign insurers in 1969. Of these

Table 2.3 *Control of banks by monopoly houses: 1970*

| | | | (Rs million) | |
	Bank	Controlling Group	Deposits	Loans and Advances
Habib Bank		Habib	4270.8	2622.7
United Bank		Saigol	3234.5	2032.4
Muslim Commercial Bank		Adamjee	1326.4	843.7
Commerce Bank		Fancy	375.4	312.9
Australasia Bank		Colony (F)	338.8	245.0
Premier Bank		Arag	41.9	23.7
Sarhad Bank		Faruque	20.2	7.1
(a)	Total controlled by monopoly houses		9608.0	6087.5
1 (a)	as per cent of all banks, domestic and foreign		59.3	51.0
2 (a)	as per cent of all domestic banks		65.4	57.0
3 (a)	as per cent of all domestic private banks (i.e. excluding those which were state-controlled)		86.9	84.2

Source: Calculated from State Bank of Pakistan (1972)

26 It should be pointed out that the smallest of these seven, Sarhad Bank, controlled by the Faruque group, was launched in the late sixties, while the others were in existence for the entire period of the sixties.

Table 2.4 *Control of insurance companies by monopoly houses: 1969*

Insurance company	Controlling group	(Rs million) Total assets
1. Eastern Federal	Arag	332.8
2. Habib	Habib	152.8
3. New Jubilee	Fancy	72.9
4. Adamjee Insurance	Adamjee	67.2
5. Premier	Premier	39.4
6. Central Insurance	Dawood	23.4
7. United	Valika	15.5
8. Eastern Insurance	A.K. Khan	14.0
9. International General Insurance	Wazir Ali	12.1
10. Crescent Star	Millwala	9.9
11. National Security	Colony (N)	9.8
12. Khyber	Zafar-ul-Ahsan	8.7
13. Union	Nishat	6.0
14. Universal	Ghandara	4.4
(a) Total		768.9
1. (a) as per cent of all insurance companies domestic and foreign		50.4
2. (a) as per cent of domestic insurance companies		76.1

Source: Based on Controller of Insurance (Karachi, 1971, pp. 334-9 and 512-27).

companies, 14 were controlled by the monopoly houses and their share came to over 50 per cent of assets of all insurance companies (i.e. those incorporated in Pakistan or abroad) and 76 per cent of all assets of insurance companies in Pakistan.

Besides their dominant control over the banking and insurance sectors, the monopoly houses were also represented on the boards of a number of important financial institutions, including those controlled by the government. The number of representatives of the monopoly houses sitting on the Board of Directors of these institutions is given in table 2.5. Most important were the links which the monopoly houses had with P.I.C.I.C., the principal foreign aid loan disbursing agency in the country. Seven leading monopoly houses were represented on the board of P.I.C.I.C. while one of them, Mr Adamjee (from the third largest monopoly house) was the Chairman; and almost 65 per cent of total loans

Table 2.5 *Representation of monopoly houses on financial institutions 1970*

Institution	Total number of directors	Number belonging to monopoly houses	
P.I.C.I.C.	25	7	(Adamjee, Dawood, Fancy, Valika, Rangoonwala, Crescent, A. K. Khan[a]).
I.D.B.P.	11	1	(Ferozesons)
I.C.P.	13	5	(Habib, Arag, Saigol,[b] Adamjee, A. K. Khan).
N.I.T.	13	6	(Dawood, Habib, Bawany, Adamjee, Saigol[b]).

Note: [a] A. K. Khan came on the Board of Directors in 1969. Before him for the entire period of the sixties, A. Jalil of the Amin Group was on the Board of Directors.

[b] They were not represented by family members of the group but by the managing directors of banks and insurance companies controlled by the group.

Source: Annual Report 1970 of (i) P.I.C.I.C. (ii) I.D.B.P. (iii) I.C.P. and (iv) N.I.T.

disbursed by P.I.C.I.C. in the period between its inception in 1958 and 1970 went to 37 monopoly houses with 13 of the larger monopoly houses getting about 70 per cent of this amount. The I.D.B.P. which was set up principally to finance medium sized investors with foreign loans was not dominated to the same extent and had only one director who belonged to the monopoly houses. However, over 30 per cent of loans disbursed by I.D.B.P. in the sixties went to only 30 monopoly houses and of these, seven accounted for 70 per cent of this amount (see table 2.6).

In order to mobilise savings of the household sector and channel them into industry, the government set up the National Investment Trust (N.I.T.) in 1963 and the Investment Corporation of Pakistan (I.C.P.) in 1965. As table 2.5 shows, the boards of these two financial institutions were also dominated by representatives of the monopoly houses; and again the chairman of one of the institutions came from a monopoly house.[27] Of the total investment by N.I.T. in shares of all quoted companies,

27 A. Dawood of the Dawood group was Chairman of N.I.T.

Table 2.6 *Loans from P.I.C.I.C. and I.D.B.P. to monopoly houses*

(From 1958 to 1970 in the case of P.I.C.I.C. and from 1961 to 1970 in the case of I.D.B.P.)

P.I.C.I.C.	(As % of total loans disbursed)	I.D.B.P.	(As % of total loans disbursed)
13 Monopoly houses	44.7% (Rs 640.9 million)	7 Monopoly houses	22.1% (Rs 260.2 million)
37 Monopoly houses	63.5% (Rs 911.3 million)	30 Monopoly houses	31.9% (Rs 374.5 million)

Source: Appendix B, table B.3

over 60 per cent was invested in companies controlled by the monopoly groups; the figure is 73 per cent if we exclude foreign-owned and government-controlled companies. The investments of I.C.P. in shares of companies controlled by the monopoly houses was much lower (about 40 per cent of their total investment), but this is explained by its large share of investments in foreign controlled companies. If these are excluded, the share of the monopoly house companies in total investment of I.C.P. increases to over 90 per cent (see Appendix B, tables B.4 and B.5).

2.2.4 Interlocking directorates

A further important feature of the corporate sector was the close links which existed between the monopoly houses, with members of one monopoly house sitting on the Board of Directors of a company controlled by another monopoly house.

The existence of these interlocking directorships between monopoly houses is illustrated in figure 2.1. In 1970, we were able to establish the existence of 78 such interlockings between quoted companies belonging to monopoly houses. The Adamjee group had the maximum (13) such arrangements with different monopoly houses.

Figure 2.1. Interlocking directorates 1970

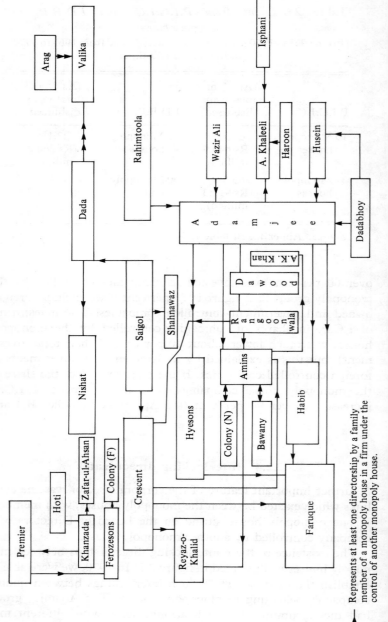

Represents at least one directorship by a family member of a monopoly house in a firm under the control of another monopoly house.

To conclude, the striking feature of the corporate environment in the sixties was not just the extreme concentration in the ownership of industrial assets by a small number of family controlled conglomerates but the way in which they also dominated the financial structure and the close connections which they had with each other.

2.3   The financial institutions

The importance of the two major financial institutions, P.I.C.I.C. and I.D.B.P., lies in the dual role they played in the sixties. Not only did they provide the foreign exchange required to import industrial machinery to the private sector, but, by providing this foreign exchange at the cheap official exchange rate *and* in the form of loans on favourable terms, they greatly influenced the profitability and financial position of the recipients. They were able to do this because the government channelled all foreign aid, loans and grants for the import of industrial machinery through these institutions and did not require them to maximise their profits by raising their interest income much above their interest payments.

In this section, we first show that these two institutions provided the major portion of the foreign exchange spent on importing industrial machinery in the sixties. We then see the sources of foreign aid and loans by countries and foreign institutions to these two banks. Finally, we show the advantages to the investor if he was able to get the foreign exchange cum cheap credit from these institutions.

2.3.1   Financing the foreign exchange component of private industrial investment in the sixties

During the sixties, the foreign exchange required for the import of industrial machinery by the private sector was provided from the following sources:

(1) The amount made available to the industrial sector by the government from Pakistan's own foreign exchange earnings. These were called 'cash licences' and were distributed through the provincial governments.

(2) Private foreign loans to Pakistani firms approved by the government.

(3) Private foreign investment in foreign subsidiaries and branches of firms in Pakistan.

(4) Deferred payments on the 'Pay As You Earn Scheme' (P.A.Y.E.). This scheme covered those investments where the investor purchased his machinery on credit from abroad and paid for it from his export earnings.

(5) Utilisation of bonus vouchers for import of machinery at the unfavourable market rate.

(6) Foreign exchange loans and grants to the government from aid-giving countries or from international institutions like the International Bank for Reconstruction and Development (I.B.R.D.), or the International Finance Corporation (I.F.C.). These were disbursed through the P.I.C.I.C. or I.D.B.P.

A detailed breakdown of the foreign exchange provided from each of these sources is unfortunately not available for the *actual* investments undertaken during the sixties. The only breakdowns which are available are for the investments which were *sanctioned*[28] during the Second Five Year Plan for both West and East Pakistan. Figures for the Third Plan period have not been officially released but the information was compiled by the author for West Pakistan[29] from the I.P. and S. Department.

Table 2.7 shows that the foreign exchange provided by the government (from the nation's own foreign exchange earnings) to the industrial sector for the import of industrial machinery made up a very small proportion of the total during the Second Plan and was almost non-existent during the Third Plan. Although detailed figures are not available for the industrial sector, imports of capital goods on bonus vouchers were higher during the Third Plan period.[30] Similarly, imports of industrial machinery with the

28 The sanctions very closely reflect the recorded investment which took place in the period not only because the official C.S.O. series for industrial investment is mainly based on these figures but also because almost all investment undertaken had to receive official clearance from either the financial institutions or a government agency, as described in Section 2.1; and being so profitable, sanctions rarely went unused.

29 Figures for East Pakistan were not shown to the author. This is mainly because of the unresolved problem of the division of assets and liabilities between Bangladesh and Pakistan and these data, which would show amount of industrial investment in East Pakistan based on loans etc., are being withheld.

30 Imports on bonus vouchers of machinery and spare parts more than doubled from Rs 342.2 million during the Second Plan to Rs 710.5 million in the Third Plan. (Source: Ministry of Finance, Pakistan Economic Survey, various issues.)

Table 2.7 *Private industrial investment sanctions during the Second Five Year Plan 1960/61–1964/65 (percentages)*

| | West Pakistan | | East Pakistan | |
	Foreign exchange component	Total invest-ment	Foreign exchange component	Total invest-ment
1. Provincial government i.e. cash licences	3.6	2.9	11.0	14.4
2. Foreign loans, foreign investment, P.A.Y.E.[a]	23.9	27.4	23.5	22.8
3. Bonus vouchers	4.2	5.8	6.4	8.1
4. P.I.C.I.C.	42.6 }68.3	40.9 }63.9	29.9 }58.1	29.0 }54.7
5. I.D.B.P.	25.7	23.0	28.2	25.7

[a] Pay As You Earn Scheme.
Source: Compiled from I.P. & S. (1966a)

Table 2.8 *Private industrial investment sanctions during the Third Five Year Plan 1965/66–1969/70 (percentages)*

	West Pakistan foreign exchange component	Total investment
1. Foreign loans, foreign invest- ment and bonus vouchers [a]	36.1	33.8
2. P.A.Y.E.	6.7	6.0
3. P.I.C.I.C.	38.0 ⎫	40.7 ⎫
4. I.D.B.P.	19.2 ⎭ 57.2	19.5 ⎭ 60.2

[a] Breakdown for each of these items was not available.
Source: Data compiled by the author from the I.P. & S. Department.

firm's own export earnings (through the 'Pay As You Earn Scheme') were also higher. But, during both the plan periods, these still amounted to a small proportion of the total as compared to P.I.C.I.C. and I.D.B.P. which provided the bulk of the foreign exchange for the imports of industrial machinery.

In West Pakistan, P.I.C.I.C. and I.D.B.P. combined provided almost 70 per cent of the foreign exchange component of total investment sanctioned and projects of these institutions accounted for about 65 per cent of total investment[31] sanctioned during the Second Plan period (table 2.7). During the Third Plan, the figure had come down to about 60 per cent but this was mainly due to the decline in the amount of foreign exchange provided for by I.D.B.P. as compared to the Second Plan. Also a large number of foreign loans[32] from private investors abroad were made available to the private sector through P.I.C.I.C. during the sixties and these amounted to almost 30 per cent of total direct credit received by it. In the case of East Pakistan, the two financial institutions provided about 60 per cent of the foreign exchange during the Second Plan for private industrial investment – the figure being slightly lower than that of West Pakistan, mainly

31 By total investment we mean the foreign exchange plus the rupee component of the investment. P.I.C.I.C.'s contribution to the rupee component of this investment was extremely small (see p. 58). This figure is only meant to illustrate the importance of the projects set up by the private sector with the help of P.I.C.I.C. in this period.
32 See Appendix B, Table B.6.

because P.I.C.I.C.'s activities were concentrated more in the West and the provincial government's share of investment was larger in the East. Also, the relative shares of P.I.C.I.C. and I.D.B.P. were about the same in the East, compared to the much greater share of P.I.C.I.C. in the West. This was because I.D.B.P. provided for the medium and small investors as compared to P.I.C.I.C. which provided for the larger ones whose investments were mostly in the West.

2.3.2 Sources of foreign credit for P.I.C.I.C. and I.D.B.P.

The major sources of foreign credit for P.I.C.I.C. and I.D.B.P. are given in tables 2.9 and 2.10. In the case of P.I.C.I.C. the major source of foreign credit was the I.B.R.D.[33] which provided almost 45 per cent of total credit made available to it after its inception in October 1957. Other major suppliers each providing between 6 and 11 per cent of the total were West Germany, Japan, the U.K., U.S.A. and Italy. Besides channelling foreign aid to the private sector P.I.C.I.C. has also played an important part in getting direct foreign loans to the private sector. These in

Table 2.9 *P.I.C.I.C. – foreign lines of credit (from inception to December 1970)*

Country/agency	Amount (U.S. $ million)	% of total
I.B.R.D.	183.36	44.8
West Germany	46.76	11.4
Japan	31.52	7.7
U.K.	31.05	7.6
U.S.A.	30.04	7.3
Italy	25.62	6.3
France	17.39	4.2
Asian Development Bank	15.12	3.7
Others [a]	28.85	7.0
Total	409.71	100.0

[a]These are Czechoslovakia, U.S.S.R., Belgium, Holland, Saudi Arabia, Poland, Switzerland and Denmark.
Source: P.I.C.I.C., 13th Annual Report, December 1970

33 International Bank for Reconstruction and Development/World Bank, Washington, U.S.A.

Table 2.10 *I.D.B.P. – foreign lines of credit (from August 1961 to 30 June 1969)*

Country/sources	Amount (U.S. $ million)	% of total
U.K.	75.10	26.2
West Germany	76.71	26.8
Japan	61.36	21.4
U.S.A.	23.05	8.0
Italy	11.72	4.1
Yugoslavia	9.29	3.2
Others [a]	29.52	10.3
	286.75	100.0

[a] These are France, Belgium, U.S.S.R, Switzerland, Denmark, Poland, Asian Development Bank.
Source: I.D.B.P. (Annual Reports).

December 1970 amounted to 34.5 per cent of the total foreign credit P.I.C.I.C. had so far received, with Japan providing the major portion (51.7 per cent), France, Saudi Arabia and West Germany also making significant contributions of about 7 per cent (see Appendix B, table B.6).

In the case of I.D.B.P. the major proportion of its foreign exchange credits have come from the U.K., West Germany, Japan and the U.S.A.

Loans in local currency have not been a major portion of the P.I.C.I.C./I.D.B.P. lending operation. In the case of P.I.C.I.C. until December 1970, they were only one twentieth of the size of total foreign credit; the figure for I.D.B.P. was higher, being about one third.

2.3.3 Advantages of getting loans from P.I.C.I.C. and I.D.B.P.

There were three main advantages of getting the foreign exchange to import industrial machinery as loans from P.I.C.I.C. and I.D.B.P.

(1) The foreign exchange was provided at the official rate of exchange which was between two and two and a half times cheaper than the market rate.

(2) Getting the foreign exchange at the official rate also provided the investor with the opportunity of over-invoicing the cost of machinery and then remitting back the foreign exchange at the market rate. The system worked as follows. An industrialist whose foreign exchange had been sanctioned at the official rate would arrange with a foreign supplier to sell him the equipment at a fictitious invoice price higher than the one he actually paid. The portion of the over-invoiced amount that represented over payments was then deposited by the supplier to the industrialist's account in a foreign bank and it could then be sold for rupees at the higher black-market rate.

Winston (1970) has estimated that, in 1966, the typical magnitude of over-invoicing being about 10 per cent, the financial profit on an import of machinery of Rs 1 million was Rs 76,514. By 1970, the typical level of over-invoicing had increased to about 20 per cent and the financial profit from over-invoicing on Rs 1 million invoiced capital goods was Rs 351,540.[34]

(3) The foreign exchange was always provided as a loan and the rate of interest on these from both P.I.C.I.C. and I.D.B.P. varied between $7\frac{1}{2}$ to $8\frac{1}{2}$ per cent during this period. The rate was no higher than that charged by commercial banks on short-term loans, but this was kept low as part of government monetary policy.[35] In relation to the rate of return on investment (which averaged about 20 per cent, i.e. gross profits as a percentage of net assets[36] and excluding profits from over-invoicing), the rate of interest charged was very low; and the repayment period for the loans was very long – on the average between 10 and 15 years.

2.4 Conclusions

The object of this chapter has been to assess, quantitatively where possible, some of the characteristics of the corporate environment in Pakistan in the sixties. The three key points which emerge are the dominant role of the monopoly houses in

---

34 In 1966, the black market rate of exchange was about Rs 10 per dollar and the official exchange rate was Rs 4.75 to the dollar. By 1970, the black market rate had risen to Rs 15 per dollar, but the official exchange rate remained unchanged (Winston, 1970, p. 408).

35 The government had pegged all rates of interest at levels that were generally far below the market equilibrium rate (See I.B.R.D., 1970, Vol. II, pp. 42–3).

36 See table 3.1, p. 67.

the economy, the great advantages, in terms of profitability and supply of finance, which accrued to those who could get cheap foreign exchange-cum-loans from P.I.C.I.C. and I.D.B.P., and the evidence that the monopoly houses both had a strong position in the running of these two agencies and got a large part of the foreign exchange-cum-loans provided by them. In Part III, we shall empirically investigate the influence of some of these factors on investment behaviour at the firm, monopoly house and industry level.

PART II
PROFITABILITY IN THE MANUFACTURING SECTOR

3

A TIME SERIES ANALYSIS OF
PROFITABILITY

It could be argued that, although the overall level of profitability was high in the beginning of the sixties, over the period the level began to fall and that this was one factor which contributed to the decline in private industrial investment in the second half of the sixties. Our aim in this chapter is therefore to measure profitability in the large-scale manufacturing sector in the sixties and see whether there was any appreciable change during the period under study. The study was carried out separately for West and East Pakistan.

This study is based on balance sheets of companies which were quoted on the Karachi Stock Exchange. Although the size of the sample in relation to the entire large scale manufacturing sector is not large (see Appendix C, table C.3) it is quite representative of the major industries. We decided to base our study for the period both for an all firm sample of quoted firms, and one based on a continuous firms sample. The latter was included since the all companies sample includes new companies which have either just been floated on the Stock Exchange or are still in the early stages of production, with the result that the profitability ratio is biased downwards. A comparison of overall profitability between West and East Pakistan is also given, as well as a discussion of the major industries, which helps explain movements in the aggregate series.

3.1 Indicators used [1]

We have used the following three indicators of profitability in the

---

1 The problems involved in using company accounts for measurement of profitability are discussed in Appendix I (pp. 80–83) which also explains how these dictate our choice of the indicators of profitability. In brief the main points are these: (i) we, like authors of previous studies, have been driven to use pre-tax profits gross of depreciation because of the tax incentives for investment and the accounting provisions for depreciation, as these had effects on post-tax profits which cannot be measured; (ii) for want of evidence, one is driven to make the assumption that under-reporting of profits, which is known to have been common, did not vary significantly over time or between firms; (iii) inflation was relatively low in Pakistan in the 1960s and so did not greatly disturb the significance of accounting profits, as traditionally measured.

manufacturing sector:

(i)   Gross profits (minus interest)/net worth
(ii) Gross profits/net assets
(iii) Gross profits/sales

where gross profits = net pre-tax profits + depreciation + interest charges

net worth   = share capital + preference shares + reserves

net assets   = net worth + long-term liabilities (including debentures)

The first ratio shows the rate of return from the shareholders' point of view, as net worth reflects their interest in the company; and the second shows the rate of return on total capital employed by the firm. The third ratio is the price–cost margin and, assuming capital–output ratios are fairly steady, it will be influenced over time mainly by factors like foreign competition, domestic competition or changes in capacity utilisation.

The relationship between the rate of return (net of interest) on net worth and the return (gross of interest) on net assets depends upon two factors – the gearing ratio and the divergence between the rate of interest and the rate of return on net assets. Since during this period the gearing ratio increased considerably, especially in the first half of the sixties and the rate of interest was low in relation to the rate of return, it is interesting to see to what extent this influenced the rate of return on net worth.

It is, of course, impossible to say precisely how far investment behaviour will respond to one ratio rather than the other. An increase in the return on net worth due to higher (and cheap) gearing is a genuine gain to the shareholder and should be an incentive, but it has the offsetting disadvantage of increased risk and that may become important when gearing goes above what is regarded, perhaps conventionally, as a prudent limit.

For this reason, we have used both ratios as our indicators of profitability in the manufacturing sector.

3.2   Behaviour of profitability in the sixties[2]

Our three indicators give a reasonably clear picture of profitability for the period 1961–70, whether one takes the sample

2 A brief summary of previous results is given in Appendix C, table C.1.

for all quoted companies or that for the 39 continuous ones (figure 3.1).[3] The general movement of all three indicators is similar and the year 1963 represents a distinct peak in profitability.

In the case of all quoted companies, there is a slight increase in price–cost margins between 1961–63, but, for the other two indicators, profitability falls slightly in 1962 but then shows a large increase. There is a large fall in profitability between 1963 and 1965 although this is not so pronounced in the case of the price–cost margin. For the period 1965–70, and if we ignore 1967 (which was an abysmally bad year for the jute and sugar industry), profitability shows a slightly rising trend except for the price–cost margin which remains quite steady.

In the case of the 39 continuous companies sample, the turning point in profitability is also in 1963 but there is a large increase in profitability in the years 1961–63. Profitability declines between 1963 and 1965 and then, excluding 1967, shows, as in the previous sample, a slight rising trend in profitability except in the case of the price–cost margin where it remains fairly steady.

Table 3.1 compares the profitability ratio for the average of the five years 1961–65 with the four years 1966–70 (excluding 1967) which correspond roughly to the Second and Third Plan periods.

The comparison between the Second and Third Plan periods does show a fall in profitability. Changes in the gearing ratio, the result of a drastic increase in long-term borrowings in the first half of the sixties, are responsible for a much larger fall in profitability on net assets than in profits on net worth. In the case of all quoted companies, the average gearing ratio increased dramatically from 7.3 per cent in 1961 to 25.7 per cent in 1965 and then a lesser increase to 30.6 per cent in 1968 at which level it remained until 1970. For the 39 continuous firms, it increased from 7.9 per cent to 17.1 per cent in 1965 and then there is a slight increase to 19.9 per cent in 1970.

This large increase in the average gearing ratio in the second half, mainly the result of very large increases in borrowing in the first half of the sixties, combined with the low rate of interest charged by the major financial institutions P.I.C.I.C. and I.D.B.P. (average 8%) in relation to the much higher rate of

3 The number of firms in the all quoted companies sample increased from about 60 in 1960 to about 200 in 1970.

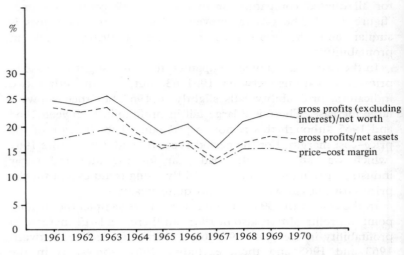

Figure 3.1(a) Behaviour of profitability in the sixties–All quoted companies

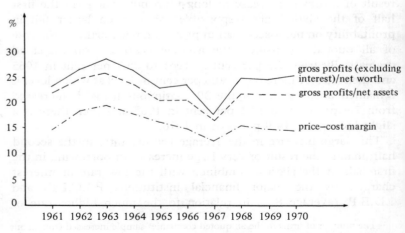

Figure 3.1(b) Behaviour of profitability in the sixties–39 continuous companies

Table 3.1 *Comparison of profitability between Second and Third Plan periods*

	Average[a] 1961–65	Average[a] 1966–70 (excluding 1967)	Per cent change
ll quoted companies			
. Gross profits (minus interest)/ net worth	23.1	21.2	− 8.2
. Gross profits/net assets	21.1	17.3	− 18.0
. Price–cost margins	17.9	15.8	− 11.7
. Gearing ratio	15.4	29.7	+ 92.8
9 continuous companies			
. Gross profits (minus interest)/ net worth	25.3	24.4	− 3.6
. Gross profits/net assets	23.2	21.4	− 7.8
. Price–cost margins	17.2	15.0	− 12.8
. Gearing ratio	12.4	19.0	+ 53.2
6 continuous companies			
. Gross profits (minus interest)/ net worth	—	23.1	—
. Gross profits/net assets	—	20.3	—
. Price–cost margin	—	14.6	—
. Gearing ratio	—	18.9	—

Weighted average
ource: Appendix C, table C.4.

return, meant that the return on net worth fell far less than that on net assets.

Our study also shows that the rate of return in both periods was higher for the continuous companies sample. Although the difference was not very large in the first period (about 10 per cent on net assets), it was much greater in the second period (about 20 per cent). This indicates that new companies which were started in the second half of the sixties had a lower rate of return. The reason for this appears to have been low capacity utilisation associated with 'starting up',[4] and aggravated in some cases (e.g. chemicals) by power failures and by costs incurred in sorting out snags.[5]

4 See Amjad (1973, p. 41) for details.
5 These are discussed in Section 3.3.

3.2.1 Province-wise study

Profitability as measured by all three yardsticks was lower in the second half of the sixties than in the first for both West and East Pakistan (table 3.2). But the decline was less in the East than in the West.

Our results for East Pakistan are quite contrary to those of an earlier study, Alamgir and Rahman (1974), who reported a large decline, of about 50 per cent, between the first and second half of the sixties. A part of the difference is explained by the fact that they exclude interest costs in their rate of return on net assets. But the main reason for the difference is that they also cover the sugar, engineering and chemical industries, which we do not, and these industries (which were mainly set up in the second half of the sixties) had very low rates of return (see Alamgir and Rahman, 1974, p. 152). However, most of the firms in these industries were in the public sector. Our results give a better picture of the performance of the private sector during this period.

Table 3.2 *Province-wise comparison of profitability during Second and Third Plan periods*

	Average 1961–65	Average 1966–70 (for East Pakistan excluding 1967)	Per cent change
Gross profits (minus interest)/net worth			
1. West Pakistan	23.5	20.5	− 12.8
2. East Pakistan	21.9	19.9	− 9.1
Gross profits/net assets			
1. West Pakistan	22.4	16.8	− 25.0
2. East Pakistan	19.9	17.3	− 13.1
Gross profits/sales			
1. West Pakistan	18.2	14.9	− 18.1
2. East Pakistan	17.1	16.7	− 2.3
Gearing ratio			
1. West Pakistan	14.9	28.8	+ 93.3
2. East Pakistan	15.0	32.1	+ 114

Source: Appendix C, table C.5.

3.3 Analysis by major industries

We now consider separately – or in groups – the major industries listed (which account for the greater part of the population of companies we have examined in the previous section) noting the main points which are germane to the interpretation of the aggregate series.

3.3.1 Cotton textile industry

Table 3.3. shows our estimates of the profitability in the cotton textile industry for the period 1961–70, and also gives the results of an earlier study by Haq and Baqai (1967) in order to achieve a link, albeit an imperfect one, with two earlier years. Their figures have a rather wider coverage and also underestimate the rate of return on net assets.[6]

The picture which emerges from table 3.3 is that there was a decline in profitability between 1961 and 1967 of about 39 per cent on net worth and 44 per cent on net assets. Since profitability was higher in 1959 as compared to 1961, as shown by Haq and Baqai's figures, the fall in relation to 1959 would be even greater. After 1967, there is an improvement in profitability rate, with a sharp rise in 1969, but profitability again fell in 1970.

One possible reason is the variation in the bonus rate and the volume of exports for cotton textiles. Profitability was highest in 1959 and 1960 after the export bonus scheme had been introduced in January 1959 with a bonus of 20 per cent on yarn and cloth. In response to domestic shortages in the home market the bonus on yarn was reduced to 10 per cent in February 1960 and was withdrawn in January 1961. This resulted in a decline in profitability in 1961 and a sharp fall in 1962. The bonus rate on yarn was re-introduced at 10 per cent in July 1962 and raised to 15 per cent in December 1963 and subsequently to 20 per cent in June 1964. The effect of this was a healthy increase in exports but no increase in profitability. This appears to have been due to the increase on the one hand in foreign competition especially from Hong Kong[7] and, on the other hand, in competition among

---

6 Haq and Baqai's study of the textile industry includes woollen, silk, synthetic and rayon where profitability was lower than that in the cotton textile industry (see Amjad, 1973, p. 431) and their figure for gross profits excludes interest payments.

7 See section dealing with problems of cotton textile exports in Tareen (1970, p. 20).

Table 3.3 *Profitability: cotton textile industry*

	1961	1962	1963	1964	1965	1966	1967	1968	1969	1970	Average 1961–65	Average 1966–70
1. Gross profits (minus interest)/net worth	31.3	24.3	22.6	22.6	19.9	19.2	19.2	21.3	26.4	22.8	24.1	21.8
2. Gross profits/net assets	29.9	22.8	20.3	20.1	17.6	17.0	16.7	18.3	21.8	18.8	22.1	18.5
3. Gross profits/sales	26.1	19.6	19.1	18.4	17.1	15.8	16.8	17.8	19.3	17.4	20.1	17.4
4. Gearing ratio	5.9	9.8	15.4	17.3	18.9	19.7	21.2	22.4	24.4	27.1	13.5	23.0

Haq and Baqai

	1959	1960	1961	1962	1963
Gross profits (minus interest)/net worth	31.8	33.5	30.1	24.3	22.2
Gross profits/net assets	20.9	22.8	19.8	15.5	13.9
Gross profits/sales	25.0	24.5	24.0	19.9	18.4

Note: Haq & Baqai's (1967) figures are not directly comparable with ours (see text).
Source: (i) Calculated from State Bank of Pakistan, *Balance Sheet Analysis of Joint Stock Companies Listed on the Karachi Stock Exchange* (Karachi, various issues).
(ii) Haq & Baqai (1967, p. 312)

Table 3.4 *Exports, bonus rates and profitability in the cotton textile industry*

| Year | Exports | | | | Bonus | | Profit-ability |
| | Yarn | | Cloth | | Yarn | Cloth | |
	Volume (million lbs)	Value (Rs million)	Volume (million lbs)	Value (Rs million)			(Gross profits*/ net worth)
58/59	28.0 (7.6)	42.5	n.a.	16.5	20%	20%	31.8
59/60	123.1 (30.6)	175.3	n.a.	56.1	10%	20%	33.5
60/61	39.0 (9.6)	73.6	60.7 (8.9)	44.6	—	20%	31.3
61/62	5.0 (1.2)	10.2	43.6 (6.2)	30.9	—	20%	24.3
62/63	11.5 (2.6)	20.4	112.2 (15.4)	67.6	10%	20%	22.7
63/64	60.8 (12.1)	98.8	143.7 (19.4)	90.4	15%	30–40%	22.6
64/65	76.9 (14.8)	138.4	195.0 (25.5)	132.8	20%	30%	19.9
65/66	55.3 (11.0)	104.9	196.1 (28.4)	149.3	20%	30%	19.2
66/67	66.6 (12.5)	117.8	212.0 (28.7)	159.1	30%[a]	40%	19.2
67/68	135.8 (23.7)	216.2	281.2 (36.7)	200.3	30%	40%	21.3
68/69	139.1 (22.4)	215.2	n.a.	244.3	30%	40%	26.4
69/70	169.6 (24.0)	268.4	n.a.	269.8	30%	40%	22.8

* Less interest

[a] Introduced in November 1967.

Note: (i) Figures for profitability refer to the calendar year i.e. profitability is for 1959 while figures for exports are for 1958/59.

(ii) Figure in parentheses give volume of exports as percentage of domestic production.

Sources: (i) Figures for production and exports from C.S.O. (1972, pp. 113–14, 445).

(ii) The bonus rate is given in Ministry of Finance, *Pakistan Economic Surveys*, various issues.

Pakistani producers in both the domestic and foreign market as a large number of new mills sanctioned in the investment boom of 1960 and 1961 came into production.[8]

It was only after 1967 that profitability began to reverse its downward trend. This, to some extent, was due to the increase in the bonus on yarn, which was raised to 30 per cent, but was mainly the result of a very large increase in exports in 1968, which rose by about 50 per cent over 1967. This is reflected in a substantial increase in profitability in 1969, when for the first time it reached a level higher than in 1962. In 1970, profitability fell slightly, although it was still higher than in the years 1963–68, mainly because of labour unrest and a number of mills reported a large number of working days lost because of it.

Province-wise breakdown

If we compare the profitability of the cotton textile industry (table 3.5) in the two provinces, we clearly see that, whereas the trends are very similar (see Appendix C, table C.6), the overall level was lower in the East, especially during the Second Plan period, as compared to the West. The explanation lies mainly in the higher prices of raw cotton in the East which had to import cotton from either the Western province or abroad. In addition, the textile industry in the East catered mainly for the home market in the first half of the sixties but towards the end of the sixties it achieved a substantial increase in exports, accompanied by a large increase in profitability.

3.3.2 Jute industry

Jute processing, the second big traditional manufacturing industry in Pakistan is another case where government measures can be seen to have influenced profitability, but in this case the role was partly to offset instabilities inherent in the structure of the industry. The jute processing (as well as the jute growing) industry was principally located in East Pakistan where it contributed about 25 per cent of value added and about 40 per

---

8 The number of looms increased by about 25 per cent between 1959/60 and 1963/64 and spindles by 21.1 per cent over the same period (see C.S.O., 1972, p. 113).

Table 3.5 *Comparison of profitability in cotton textile industry between East and West Pakistan*

		Average 1961–65	Average 1966–70
Gross profits (minus interest)/ *net worth*			
	West Pakistan	24.6	21.8
	East Pakistan	13.6	17.3
Gross profits/*net assets*			
	West Pakistan	22.7	18.9
	East Pakistan	12.6	15.3

Source: Appendix C, table C.6.

cent of employment in the large-scale manufacturing sector of the province.[9]

Profitability in the jute industry fluctuated widely (table 3.6). Pakistan accounted for 25 per cent of world exports of jute manufactures and for 60 per cent of world exports of raw jute. Consequently, Pakistan's production of raw jute and manufactures influenced to a substantial extent the supply position in the world jute economy. Since the production of raw jute was considerably influenced by weather conditions (especially floods and cyclones) and world demand trends were also subject to cyclical fluctuations (mainly because of changes in

9 The experiment to set up a jute industry in West Pakistan, in the late sixties, proved to be a dismal failure, at least in the first three years of its production. All the four jute mills that were set up incurred heavy losses. There were many reasons for its failure but the main one was that it could not compete with jute products from East Pakistan. A committee set up by the West Pakistan Jute Mill Association in 1970 to enquire into the problems of the jute industry pointed to several causes like the dearth of skilled labour, heavy cost of importing machinery and an irrational tax structure.

Gross profits (minus interest)/net worth

1968	1969	1970
−35.7	−5.0	−1.5

Gross profits/net assets

| −15.0 | −2.2 | −0.6 |

Source: Balance sheets of Amin Fabrics, Crescent Jute and Thal Jute Companies.

Table 3.6 *Profitability: jute industry*

Indicator	1961	1962	1963	1964	1965	1966	1967	1968	1969	1970	Average 1961–65	Average 1966–70
1. Gross profits (minus interest)/net worth	11.1	33.3	29.2	21.6	17.4	25.3	10.0	14.7	18.2	17.7	22.5	17.2
2. Gross profits/net assets	10.8	31.1	26.8	19.3	15.7	22.0	9.5	12.9	15.4	14.4	20.7	14.8
3. Gross profits/sales	6.2	21.3	18.9	16.0	14.5	16.4	8.9	12.1	11.5	13.9	15.4	12.6
4. Gearing ratio	10.0	8.7	11.1	16.8	18.6	19.4	23.7	27.5	27.5	34.4	13.0	26.5

Haq & Baqai

	1959	1960	1961	1962	1963
Gross profits (minus interest)/net worth	35.0	40.5	15.2	24.7	34.4
Gross profits/net assets	16.7	18.0	8.3	19.0	17.2
Gross profits/Sales	21.3	19.6	6.9	20.4	19.9

Note: Haq & Baqai's (1967) estimates are not directly comparable with ours (see text).
Source: (i) State Bank of Pakistan, *Balance Sheet Analysis of Joint Stock Companies* (Karachi).
(ii) Haq & Baqai (1967, p. 312.)

inventories), these both combined together to lead to sharp fluctuations.

The effect of these wide fluctuations in prices can be seen most clearly in 1961 and 1967 when profits of the jute mills fell drastically. In 1961, the average unit value for jute (per bale) went up from Rs 142 in the first quarter of 1960 to Rs 357 in January–March 1961. Since contracts for manufactures are generally made fairly far in advance, based on the ruling price of jute, mills which had not covered themselves lost considerably in the process (Haq and Baqai, 1967, p. 295). In 1967, first the devaluation of the pound sterling in November 1967 resulted in short realisation of sale proceeds of exports[10] and, secondly, India reduced considerably its export duties on jute manufactures, causing cut-throat competition in the export market, which, in the case of sacking, was so severe that its price was almost as low as that of raw jute.[11]

As in the case of the cotton textile industry, profitability was at its peak in 1960, when a bonus of 20 per cent on exports of jute was introduced. Ignoring 1961, profits were still high during 1962 and 1963[12] but fell drastically in 1964 and 1965. A major reason for this decline was the rise in raw jute prices which increased by almost 40 per cent in these two years.[13] In 1966, profits increased, mainly in response to an increase in exports which rose from Rs 317.8 million to Rs 575.1 million. After a disastrous year in 1967, the government increased the bonus on exports of jute manufactures to 30 per cent[14] and also abolished the export duty on raw jute in November 1967. As a result of these measures, profitability rose slightly in 1969 and 1970 but was still far below what it had been in the earlier years of the sixties.

10 It was estimated that because of this the industry lost almost Rs 20 million in foreign exchange (Haidari, *Corporate Companies at a Glance*, 1969, p. 31).
11 Ibid., p. 31.
12 During the period 1959–63, the jute industry had the highest profitability amongst all industries (Haq and Baqai, 1967, p. 295).
13 The index of raw jute prices was as follows:

    1959/60 = 100   1965/66 = 149.2
    1963/64 = 103.6   1966/67 = 159.3
    1964/65 = 141.2   1968/69 = 152.3

Source: C.S.O. (1972, p. 315).
14 In the case of certain jute products, such as carpets and matting, the rate of bonus was increased to 40 per cent.

3.3.3   Sugar industry

Our figures for the sugar industry are confined to West Pakistan only, since most of the firms in East Pakistan were in the public sector and profitability was extremely low[15] (table 3.7).

Prior to 1962, the government completely regulated the profitability in the sugar industry by fixing both the prices of sugar cane and the price paid for sugar, as well as the actual distribution of sugar in the market through its ration depots.[16] Under this regime, profitability of the sugar industry was very low during the early years of the sixties.

The sharp increase in profitability in 1963 occurred when, in a major change in policy, the government allowed the sugar industry to sell a part of its produce in the open market. The mills were still required to supply a specified quantity of sugar to the government every year at a fixed price, but if the mills output exceeded this amount, they could sell the extra on the open market.

Profitability in the sugar industry fluctuated considerably in response to the varying rate of recovery from sugar cane in different years. The large drop in profitability in 1967 was due to the poor crop of that year when the average rate of recovery dropped by as much as 30 per cent for some mills.[17]

In reaction to the high profits of 1963 and 1964, the government sanctioned, and the private sector eagerly constructed, a large number of new mills with the result that production almost doubled between 1964 and 1966 and profitability came down.

15 Alamgir and Rahman's study of the sugar industry in East Pakistan shows its very low profitability in the sixties.

	1963/64	1964/65	1965/66	1966/67	1967/68	1968/69
Gross profits[a]/net assets	5.8	4.5	5.0	1.5	0.8	−2.3

[a] gross of interest

Source: Alamgir and Rahman, 1974, p. 152.

   The main reasons for this low profitability were the very low sugar yields, poor location of mills and unusually small land holdings which resulted in buying from a very large group of farmers (about 100,000 per season). *Source:* I.B.R.D., 1970, Vol. II, p. 53.

16 The manner in which this was done is described in Anwar (1970, pp. 244–5).

17 See Annual Reports of Companies in the sugar industry.

Table 3.7 *Profitability: sugar industry*

Indicator	1961	1962	1963	1964	1965	1966	1967	1968	1969	1970	Average 1961–65	Average 1966–70
1. Gross profits (minus interest)/net worth	16.0	12.0	40.0	41.9	22.1	24.8	15.5	28.8	27.2	27.9	26.4	24.8
2. Gross profits/net assets	n.a.	n.a.	28.0	32.6	16.6	18.8	12.5	22.2	21.1	22.1	25.7 (Av.:1963–65)	19.3
3. Gross profits/sales	9.3	9.1	19.7	25.4	21.9	18.2	12.6	22.5	21.6	17.7	17.1	18.5
4. Gearing ratio	n.a.	n.a.	37.5	27.4	34.8	35.9	26.5	31.6	32.0	29.0	33.2 (Av.: 1963–65)	31.0

Source: (i) For 1961 and 1962 from Haq and Baqai (1967, p. 297).
(ii) For other years, calculated from State Bank of Pakistan, *Balance Sheet Analysis of Joint Stock Companies* (Karachi).

3.3.4 Other industries

Table 3.8 *Summary table: comparative profitability (gross profits minus interest as % of net worth)*

Industry	All Pakistan Average 1961–65	Average 1966–70	Per cent differenc
1. Other textiles (woollen, silk, synthetic and rayon textiles)	17.0 (13.0)[a]	14.6	– 14.1
2. Chemicals			
(i) All quoted	14.6	13.5	– 7.5
(ii) 8 continuous companies	—	21.2	—
3. Paper and board	22.8	20.2	– 11.4
4. Engineering	21.3	22.8	+ 7.0

[a] Average 1962/65
Source: Appendix C, table C.7.

As table 3.8 shows, profitability as measured on net worth was lower in the second half of the sixties for other textiles, chemicals and paper and board industry and slightly higher for the engineering industry.

In the case of other textiles, profitability declined very sharply after 1961, and was extremely low in the period 1962–65, but recovered slightly in the period 1965–70. The decline in profitability after 1961 can be attributed to the very low profitability in the rayon industry which accounted for over 50 per cent of the net worth of all industries included in this group. This was mainly the result of technical problems which arose in the industry's largest firm (Kohinoor Rayon) because of faulty initial design and project analysis, especially in the use of local raw materials. This situation was worsened by an unfavourable government import policy for yarn.

The low profitability in the Chemical industry was mainly the result of heavy losses incurred by some of the new larger firms which were set up in the sixties (especially Valika Chemicals and Esso Fertilizer). These losses were due to low capacity utilisation of these firms and were blamed on very frequent power failures faced by them. If we exclude these new firms, we find that the profitability of the existing firms was much higher.

The slight decline in the paper and board industry occurred as new firms, under government pressure, were set up in West Pakistan, whereas formerly the industry had been entirely located in the East. Profitability was lower for these firms, especially those which came into production in the last few years of the sixties.

An interpretation of the sixties

We can now interpret the movement in overall profitability in manufacturing in the light of these developments in individual industries. If we combine Haq and Baqai's study for the years 1959 and 1960 with our evidence for the years 1961–70, we can see the following broad movements which took place in this period.

Profitability was at its highest in the years 1959 and 1960, when the bonus scheme was introduced on exports of the cotton textile and jute industry. It fell sharply in 1961 because of the removal of the bonus on cotton yarn and a large increase in raw jute prices which led to a major fall in the profits of these two industries. Profitability rose again in 1962 and 1963. This increase can be attributed to the high profits of the jute and sugar industry in these two years (the latter because of the government's policy to de-control the price of sugar) but another factor was the increase in capacity utilisation[18] because of the more liberal import policy of the government and the increase in imported raw material inputs that it made possible.

Profits then declined in the next two years, i.e. 1964 and 1965. This period coincided with the introduction of the free list in 1964 and it could be said that the increase in imports of finished products allowed under this scheme acted as a dampening influence on domestic profits. This scheme, however, was subject to considerable government restrictions after September 1965.[19]

During the period 1965–70, profitability showed a slight upward trend. This was a period in which the industrial sector faced

18 See Brecher & Abbas (1972, p. 234).
19 See Section 2.1.2 for details.

rising costs. There were large increases in agricultural prices[20] after the bad harvests of 1965 and 1966; and prices of imported raw material inputs increased as they had now to be imported at the cash-cum-bonus rate,[21] rather than the cheaper official rate at which they were allowed earlier. The fact that the manufacturing sector was able to maintain profits (including stock appreciation) in the face of higher costs implies that it was able to pass them on (on a historic cost basis) in the form of higher prices.

To sum up, there was little difference in the level of profitability on net worth for manufacturing as a whole between the averages for the first and second halves of the 1960s; on net assets, there was more difference, but not a large one. In individual industries and in the average, for the odd year, there were major changes. These can be attributed in considerable part to changes in government measures affecting industries and to the vagaries of primary output and prices, notably in jute and sugar.

Appendix I

Problems with using corporate profits as an indicator of trends in profitability

There are a number of problems associated with using company accounts' reported profits as a measure: (a) of the overall *level* of profitability and (b) as an indicator of the underlying *trend* in profitability. The former problem was illustrated in our study of monopoly houses (Chapter 2, p. 43) when we saw how monopoly houses spread out their pre-tax profits from sales by forming a number of semifictitious companies which charge commissions on sales. Also there are the fees paid out to managing agents who do not seem to be performing any useful function. Finally, there is the problem of under-reporting of sales so as to save on excise and capacity duty as well as direct taxes on profits. It is impossible to gauge the extent of the underestimation of profits because of practices of this sort. A figure between 20 to 40 per cent was mentioned to the author in his interviews with different

20 Agricultural prices increased 10 per cent in West Pakistan between 1964/65 and 1966/67 and about 30 per cent in East Pakistan in the same period (Lewis, 1970b, p. 392).
21 See Section 2.1.2 for details.

businessmen and government revenue collecting officials. However, so long as the understatement of profits does not change from year to year or across industries, comparative figures are still useful.

The second problem arises because of the manner in which company profits are measured. According to Nordhaus (1974) raw movements in corporate profits may be a misleading indicator of underlying trends in profitability because of changes (1) in accounting conventions and depreciation provisions (2) in the burden of corporate taxation (3) in the price level and (4) in the financial structure of corporations. Let us see how these changes affect our data and what corrections can be made for them.

As regards the first correction, the company accounts' definition of profits subtracts the tax-allowable depreciation (i.e. capital allowances) in calculating profits and changes in corporate depreciation may merely reflect changes in tax law. Secondly, since depreciation is taken on book value rather than replacement cost, economic depreciation will be understated when there is inflation if tax allowances equal economic depreciation in the absence of inflation. As far as the first problem is concerned, the government gave very generous accelerated depreciation allowances which would enable a company to recover between 57 and 78 per cent of plant cost in a five-year period (see Chapter 2, p. 36) and this allowance was not changed during the period of the sixties. A difficulty arises, however, because companies, rather than opting for the accelerated depreciation allowances, could opt for the tax holiday scheme under which firms were let off all tax on profits arising from new projects for periods which varied from two to six years, depending on whether the industry was established in developed areas, semi-developed areas or undeveloped areas. A firm would show higher net profits before tax if it had gone for the tax holiday scheme rather than for the accelerated depreciation allowances. We have, therefore, included depreciation in our figures for gross profits on the grounds that variations in gross profits (including capital allowances) will indicate variations in the incentive to invest (which is our concern) better than profits net of capital allowances, if, as is the case here, the variation in capital allowances measures not a true variation in depreciation costs resulting, say, from variation in the capital–output ratio, but instead reflects differences in tax treatments of depreciation.

As far as making adjustments for changes in taxation are

concerned, corporate tax remained constant at 60 per cent during the sixties. But what did change during the period were rebates that were given on corporate tax for reasons like encouragement of exports, broad-basing of industries, maximum distribution of profits, preferential treatment for small industries etc., and, as noted above, the tax holiday varied by regions. Therefore, we would find that post-tax rates would vary, depending on whether at the moment observed firms were enjoying a tax holiday or not or whether they qualified for rebates. Since our data do not provide information on which firms were getting rebates it is not possible to adjust post-tax profits for changes in these rebates. This is another reason for taking the pre-tax profit rate as our basic measure of profitability in the industrial sector.

However, from the point of view of the overall profitability of the manufacturing sector, the post-tax return is still important, as it would have reflected changes in the tax burden on the corporate sector, especially the effect on post-tax profitability of the tax holiday scheme as those firms enjoying the benefits of the scheme came into production. The problem with the construction of such a series, however, is that the definition of tax provision of the State Bank data changed mid-way through the sixties, thus making it impossible to construct a consistent post-tax series for the whole period. In the earlier series for the period 1961–66, the figure for tax provision included, besides provision for current year tax payments, additions to tax reserves and provision for deferred taxation, whereas, in the later series 1965–70, tax provision excluded addition to tax reserves and deferred taxation. Since breakdown of the tax provision figures for the earlier years is not available, it was not possible to construct a post-tax profitability series for the whole period.

The third problem in considering corporate profits is the effects of the movements in the price level. During a period of inflation the figure for profit on historic cost measured in the accounts will exceed the figure on replacement cost and, as inflation proceeds, it can be expected that entrepreneurs will begin to shift towards replacement cost calculations even if they do this implicitly by merely raising their required rate of return on a historic cost basis. Fortunately, since adjustments would have had to be made, prices of manufactured goods and imported raw material inputs were quite stable until about the last few years of the sixties. As regards fixed assets, most of the industrial machinery imported during this period was at the official exchange rate and this was not changed in the sixties. In fact, during the second half of the sixties, prices of imported machinery and transport equipment in fact fell so that our measure would to some extent overestimate profits on replacement cost.

Finally, changes in the financial structure of corporations can influence the trend in profitability. This can arise either through changes in interest rates charges on borrowed capital as well as through changes in gearing ratio (defined as the ratio of long-term liabilities to net assets of the company). The rate of interest remained fairly steady during the sixties, at about 8 per cent, both for loans from P.I.C.I.C. and I.D.B.P. as well as those from the commercial banks. What did increase dramatically in this period was the gearing ratio, especially during the first half of the sixties. This being so, we decided to measure profits both before and after deducting interest, but the State Bank data which we used did not provide separate figures for interest charges. We, therefore, calculated the interest charges by multiplying the gearing ratio by the prevailing rate of interest (8 per cent) and then adding it to the gross profitability figure. This method should give us a fairly good estimate of interest costs, principally because of the very small change which took place in interest charged by the financial institutions during this period.

4

FACTORS INFLUENCING PROFITABILITY AT THE INDUSTRY LEVEL

The corporate environment created conditions which led to a high overall rate of return in the manufacturing sector in the sixties. In this chapter we analyse the factors which could explain inter-industry differences in profitability, notably the effects of protection and related government policies in differing market structures and the effect of varying degrees of capacity utilisation. We first consider theoretically the impact of these factors across industries and then empirically test the relationship between profitability and these factors for a sample of industries for the period 1965–70 for which data are available. Our results suggest that profitability is not only influenced by measures taken by the government but that factors like market structure and links between the industrial and trading interests are also extremely important in influencing profitability at the industry level.

4.1 Some theoretical considerations

4.1.1 Protection

In Pakistan in both the fifties and the sixties the amount of protection given to an industry was determined *not* by the tariff structure but by quantitative restrictions, which were generally the effective constraint on imports. The way in which prices will be influenced when quantitative restrictions *dominate* tariffs can be illustrated by what we call the *Pal–Lewis Model* (Pal, 1964 and 1965; Lewis, 1969 and 1970a). Three different situations are considered, namely (a) quantitative restrictions on imports; (b) quantitative restrictions on imports together with monopoly in the import trade; and (c) quantitative restrictions on imports combined with existence of a domestic industry.

In figure 4.1, DD is the demand curve and $S_m S_m$ is the supply curve for imports (including tariff). With no import restrictions OM_1 will be imported and the price would be OP_1. If, however, because of import restrictions only OM_2 is imported into the

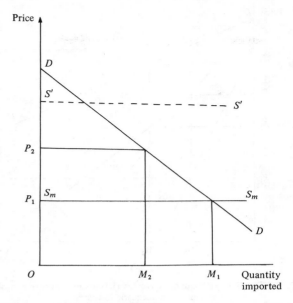

Figure 4.1. Pal–Lewis model: quantitative restrictions on imports

country, then the equilibrium price will increase to OP_2 and P_1P_2 will be the licensed-created profits per unit going to the licence holder. It can be seen that if licensed created profits are large, changes in landed costs (e.g. if tariffs are applied as well as quotas) do not influence domestic market prices over a fairly wide range – and therefore changes in domestic prices are determined by changes in quantity licensed. Only in the extreme case, if the tariff was to raise the landed cost to that implied by $S'S'$ would the tariff be the determinant of domestic price and not the quantity of licensed imports.

In Figure 4.2, we see the effect on domestic prices of the existence of monopoly in the import trade. The monopolist would maximise profits where $MR = MC$ and, therefore, the quantity imported will fall short of the amount permitted by the government allocation (i.e. OM_2) by the amount M_3M_2 and there would be monopoly profits (in excess of profits in the competitive case) to the extent P_3P_2. If such a situation exists, then we would expect 'liberalisation' of import policy, i.e. allowing goods to be imported by other than those who have a licence, to increase

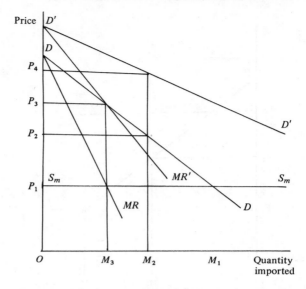

Figure 4.2. Pal-Lewis model: quantitative restrictions on imports combined with existence of a domestic industry

competition and reduce the price. However, if demand is higher in relation to import quotas so that the monopolist was using all the import allocations offered by the government (the situation shown by the demand curve $D'D'$ when monopolist and competitive price are the same at OP_4) then the domestic price of imports will not be affected simply by the entry of new firms – unless there is an increase in the import quota.

In figure 4.3, the domestic supply curve is shown as S_dS_d. If OM_2 is the licensed imports allowed then the total supply curve is shown by S_MLRS and the equilibrium price will be OP and M_2X will be supplied by the domestic industry. In this case, domestic supply will bring down prices from OP_2 to OP and licensed created profits for importers will fall. Even in this case the domestic price is not influenced by the imported price S_MS_M (including tariff) and it would only influence the domestic price if the landed costs (including tariff) were to increase above OP or if the quota were expanded to OM_1 or beyond. If the amount of licensed imports were to decrease (below OM_2) the domestic price would increase and lead to increased protection for the domestic industry.

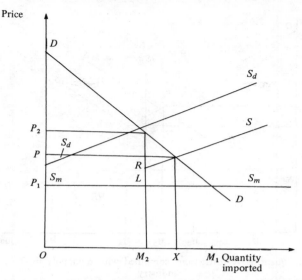

Figure 4.3. Pal–Lewis model: quantitative restrictions on imports together with monopoly in the import trade

4.1.2 Market structure

The Pal–Lewis model does not take into account the existence of monopoly in the domestic market. This situation is shown in figure 4.4. In the absence of any quantitative restrictions and under competitive supply conditions the domestic supply curve is $S_d S_d$, OM_1 is produced domestically and $M_1 M_5$ is imported. If $M_1 M_2$ is the amount of licensed imports, then the domestic supply curve is represented by $S_d LKS'_d$ and at the equilibrium price OP_3 domestic production now becomes OM_1 plus $M_2 M_4$.

If domestic supply was controlled by a monopolist (and assuming the special case where the monopolist's marginal cost curve coincides with the supply curve in a competitive situation) then he would maximise his profits where $MR = MC$ and the resulting price OP_2 will be higher than in the competitive situation (i.e. OP_3) and domestic output will decrease by the amount $M_3 M_4$. However, an increase in the amount of licensed imports ($M_1 M_2$) will decrease the price as well as monopoly profits, as the domestic supply curve will shift further downwards by the extent of the increase in quantity imported.

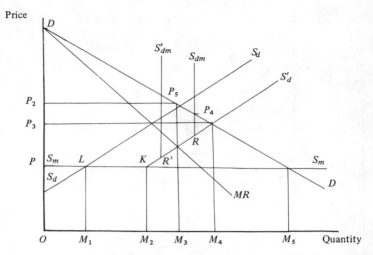

Figure 4.4. Quantitative restrictions combined with monopoly in the domestic industry

4.1.3 Government policy towards imported raw material inputs

We have so far only looked at the factors which would influence output price of an industry. Government policy towards the raw material inputs required in that industry would also have an important influence on costs and profits. A high tariff on inputs would lower the rate of effective protection given to that industry and be reflected in higher costs. Also an industry could find its output restricted below the profit maximising one because of government stringency in the licensing of raw material imports. This situation is also illustrated in figure 4.4 where, because of shortage of raw materials inputs, the industry's supply curve is restricted to $S_d LKRS_{dm}$ and the prevailing price OP_4 will be higher than the one OP_3 in a competitive situation. However, it would be lower than the one in a monopolistic situation OP_2, but, if output was restricted to the level shown by $S_d LKR'S'_{dm}$ because of raw material shortages, then the price would be higher at OP_5 even though total profits would be less.

4.1.4 Capacity utilisation

The above analysis shows in a formal geometric way the relationship of quotas and varying conditions of competition on prices and profits. But so far we have ignored variations in capacity utilisation and their effect on profitability.

There is strong evidence from various countries (Neild (1963), Nordhaus & Godley (1972) and Eichner (1973)) – though admittedly not on Pakistan or other developing countries where the data are limited – that manufacturers set their prices according to costs when operating at some normal level of capacity utilisation rather than varying prices to clear the market, and adhere to their mark-ups on normal costs with greater or lesser rigidity as demand changes from year to year. Given this pattern of behaviour and the fact that overhead costs, while varying in importance, are large in all manufacturing industries, one would expect profits per unit to be positively associated with capacity utilisation.

4.1.5   Other factors

We need next to consider export subsidies in the form of the export bonus scheme. Whether these would increase profitability would depend on the amount of the industry's output that is exported and the extent of competition it faces in the world market. If the latter is very great, then the subsidy might well have to be passed on completely in the form of lower prices, but the rise in capacity utilisation associated with high exports (assuming given capacity) would lead to higher profits per unit for the reasons indicated above.

Some evidence has been put forward in studies on advertising expenditure and profitability in advanced industrial countries which suggest that they are significantly related to each other. (For recent studies in the U.K., see Holterman (1973) and Khalilzadeh (1974).) One of the major reasons for this relationship is that advertising expenditure can act as a barrier to entry to new firms, hence increasing concentration and leading to higher profitability. We therefore look at this variable too.

4.2   Empirical analysis[1]

Data limitations have restricted our empirical analysis only to

1 Because of these severe limitations of data coverage and availability, we have

West Pakistan for four years between 1965/66 and 1969/70 (i.e. excluding 1968/69). There was a risk that this would distort the results. In those cases where transport costs were high and cut trade between West and East (which were separated by 1000 miles by air and more than 3000 miles by sea), it can be argued that it is an advantage to consider either the West or the East, because there was no competition between them. But where transport costs were not so high as to preclude trade, the lack of figures for production in the East may bias the observed degree of concentration. Most of the industry was, however, in the West; and, of those in the East, almost 80 per cent were in the food, beverage and textile industries and did not send exports to West Pakistan. However, what we did take into account was the fact that in the case of a very few industries, namely, jute, tea, paper and paper products, the major portion of production was in the East and the West was dependent on inter-wing imports.[2] These industries were excluded from the study.

The indicator of profitability used by us, the price–cost margin, was calculated in two different ways. In the first measure PC_1, both direct and indirect costs were subtracted from gross sales whereas in the second measure PC_2 only direct costs were subtracted.[3] The reason being that PC_1 to some extent under-

had to use two different sources and this has meant using slightly different measures of profitability in Part II and Part III of our study. In our study involving inter-industry differences in profitability (and later investment behaviour at the industry level in Chapter 7), we have used the Census of Manufacturing Industries data because of their much wider coverage of different industries. However, in our time series study of profitability in Chapter 3 and study of investment behaviour at the firm and monopoly house level, i.e. Chapters 5 and 6, we have used quoted company accounts data published by the State Bank of Pakistan.

The definitions of the different indicators used are discussed in detail in either the main text or appendices and the merits and de-merits of the indicator together with the differences from other indicators are also clearly explained.

2 In the case of the jute industry in West Pakistan, production did not start until 1968/69 and was therefore completely left out. According to the C.M.I. 1964/65, 70 per cent of paper and paper products production was in East Pakistan and 100 per cent for tea manufacturing. (Breakdown of tea blending production was not given because of problems of firms identification.)

3 $PC_1 = ($sale value of output^a–employment costs–material costs^b–depreciation–rent–interest–advertising–other overhead costs$^c)/$sale value of output^a.

$PC_2 = ($sale value of output^a – employment costs – material costs$^b)/$sale value of output^a

estimates profits because depreciation costs included in fixed costs are the accounting rate of depreciation, which, in the presence of fiscal incentives given in the form of accelerated depreciation allowances during this period, would be in excess of the actual 'economic' depreciation.

Our measure of concentration is the share of the four largest firms in total sales or output of the industry in 1968 (detailed calculations and methodology are discussed in Appendix D, table D5). Our study covers 25 industries, except for 1965/66, where our sample consists of only 24 industries and excludes the petroleum and petroleum products industry which started production from 1966/67. Each of these industries contributed at least one per cent of total value added in the large-scale manufacturing sector in 1969/70 and the sample accounts for 80 per cent of the value added of the large-scale manufacturing sector of West Pakistan in the same year.

The results for only the average of the four years have been reported. Given the fact that in certain industries the price–cost margins were subject to wide fluctuations these are perhaps the most representative of the relationship between price–cost margins and the different variables for which the models were tested. However, the results of the individual years in almost all cases were very similar and are given in the appendix.[4]

4.2.1   Model A1: price–cost margins and concentration[5]

The relationship between price–cost margins and concentration was tested in both the linear and non-linear form. The capital–output ratio[6] was included as an independent variable

[a]   Less indirect taxes
[b]   Raw material, fuel and electricity costs
[c]   These include business insurance premiums, postage, telegraphs and telephone, printing and stationery, water charges, royalties and fees for technical advice.
4   See Appendix D, tables D.1 to D.4 for results of different models tested for individual years.
5   For a previous study on Pakistan see White (1974a and b) and for a criticism of his work Amjad (1977). Also see Schwartzman (1959), Collins and Preston (1968), Holterman (1973) and Khalilzadeh (1974) for studies on advanced industrialised countries on the relationship between price–cost margins and concentration. For the manufacturing sector in India see Sawhney and Sawhney (1973).
6   The price–cost margin as an indicator of profitability is subject to criticism

because it would influence the price–cost margin, although this influence would be diminished in our first indicator PC_1 as it excludes depreciation and other fixed costs from profits. Also, to the extent that a high capital–output ratio may be associated with high absolute capital requirements it may constitute barriers-to-entry and hence further influence the relationship between concentration and price–cost margins.

The results were as follows:

$$PC_1 = \ \ 2.45 + 0.22^a CR_4 - 0.89 \ K/O$$
$$\qquad\qquad (4.26) \qquad\quad (0.32) \qquad\quad R^2 = 0.49$$

$$PC_2 = 13.74 + 0.24^a CR_4 + 4.61^c \ K/O$$
$$\qquad\qquad (4.236) \qquad\quad (1.509) \qquad R^2 = 0.60$$

$$\text{Log } PC_1 = \ \ 1.52 + 0.41^a CR_4 + 0.12 \ K/O$$
$$\qquad\qquad\quad (4.131) \qquad\quad (1.180) \qquad R^2 = 0.57$$

where PC_1 and PC_2 = measures of the price-cost margin

$\quad CR_4 \qquad\qquad$ = four firm concentration ratio

$\quad K/O \qquad\qquad$ = capital–output ratio

Note: Figures in parentheses are *t*–ratios.
$\quad$[a]Significant at the 1 per cent level.
$\quad$[c]Significant at the 10 per cent level.

There is a significant relationship between price–cost margins and concentration for all three forms of the model tested and the regression coefficient of the concentration ratio is significant at less than the 1 per cent level.

The regression coefficient for the capital–output ratio variable is positive with PC_2 as the dependent variable although it is only significant at the 10 per cent level. Given the fact that there does exist a slight correlation between capital–output ratio and concentration we also regressed PC_2 with the capital–output ratio

because it is influenced by variations in the capital–output ratio (See Benishay, 1967 and Mann & Meehan, 1969, pp. 389–90). This influence can be diminished by excluding depreciation and other fixed costs from profits. But even then the influence of the capital–output ratio will remain in so far as it is associated with variations in the equity interest (including reserves) of firms in relation to their sales. In order to take this into account, we include the capital–output ratio as an independent variable in our model along with the other variables whose significance we wish to test.

The capital–output ratio for each industry was calculated by dividing the book value of fixed assets by the value of production.

alone and did get a positive and significant relationship.[7] In the case where our profitability measure excludes fixed costs (and hence depreciation costs), the regression coefficient is not significant and indicates that capital intensity of the industry as reflected in the capital–output ratio is not significantly related with the profitability measure that excludes fixed costs.

As an alternative measure of the degree of competition, we used the number of firms in each industry. The relationship of price–cost margins to this variable was tested in the form of a simple regression analysis between our two measures of the price–cost margin and the number of firms in each industry. The results were as follows:

$$PC_1 = 26.18 - 0.07^a F_N$$
$$(2.555) \qquad R^2 = 0.22$$
$$PC_2 = 35.2 - 0.09^a F_N$$
$$(2.647) \qquad R^2 = 0.23$$

where PC_1 and PC_2 = measure of the price–cost margins
  F_N = number of firms in each industry

Note: Figures in parentheses are t–ratios.
[a]Significant at the 1 per cent level.

The negative sign of the regression coefficient is consistent with the theoretical expectation that an increase in the intensity of competition tends to reduce profitability. The correlation coefficient is lower than the previous results using the concentration ratio, as one would expect: the concentration ratio reflects better the degree of existing competition since it takes some account of the relative size of firms and the market power of the largest, whereas the number of firms indicator does not do so. However, to the extent that for the average of the four years the regression coefficient for the number of firms variable is significant at the one per cent level, our previous results of a significant relationship between the degree of competition and price–cost margins are confirmed.

7 The simple correlation coefficient between capital–output ratio and concentration is between 0.40 and 0.50 for different years. The result of the regression analysis between PC_2 and capital–output ratio (K/O) for the average of the four years was as follows:

$$PC_2 = 23.2 + 10.65^a K/O$$
$$(2.993) \qquad R^2 = 0.23$$

[a]significant at the 1 per cent level.

4.2.2 Model A2: impact of foreign competition on price–cost margins[8]

(A) Level of protection

In order to see the effect of the level of protection afforded to a domestic industry on price–cost margins, we tested the model in the following form:

$$(PC_1)_i = a + b_1(P)_i + b_2(CR_4)_i + b_3(K/O)_i + e$$

where $(PC_1)_i$ = price–cost margin of the ith industry
$(P)_i$ = level of protection in 1963/64 of the ith industry
$(CR_4)_i$ = four-firm concentration ratio of the ith industry
$(K/O)_i$ = capital–output ratio of the ith industry
e = error term

For the level of protection we used all three measures calculated for 1963/64 by Lewis and Guisinger (1971), namely for each industry the difference between domestic and c.i.f. import price of the product, the effective rate of protection and the effective rate of protection from all sources[9] for 18 out of the 25 industries for which they were given. The results for the average of the four years are given in table 4.1. Because of the existence of strong multi-collinearity between protection and concentration ratio, the results are also given separately just for protection and the price–cost margin.

The results show that in the case of all three measures of protection the sign of the regression coefficient was negative and in two out of the three cases was significant at less than the one per cent level.

There can be three possible reasons for not expecting any association between Lewis and Guisinger's estimates of protection and profitability.

---

8 For the rest of the study we have used only our first measure of profitability, i.e. PC_1, because by taking into account fixed costs it is the better indicator to use. For results using PC_2 as the indicator of profitability, see Amjad (1975) for the different models tested in this chapter. The results were, however, not substantially different.

9 The rate of effective protection is defined as the per cent of value added 'due to' protection, or $(w-\hat{w})/w$, where w is value added at domestic prices and $\hat{w}$ is value added at 'world prices' (Lewis, 1970a, p. 80). The difference between the rate of effective protection and effective protection from all sources is that, whereas the former is based on prices implied by the tariff structure alone, the latter is based on the actual differentials between world and domestic prices.

Table 4.1 *Result of regression analysis: impact of effective protection on profitability (number of industries: 18)*

Dependent variable (PC_1)	Protection			Concentration ratio (CR_4)	Capital-output ratio (K/O)	Constant	R^2
	Per cent by which domestic price exceeds 'world' price (P_1)	Effective tariff protection (P_2)	Protection from all sources (P_3)				
Four years average 1965–70 (excluding 1968–69)	−0.02 (0.974)	—	—	—	—	25.3	0.06
	−0.004 (0.181)	—	—	0.16 (2.525)	0.66 (0.231)	13.2	0.41
	—	−0.11[a] (2.851)	—	—	—	25.7	0.34
	—	−0.08[b] (1.748)	—	0.11[c] (1.695)	1.34 (0.518)	17.2	0.51
	—	—	−0.09[a] (2.713)	—	—	29.5	0.32
	—	—	−0.05 (1.288)	0.11[c] (1.536)	1.24 (0.456)	19.1	0.41

Note: Figures in parentheses are *t*-ratios.
[a] Significant at the 1 per cent level
[b] Significant at the 5 per cent level
[c] Significant at the 10 per cent level

First that the measures of protection are inaccurate. Not only are there inherent difficulties in estimating the rate of protection but also the lines followed by Lewis and Guisinger in their calculations make it extremely difficult to place much confidence in their figures.[10]

The second reason, pointed out by Bhagwati and Desai (1970), is that measures of protection at any one point in time can be quite meaningless in themselves. This is because in an economy in which import restrictions determine the level of protection, this premium will vary considerably both with changes in the government's import policy (which were indeed very frequent) and also because of changes in supply and demand conditions.[11]

Thirdly, and this could be the most important reason, it is a basic mistake to assume that effective protection would be reflected in profitability differences amongst industries. There is no 'a priori' reason why this should be so. The 'efficiency' of the domestic industry when compared with foreign competitors can show considerable variation and will be determined mainly by its

10 For their calculation of the rates of protection Lewis and Guisinger relied heavily on Pal's two surveys carried out in 1963/64 and 1964/65. In his surveys, Pal had collected data on domestic prices of commodities from wholesalers and purchasers of goods and the c.i.f. prices of identical commodities from custom records. This is an extremely difficult task, especially in trying to find 'identical' goods and differentiating for different grades or sizes of items. (For details of how this survey was carried out, see Pal, 1964 and 1965.) In the case of a few other industries, Lewis and Guisinger used direct comparisons between domestic and 'world' prices which again involves making a number of assumptions in finding identical goods. (See Lewis and Guisinger, 1971, Appendix E, pp. 362–3 for details of how their different rates of protection were worked out.)

11 This can be illustrated by the accompanying diagram. A given quota level ($AB = CD$) leads to a higher implicit tariff level (QM/MO) than earlier (NM/MO) if domestic demand increased from $D_1 D_1$ to $D_1 D_2$, with foreign supply FS and domestic supply SS remaining unchanged (see Bhagwati and Desai, 1970, p. 334).

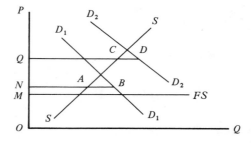

cost structure. Therefore, even though a domestic industry has high protection relative to world prices, it can still earn low profits because of high costs which could be the result of a number of factors like technical inefficiencies, frequent stoppages,[12] unskilled labour, low capacity utilisation, all of which result in higher costs. The high degree of protection, therefore, may be precisely to protect an inefficient industry.

Given the poor nature of the data on protection and the fact that our profitability estimates are for later years, it is not possible to read much into the strong negative result. However, what can be said with some confidence is that effective protection, as measured by Lewis and Guisinger, is not reflected in profitability differences amongst industries.

(B) Competitive imports

Another proxy – though admittedly an imperfect one – for the degree of foreign competition is the proportion of imports in total domestic supply. In the Pal–Lewis model illustrated earlier (figure 4.4), the effect of imports will be strong where the domestic supply curve either started higher than the supply price of imports (including tariff), or only a small portion of the domestic supply curve lay below it. To test the relationship between price–cost margins and competing imports, we measured imports as a percentage of total domestic supply[13] as well as in the form of a dummy variable with a value equal to zero when imports are less than 20 per cent of domestic sales and otherwise equal to one.

Our results were as follows:

$$PC_1 = 9.92 + 0.27^a CR_4 - 0.81 \ K/O - 0.12^c M$$
$$\quad\quad (4.629) \quad\quad (0.303) \quad\quad (1.669) \quad\quad\quad R^2 = 0.55$$

$$PC_1 = 9.72 + 0.28^a CR_4 - 1.03 \ K/O - 7.6^b M_D$$
$$\quad\quad (5.104) \quad\quad (0.406) \quad\quad (2.251) \quad\quad\quad R^2 = 0.59$$

where PC_1 = price–cost margin
$\quad\quad CR_4$ = four–firm concentration ratio
$\quad\quad K/O$ = capital–output ratio

12 This was a common complaint made by firms in the chemical industry, which incurred heavy losses because of frequent electricity failures (Annual Reports of firms in the Chemical Industry).

13 See Appendix D, table D.8 for imports as a percentage of domestic supply.

M = competing imports i.e. imports as a percentage of total supply

M_D = dummy variable for competing imports of the ith industry, i.e. $M_D = 0$ when imports are less than 20 per cent of domestic sales, otherwise $M_D = 1$

Note: Figures in parentheses are *t*-ratios.

[a]Significant at the 1 per cent level.
[b]Significant at the 5 per cent level.
[c]Significant at the 10 per cent level.

In the first case the import variable has a negative sign but is significant at the 10 per cent level. However, when we divided the industries into two different categories, those where imports are less than 20 per cent and those with more and used the dummy variable for competing imports, the results are improved, suggesting that for those industries in which competing imports were a very small proportion of total domestic sales they made hardly any difference to the profitability in the domestic industry but where they were a significant proportion (taken in this case as more than 20 per cent) they did act as a check on profitability of the industry. The results, however, suggest that the check was only a weak one.

In order to examine the influence of market structure on profitability, one has to examine not just the level of imports, per se, but the amount of imports in combination with the level of concentration which exists in that domestic industry. That is, in those industries in which there was a higher level of concentration as well as a low level of imports, one would predict that the price–cost margin was higher, compared with an industry in which the level of concentration was high but the existence of a large quantity of competing imports weakened the impact of concentration on domestic profitability. To take into account this interaction, the relationship was tested with the dummy variable for competing imports together with the concentration ratio with the following result:

$$PC_1 = 8.64 + 0.30^a CR_4 - 0.06\ K/O + 0.10^a M_D CR_4$$
$$(5.316)\qquad(0.032)\qquad(2.520)\qquad R^2 = 0.61$$

where PC_1 = price–cost margin
CR_4 = four-firm concentration ratio
K/O = capital–output ratio

$M_D=$ dummy variable for competing imports i.e. $M_D=1$ when imports are less than 20 per cent of total domestic sales, otherwise $M_D=0$

Note: Figures in parentheses are *t*-ratios.
[a]Significant at the 1 per cent level.

The results are now significant at the 1 per cent level, and show that in testing the impact of competing imports on domestic profitability the best results are obtained when we combine the level of imports with the level of concentration existing in the domestic industry. However, although competing imports do have an inverse association with domestic profitability, the fact that the results are not all that significant in some of the models tested suggests that the impact of competing imports on domestic profitability was not as great as the theoretical considerations given above and earlier analysis by Pal and Lewis might have led us to expect.

Imports and domestic profitability: an alternative explanation One important reason why the relationship between competing imports and domestic profitability was not as strong as expected could be the existence of a very strong linkage between the traders and the industrialists in Pakistan. It is well known that most of the industrialists, especially the big industrial houses, were originally traders who moved into industry following the collapse of the Korean boom and the imposition of tariffs on the imports of manufactured goods (see Papanek (1967); Amjad (1974)). Most of the new class of industrialists, in fact, continued to have large interests in trade and the manner in which the import trade in Pakistan was regulated[14] through entitlements to import-licences on the basis of performance in the Korean boom, i.e. 'category holders' meant that they continued to have virtual monopoly in the import trade. To quote from the Report of the Anti-Cartel Law Study Group (Government of Pakistan, 1965, p. 55):

The categorisation of imports is another important source of concentration of wealth and economic resources in a few hands in this country. Industrial category holders mostly got their categories fixed on the basis of an industrial survey carried out in 1955. As far as com-

14 See Section 2.1.

mercial category holders are concerned their entitlement is based on their performance during the Korean boom period. To the extent that our import trade is regulated in accordance with the entitlement of category holders on the basis of past performance, new comers are kept away.

An idea of the position of category holders in the import trade[15] can be had from table 4.2, showing the position in the period January–June 1963. (The figures are for actual imports.)

It could be argued, however, that the influence of monopoly in the import trade was considerably reduced with the policies of import liberalisation introduced by the government in the sixties. Also that, with the introduction of the free list in 1963/64, items placed on this list could be imported without having to apply for

Table 4.2 *Position of category holders in import trade*
(January–June 1963)

	Import values (Rs crores)	Percentage of total
Category holders		
(i) Commercial	16.97 ⎫	23% ⎫
	⎬ 57.2	⎬ 79%
(ii) Industrial consumers	40.24 ⎭	56% ⎭
Open General Licence (O.G.L.)[a]	6.40	9%
Bonus Vouchers	9.20	12%
Total	72.8	100

Note: [a]The O.G.L. was introduced in 1961 and it applied to specific commodities and to specific groups of commercial importers and provided for issue of licences of specified amount in each shipping period. Its purpose was to encourage new entrants in the import trade and to extend the value of licences issued in the commodities chosen. (See Chapter 2, above, pp. 38–9).
Source: Chief Controller of Imports and Exports. From Report of the Anti-Cartel Law Study Group (Government of Pakistan, 1965, pp. 56).

15 This is the total regulated import trade and accounts for about 50 per cent of the total imports into the country and about 70 per cent of total private imports. Other private imports not covered by this are either imports of machinery under foreign credits or imports under the Indus basin project.

an import licence. In 1963–64, imports on the free list accounted for only 15 per cent of total regulated imports but by 1964/65 this had increased to almost 50 per cent.[16]

During the period of the Third Plan (i.e. 1965–70), which is the one we are covering here, the policy of import liberalisation suffered a severe setback because of the foreign exchange crisis. Items on the free list were originally reduced and, although the number was subsequently increased, they were subject to varying and increasing degrees of administrative restrictions. Alamgir (1968) in his study, for example, found that in 1966/67 there was a substantial increase in the average mark-up on free list items compared to those reported in Pal's (1965) study for the year 1964/65.[17] (They rose from 29.8 per cent in Pal's study to 43.0 per cent in Alamgir's study (Ibid., p. 51).) Alamgir also suggests that free list imports may be monopolised by persons having bank support and storage facilities. Also, since under the free list a particular commercial bank was designated to handle the entire allocation for the import of a certain item, the selection was influenced by the creditworthiness of the importer and this, in general, favoured the larger importers. According to Alamgir, therefore, 'this may by way of creating private monopoly in the import trade, contribute to the existence of a very high scarcity premium in free list items' (Ibid., p. 50).

It is also worth noting that, even during the period of import liberalisation, studies carried out to see its impact found that it had made little difference to the domestic prices of imported goods. In his first study, Pal had found that there was no significant difference in profit margins between items imported by category and those on the 'Open General Licence' (Pal, 1964, p. 605).[18] In his subsequent study, Pal analysed price changes of commodities placed on the free list and found a very small decline in the weighted average price of these goods (Pal, 1965, p. 550). He also found that the increased supply effect of the free list was

16 See table 2.1, p. 40.
17 The problems mentioned earlier in calculating the rates of protection by Lewis and Guisinger based on Pal's survey are not applicable here as in this case data regarding the change of prices of the same commodity were being collected from the same source.
18 Pal took the 'normal' mark-up as 12 per cent which was taken from the Tariff Commission. The weighted average of margins on items on the free-list was 28 per cent (Pal, 1965, p. 551).

insufficient to eliminate super normal profits, and he explained this as being either due to the 'existence of monopolistic elements in the market' (Ibid., p. 551) or because of administrative and other restrictions.

It should be pointed out, however, that the discussion so far does not imply that supply restrictions on imports are not an important factor in determining domestic prices and hence in influencing profitability amongst different industries as the 'Pal–Lewis Model' suggests. What we are suggesting is that insofar as there is a monopoly in the import trade (a point which Pal admits) as well as a linkage between traders and domestic producers of the same commodity, imports will be prevented from acting as an effective check on domestic profits. The greater the monopoly in the import trade and the closer the linkage between the importers and the producers, the less we would expect the impact of imports to be. That a strong linkage existed is suggested by the fact that almost all the major industrialists had very large trading interests and were active importers.[19]

An extreme example of this linkage and how it affected domestic profits was the sugar crisis in the winter of 1968. The extremely high profits in the sugar industry generated in the earlier years of the sixties were beginning to decline because of increased domestic production as well as new entrants into the industry. By 1968, over-production became a distinct possibility and there is evidence that sugar producers deliberately cut back production in order to keep sugar scarce and maintain or even raise domestic prices.[20] The government responded to the situation by allowing the import of sugar into the country. This should have resulted in lower prices. But it so turned out that, of the five main importers, three were sugar producers themselves.[21] By holding the imported sugar back and not releasing it onto the

19 See Report of the Anti-Cartel Law Study Group (Government of Pakistan, 1965, p. 19).
20 See *Pakistan Times*, 25 May 1968.
21 The then Commerce Minister, Mr Hoti (incidentally also an owner of one of the largest sugar mills in the country) accused some manufacturers of having joined hands with 'importers' – in fact some of the principal importers were also manufacturers – to inflate sugar prices artificially to the detriment of consumers. Replying to a question, the Minister said that the five big traders were the manipulators – Adamjee*, Bawany*, Haji Hashim, Mian Bashir* and Abed. (Reported in the *Pakistan Times*, 16 December 1968). (*owned sugar mills)

market, they were able to keep sugar scarce and prices high,[22] so that for 1968/69 sugar industry profits were high, although it was a year in which large amounts of imported sugar were entering the country. Any attempt to establish a negative relationship between imports and profits in this case would be highly unsuccessful.

4.2.3 Model A3: price–cost margins, capacity utilisation, exports and advertising expenditure

We now consider the three other explanatory variables discussed in Section 4.1 which could affect price–cost margins, namely capacity utilisation, exports and advertising expenditure. The results of our regression analysis were as follows:

$$PC_1 = 2.09 + 0.24^a CR_4 - 1.90 \ K/O + 0.11^b CU - 0.20 X + 0.15 A$$
$$(4.512) \quad (0.657) \quad (1.900) \quad (0.906) \quad (0.501)$$

$$R^2 = 0.59$$

where PC_1 = price–cost margin
CR_4 = four-firm concentration ratio
K/O = capital–output ratio
CU = capacity utilisation
X = exports as a percentage of domestic production
A = advertising expenditure as a percentage of value added

Note: Figures in parentheses are t-ratios.
[a]Significant at the 1 per cent level.
[b]Significant at the 5 per cent level.

Our empirical results seem to give some support to the hypothesis of a positive and significant relationship between price–cost margins and capacity utilisation although this result must be interpreted keeping in mind the limitations of the data on capacity utilisation.[23]

The relationship between exports and the price–cost margin in our sample of industries seems to be critically dependent on two

---

22 The report in the *Observer* (6 December 1968) entitled 'Sugar Crisis', stated that, 'The crux of the matter is that mills took loans up to 75 per cent of stock value which helped them to hold back stocks.'
23 See notes to Appendix D, table D.9.

industries – cotton textiles and rubber footwear – which exported between 1965/66 and 1968/70, on average, 20.8 per cent and 15.3 per cent of their domestic production, as compared to the much lower figures for the other industries, whose average was only 1.5 per cent.[24]

The reason for the insignificant relationship was that the cotton textile and rubber footwear industries made comparatively low profits in most years. In the case of cotton textiles, there was considerable competition in the domestic market as well as in the export market, where it faced strong competition from Hong Kong and India.

In the case of advertising expenditure our results are based on data by different industries in 1966/67 which were available in the Census of Manufacturing Industries for that year.[25] In our model, advertising expenditure was taken as a proportion of value added in each industry for that year. Our results, however, showed that advertising was not significantly related to price–cost margins.

4.3　Conclusions

In this chapter we set out to test various factors (as far as we could within the limitations of the data) which might explain inter-industry differences in profitability. Because of lack of available data, the study had to be restricted to the large-scale manufacturing sector in West Pakistan for the years between 1965 and 1970. Our sample comprised 25 industries and covered over 80 per cent of the large-scale manufacturing sector.

Our main results were:

(a) When price–cost margins are used as an indicator of profitability, concentration was an important factor in explaining differences in profitability between different industries. These results were not altered whether we used gross profits (including fixed costs) or net profits (excluding fixed costs) as our indicator of profitability.

(b) The impact of foreign competition on profitability is signi-

24　See Appendix D, table D.10 for exports as a percentage of total domestic production.
25　See Appendix D, table D.11 for advertising as a percentage of value added of selected industries in West Pakistan.

ficant, although our results clearly show that the rate of effective protection is not the correct measure to see its impact. It is, however, not as strong as the 'Pal–Lewis Model' would expect us to believe. This, we feel, may be because of the linkage between the industrial and trading interests, a product of historical circumstances in the country. Imports worked best as an explanatory variable when specified in an interaction term with concentration, which suggests that arguments connecting imports and profitability may be misleading if they do not take into account the effects of concentration.

(c) Price–cost margins were positively and significantly related to capacity utilisation.

(d) The relationship between price–cost margins and exports was not significant in most cases and was dominated by the performance of the cotton textile and rubber footwear industry.

(e) Advertising expenditure (for 1966/67) had little association with profitability in the period studied.

PART III

FACTORS INFLUENCING
INVESTMENT BEHAVIOUR

5

INVESTMENT BEHAVIOUR AT THE FIRM LEVEL

The purpose of this chapter is to test how far investment by individual firms was related to profits and to sales in Pakistan in the sixties and to explore in particular how the relationship differed between the first and second halves of the decade. These periods correspond to the Second Five Year Plan (1960/61 to 1964/65) and Third Five Year Plan (1965/66 to 1969/70). Between these two periods 'boom' gave way to a 'slowing down' and the availability of loans to firms on favourable terms decreased. These loans had an important influence on the financing of investment and the behaviour of firms in Pakistan, where the institutional framework was very different from that of a market economy of the advanced industrial countries in the West.

We start by setting up a simple model of investment behaviour based on the conventionally accepted profit and accelerator theories to ascertain to what extent they provide an explanation of firms' investment behaviour in the sixties. The model is then modified to take into account the peculiar institutional setting in which firms operated in Pakistan, especially the dependence of firms on loans from financial institutions at favourable terms. This institutional setting, termed the 'corporate environment' has been explained in Chapter 2, and here we investigate the extent of dependence of firms on loans from financial institutions, especially to bring out the differences over the two plan periods. We then go on to discuss the conditions under which external funds can be incorporated in our model as a factor influencing investment behaviour. Finally, the empirical results of the model incorporating external funds are set out and the broad conclusions that can be drawn from our study are put forward.

5.1   A test of the profit and accelerator hypotheses

5.1.1   A simple model of investment behaviour[1]

We start by testing the hypothesis that entrepreneurs investment decisions were principally based on expectations of the future and that the factors determining these expectations can be represented by an index of the level of profits or changes in sales.

That profits influence the decision to invest (Kalecki, 1971; Klein, 1950; Tinbergen, 1938)[2] is based on the assumption that entrepreneurs wish to maximise the present value of expected future profits and will invest according to recent profits since they are likely to be taken as best available indicators of future profits.[3] Another view of the influence of profits on the rate of investment stresses their role as a supply of funds, as well as institutional barriers and entrepreneurial caution with respect to outside finance. Capital market imperfections may lead to limited availability of funds and there may be self-imposed restrictions on the business firm designed to avoid or limit external financing; investment will therefore be governed predominantly by the level of retained earnings the firm can generate. However, the short-run influence of profits would be diminished if profits fluctuated violently. Also, to the extent that imperfections in the capital market are overcome by government or other institutional help in the financing of investment, the long-run dependence on profits will be diminished.

The accelerator principle,[4] rigidly construed, asserts that the change in the capital stock per unit of time (i.e. net investment) is a function of the rate of change in output and is based on the critical assumption that firms, prior to an increase in output, are working at their desired level of capacity utilisation.

1 For a review of econometric studies on investment behaviour for the advanced industrial countries, see Meyer and Kuh (1959), Eisner and Strotz (1963), Kuh (1963), Jorgenson (1971) and Helliwell (1976). Jorgenson provides the most comprehensive survey on recent research on investment behaviour but mainly concentrates on time series studies for individual firms and industries.
2 See Tinbergen and Polak (1950, pp. 166–7), Klein (1950, pp. 27–32 and 34–9) and Kalecki (1971, pp. 6, 106 and 111).
3 Of course, other events may interfere – war, political and economic developments at home and abroad.
4 The earliest formulation of the accelerator principle was given by Clark (1917). In Clark's model desired capital is proportional to output. The accelerator model with an adjustment coefficient equal to unity was rejected by Kuznets (1935), Tinbergen (1938) and Chenery (1952).

Deficiencies in the dynamic adjustment process of the original acceleration principle have been largely cleared up by the flexible accelerator model of investment originated by Chenery (1952) and Koyck (1954). They have elaborated an adjustment process designed to erase gradually a disequilibrium between desired and actual capital stock according to a distributed lag pattern rather than instantaneously according to the rigid original acceleration theory.

Denoting the actual level of capital by K and the desired level by $K^\star$, capital is adjusted towards its desired level by a constant proportion[5] of the difference between desired and actual capital.

$$K_t - K_{t-1} = (1 - \alpha)(K_t^\star - K_{t-1}).$$

The flexible accelerator hypothesis might not work or might work less effectively for any one of the following reasons:

(a) Industries experience wide fluctuations in sales and, in some cases (e.g. jute in Pakistan), large ones.

(b) In the case where firms go in for the production of new products (for example rayon or chemicals) which were previously imported, this would not be reflected in any increase in previous years' sales. However, since our sample of companies used to test the model at the firm level consists for the most part of those engaged in the production of a single product (with the exception of a few conglomerates)[6] this would not significantly influence the testing of the accelerator model.

(c) There may be excess capacity, especially in firms belonging to the intermediate and capital goods industries. We have tried to take this factor into account in our model by adjusting the sales variable by the average ratio of fixed assets to sales over a three-year period. Also, to the extent that the firm's capacity utilisation was determined by the amount of licensed imported raw materials made available to it by the government, the firm might well find it more profitable to increase capacity through new investment rather than to buy imported raw materials at the more expensive bonus rate of exchange. In such cases, the problem of

5 In the Chenery and Koyck model the time structure of the investment process is characterised by a geometric distributed lag function. Actual capital is a distributed lag function of desired capital with geometrically declining weights (See Jorgenson, 1971, p. 1112).

6 Only three out of our 36 firms sample and five out of our 94 firms sample were engaged in more than one industry (See Appendix C, table C.2).

excess capacity would not necessarily act as a constraint to the working of the accelerator hypothesis.

(d) Replacement of obsolescent capital may make up a large part of gross fixed investment, and this item may not be sensitive to sales. In the case of Pakistan, where the existing capital stock at the beginning of the sixties was small in relation to the amount of investment undertaken in the sixties, this would make up a very small portion of total investment.[7]

Model B.1

The above version of the profit and accelerator hypothesis is tested in a model of the following specifications.[8]

$$I_{it}/K_{i(t-1)} = a_0 + a_1 \frac{(S_{i(t-1)} - S_{i(t-2)})}{K_{i(t-1)}} \frac{\bar{K}_i}{\bar{S}_i} + a_2 \frac{(S_{i(t-2)} - S_{i(t-3)})}{K_{i(t-1)}} \cdot$$

$$\frac{\bar{K}_i}{\bar{S}_i} + a_3 \frac{P_{i(t-1)}}{K_{i(t-1)}} + a_4 \frac{P_{i(t-2)}}{K_{i(t-1)}} + a_5 \frac{P_{i(t-3)}}{K_{i(t-1)}} + u_i.$$

where

I_{it} = gross investment of the ith firm measured as the difference in gross fixed assets at cost in year t minus that in $t-1$

$K_{i(t-1)}$ = gross fixed assets at cost of the ith firm at the end of the year $t-1$

$S_{i(t-1)}$ = sales of the ith firm in year $t-1$

$P_{i(t-1)}$ = gross profits (i.e. net pre-tax profits plus depreciation) of the ith firm in year $t-1$

$\dfrac{\bar{K}_i}{\bar{S}_i}$ = three year average of fixed assets and sales of the ith firm

u_i = error term

7 In our model of investment behaviour we did initially include the actual capital stock at the beginning of a period as an independent variable to explain replacement investment as has been done in a number of studies (see Jorgenson and Siebert, 1968, p. 682). The results, however, were insignificant for all years and the variable was therefore dropped from the model.

8 This model is in many ways similar to those used by Meyer and Kuh (1959, pp. 76–9), Eisner (1960), and Kuh (1963, pp. 263–5), for a study of investment based on cross-sectional data for the United States and that of Dimsdale and Glyn (1971, p. 164) for investment in British industry again based on a cross-section of firms.

According to the above model, investment in any period is assumed to correspond to the investment decision of the entrepreneur in some earlier period because of a time lag[9] involved between the decision to invest and the actual investment being carried out. The two main hypotheses which are tested, using the method of least squares, relating to the investment behaviour of firms are as follows:

(1) Current gross fixed investment (in period t) is a linear function of past profits (i.e. profits in periods $t-1$, $t-2$ and $t-3$ of the respective firms).

(2) Current gross fixed investment is a linear function of past changes in sales (i.e. changes in sales in period $t-1$ over those in period $t-2$, and in $t-2$ over those in $t-3$).[10]

Normalisation of data

In the above model, the change in sales variable has to be adjusted both for variation in the firm's capacity utilisation (as discussed earlier), as well as (in a cross-sectional study) across firms for inter-firm differences in capital intensity. This was done by multiplying the change in sales variable by the average ratio of fixed assets to sales in the three preceding years. The coefficient of the change in sales variable has, therefore, to be interpreted taking this adjustment into account. It would be equal to 1 only in the special case where the incremental capital–output ratio (I.C.O.R.) is equal to the average. In order to obtain the I.C.O.R., the coefficient has to be multiplied by the average ratio of fixed assets to sales.

In order to eliminate the effect of size on the relationship between gross fixed investment, profits and change in sales, all these variables were deflated by the stock of fixed assets at the beginning of the year. This would also eliminate heteroscedasticity on the assumption that the standard error of the distur-

9 This time lag would vary depending on the procedure followed to get the investment sanctioned. It would be between one and a half to two years for those involving sanctions and loans by the government or the financial institutions (Durrani, 1966, p. 18) and about a year for those investments for which machinery was imported on bonus and slightly less for investment involving domestically produced machinery.

10 A third lagged change in sales variable was included in preliminary regressions, but was dropped since it never reached significance.

bance term u_{it} would otherwise be proportional to the size of the firm.[11]

5.1.2 Data: composition of the sample and problems with testing the model

The data used to test the model consist of a sample of 39 continuous firms quoted on the K.S.E. for the period 1961–65 and 96 firms for the period 1965–70. Since it was the larger firms which sought public subscription of shares and tried to obtain the status of being included on the K.S.E., our study of investment behaviour at the firm level should only be taken as representative of larger firms in the country.

One major shortcoming of our study is that the data cover investment behaviour only for the period 1962–70 (data for the earlier years were not published by the State Bank). We therefore could not cover the first two years of the Second Five Year Plan. This is indeed unfortunate. In the early sixties, the boom in private industrial investment, especially in the cotton textile and jute industry, appears largely to have been in response to the increase in profits and sales which took place after the introduction of the export bonus scheme in 1959. Moreover, in the first two years of the Second Plan, there were hardly any direct controls over industrial investment.[12]

The other major drawback of the study is that in testing the accelerator hypothesis our figures for sales are in terms of current prices. The sales figures could not be deflated by a price index because in the case of the two major industries, cotton textiles and jute textiles, the existence of the export bonus scheme made it impossible to deflate sales figures, as the proportions of sales in the export market were not known. Our results for the testing of the accelerator hypothesis, especially in our study of investment behaviour for individual years must therefore be interpreted with caution.

11 The size deflator to be used should be one that is not subject to abrupt changes or affected by firms' differences in accounting procedures. On both these counts gross fixed assets is superior to any other alternative measure. It has also been used by Meyer and Kuh (1959, pp. 84–5), Eisner (1960, p. 8), Kuh (1963, pp. 78 and 93) and Dimsdale and Glyn (1971, p. 164).
12 See Section 2.1.1 for details.

5.1.3   Empirical results[13]

Model B.1 was tested for the individual years 1962–70, for the smaller sample of 36 firms for the period 1962–65 and for 1966–70 with the larger sample of 94 firms.[14] The results are given in table 5.1. They clearly show that the change in the value of sales variable was not significant for both samples of firms for all the years covered with the sole exception of 1965, and in fact had a negative sign for a number of years.

The profit variable was also not significant for the period of the Second Plan but it was significant at the 1 per cent level for the last three years of the Third Plan, i.e. 1968 and 1970.[15] There is

13 A number of studies to test the profit hypothesis have been carried out in India to see to what extent it explains investment behaviour at the *industry level*. Prominent among these are Bagchi (1962a and b), Krishnamurty (1964) and Sarkar (1970).

  Bagchi's earlier study (1962a) on investment behaviour for the years 1951–55 was based on cross-sectional analysis across 27 industries and tried to relate investment behaviour to changes in sales and profits after tax in the previous years. Bagchi found that past profits had a significant influence on investment (Ibid., p. 173), although he did not find much support for the change in sales hypothesis. In his later study, covering the period 1951–60, Bagchi (1962b), realising that in his earlier study he had not taken into account differences in sizes of industries, after normalising for size found that the relationship no longer held. He therefore came to the conclusion that there was no systematic relation between investment and profit or changes in sales in the case of public limited companies in India.

  The two other studies of Krishnamurty and Sarkar are both time series analyses and came to the conclusion that there was a significant relationship between investment and profits. They have, however, recently been subjected to criticism by Patnaik (1973, pp. 73–5) who has suggested that both the time series studies suffer from the existence of serial correlation in errors.

14 Out of our original sample of 39 firms, three were left out for the years 1962–65. These were Asbestos Cement, Packages and Chittagong Jute. The reason why they were left out was because their rate of growth of gross fixed assets during 1962–65 was more than double that of the highest figure in the remaining sample. For similar reasons Rana Tractors and Sandoz Ltd, were left out for the years 1966–70. Meyer and Kuh (1959, p. 44) also excluded from their sample those observations which had extremely large rates of growth (which they took as being greater than 50 per cent of gross fixed assets).

15 For the period of the Third Plan we found a high degree of multi-collinearity between the profit variables in the preceding three years. To get over this problem two alternative methods were tried. The first was to drop the profit variable for the years $t-1$ and $t-3$ and choose only profits for the year $t-2$, because in most cases the lag involved in the decision to invest was about two years. The second was to use a weighted profit variable based on a lag pattern, which gave more weight to profits in year $t-2$ and less but equal weight to profits in $t-1$ and $t-3$. The weights used to derive the profit variable were

$$P_{t\star}/K_{t-1} = (0.25 \times P_{t-1}/K_{t-1}) + (0.50 \times P_{t-2}/K_{t-1}) + (0.25 \times P_{t-3}/K_{t-1})$$

Table 5.1 *Results of regression analysis: Model B.1*

Number of firms	Year	Sales change $(t-1)$	Sales change $(t-2)$	Profits $(t-1)$	Profits $(t-2)$	Profits $(t-3)$	Constant term	R^2
36	1962	n.a.	n.a.	0.12 (0.620)	n.a.	n.a.	13.16	0.01
	1963	−0.09 (0.871)	n.a.	0.03 (0.308)	0.02 (0.122)	n.a.	12.01	0.03
	1964	0.07 (0.396)	−0.15 (0.9751)	−0.11 (0.3493)	0.08 (0.320)	0.31 (1.303)	9.76	0.05
	1965	0.18^b (2.151)	0.02 (0.2)	0.07 (0.401)	−0.12 (0.685)	0.05 (0.30)	7.46	0.26
94	1966	n.a.	n.a.	0.03 (0.307)	n.a.	n.a.	11.84	0.00
	1967	0.03 (0.836)	n.a.	—	0.07 (1.238)	—	7.30	0.02
	1968	0.03 (0.34)	−0.02 (0.546)	—	0.24^a (4.900)	—	3.14	0.25
	1969	−0.04 (0.632)	−0.03 (0.391)	—	$0.23^{a\star}$ (2.809)	—	5.94	0.10
	1970	−0.02 (0.479)	−0.004 (0.097)	—	$0.21^{a\star}$ (4.253)	—	3.74	0.18

Note: Figures in parentheses are *t*-ratios.

    —: Indicates that variable was not used in the regression analysis.

 n.a.: Data not available for that year.

[a] Significant at the 1 per cent level.
[b] Significant at the 5 per cent level.
★ Weighted profit variable (see text).

Since the weighted profit variable took into account profits in all preceding years it was thought to be the more appropriate one to use and only its results have been reported. However, using profits in $t-2$ also did not give a significantly different result. Where the profit figure for the year $t-3$ was not available, the weights used were

$$P_t^\star / K_{t-1} = (0.40 \times P_{t-1}/K_{t-1}) + (0.60 \times P_{t-2}/K_{t-1})$$

Slightly different combination of the weights were also tried but the results were almost the same. It would have been preferable to use a more sophisticated lag structure (like the Almon Lag Scheme) but since the routine was not available for calculating the lags we decided to use this approximate method. Nordhaus and Godley (1972) in calculating the effects of cost increases on prices also used a similar approximated-by-hand method as the routine for calculating the lags iteratively had not been written – though they had better independent evidence on their lag structure than we possess (Ibid., p. 882).

some support therefore that profits were significantly associated with investment behaviour in the last three years of the plan, although it must be borne in mind that the explanatory power of the model is still very limited in that the R^2 are very low and indicate that our model explained a very small portion of the variation in the levels of investment between firms.

5.1.4 Pooled data studies

In order to increase the number of observations in our sample (especially for the Second Plan period) and to obtain estimates of the coefficients which were less dependent on the particular year chosen, we decided to pool our cross-sectional data for the years in the Second and Third Plan for which it was possible to do so.[16] It was also hoped that, by pooling the data, we would diminish to some extent the multi-collinearity in the preceding year's profit variable during the Third Plan period.

The results were as follows:

Second Plan period (1963, 1964, 1965)

$$I_t/K_{t-1} = 11.0 + 0.9\alpha_2 - 3.2\alpha_3 - 0.03\, P_{t-2}/K_{t-1} - 0.05\, P_{t-1}/K_{t-1}$$
$$\phantom{I_t/K_{t-1} = 11.0 +} (0.304)\ (1.084)\ (0.355) (0.649)$$

$$- 0.03 \frac{\Delta S_{t-2}}{K_{t-1}} \bar{K}/\bar{S}$$
$$(0.604)$$

Number of observations = 108 $R^2 = 0.03$

Third Plan period (1967, 1968, 1969, 1970)

(i) $I_t/K_{t-1} = 5.64 - 1.91\alpha_2 + 0.36\alpha_3 - 1.86\alpha_4 + 0.10^b P_{t-2}/K_{t-1}$
$$\phantom{(i)\ I_t/K_{t-1} = 5.64} (1.054)\ (0.192)\ (1.022)\ (1.955)$$

$$+ 0.09^c P_{t-1}/K_{t-1} + 0.02(\Delta S_{t-2}/K_{t-1})\,(\bar{K}/\bar{S})$$
$$(1.487) (0.3621)$$

Number of observations = 376 $R^2 = 0.12$

16 In order to use the maximum number of firms in the sample in the pooled data study, we used only one variable to represent the change in sales, which for the first years in the two samples (i.e. 1963 and 1967) is the change in sales in the year $t-1$ and for the others for the year $t-2$. We also ran the model with a smaller sample (i.e. excluding 1963 and 1967) but including the change in sales in both years $t-1$ and $t-2$ – but they were still not significant for both years.

(ii) $I_t/K_{t-1} = 5.27 - 1.8\alpha_2 + 0.7\alpha_3 - 1.6\alpha_4 + 0.20^a P\star/K_{t-1}$
$\qquad$ (0.971) (0.384) (0.853) (6.632)
$\qquad + 0.001(\Delta S\star/K_{t-1})(\bar{K}/\bar{S})$
$\qquad$ (0.085)

Number of observations = 376 $\qquad R^2 = 0.11$

$\star$ weighted profit and sales variable (see text)
where $\alpha = 1$ for an observation in year i, $i = 2,3,4$
$\qquad = 0$ otherwise.

Note: Figures in parentheses are t-ratios
[a] significant at the 1 per cent level
[b] significant at the 5 per cent level
[c] significant at the 10 per cent level

The results for the pooled data study are quite similar to our individual years study. In the three years of the Second Plan for which we pooled data, the results are insignificant for both the profit as well as the change in sales variable. For the period of the Third Plan the previous two years' profits are significant at the 5 and 10 per cent levels. However, the influence of multicollinearity between the preceding year's profits, although diminished, is not completely removed and when we use the weighted profit variable it is significant at the 1 per cent level. The change in sales variable, either if we use t-2 figures, or the weighted sales variable,[17] is in both cases insignificant.

5.1.5 Average data studies

Our results for Model B.1, both for the individual years as well as the pooled data study seem to suggest that the systematic influence on investment in any particular year of the three preceding years' profits and changes in sales is quite weak. This is also true for those years in which the profit variable is significant, in that the explanatory power of the model is very limited – the R^2 are very low.

As an alternative test, we tried relating average profits and change in sales figures for a number of years to investment, also over a number of years. The justification for this procedure is that (a) one captures the profit or sales climate of a plan period, a climate which, in part, may have been anticipated where, for

---

17 The weights used to derive the weighted sales variable are the same as those for the profit variable.

example, changes in government policy were known or could be foreseen, and that one relates investment to that climate and (b) that investment decisions tended to be taken with respect to a plan period or at least a run of years within the framework of the government's investment schedule. The objection to the procedure is that causation may flow within the period from investment to profits and sales, as well as the other way round, so giving rise to 'simultaneity', but steps were taken to diminish this difficulty.

The model was specified in the following form:

Model B.2

$$\frac{\Sigma I_i}{K_{i(t-1)}} = a_0 + a_1 \frac{\Sigma P_i}{K_{i(t-1)}} + a_2 \frac{\Delta S_i}{K_{i(t-1)}} \cdot \frac{\bar{K}_i}{\bar{S}_i} + u_i$$

where

ΣI_i = sum of investments of the ith firm for the years 1962 to 1965 (or 1966 to 1970)

ΣP_i = sum of profits of the ith firm for the year 1961 to 1964 (or 1965 to 1968)

ΔS_i = change in sales of the ith firm between 1964 and 1961 (or 1968 and 1965)

$K_{i(t-1)}$ = gross fixed assets at cost of the ith firm in 1961 (or 1965)

$\bar{K}_i/\bar{S}_i$ = four-year average of gross fixed assets and sales of the ith firm, i.e. from 1961–64 (or 1965–68)

u_i = error term

The hypothesis is that a 'representative' firm which earned higher average profits over the plan period would undertake a greater amount of investment both because it would act as a greater inducement to invest, as well as making available to the firm more internal funds to finance this investment.[18]

With the increase in sales measured over the last few years, the accelerator hypothesis can now also be used to see whether during the period of greater government stringency, especially in the years of the Third Plan, firms found it more difficult to increase their capital stock in response to increases in sales than

18 Patnaik (1973, p. 200) used a very similar model to test the profit hypothesis for three five-year periods between 1951 and 1965 for India, based on cross-section of industries data. Singh and Whittington (1968) also test the relationship between growth and profitability of firms between 1948 and 1960, divided between two six-year periods.

they did in the period of the Second Plan when government controls were almost negligible.

In order to minimise the effects of a simultaneous equation bias in testing investment behaviour in this form (i.e. of aggregating data over a number of years) figures for profits and changes in sales were not taken over the entire plan period. Assuming a two-year gestation[19] period, our figures for profits and sales taken in the present form would be affected for only one year by the investment undertaken during the previous two years (i.e. 1964 and 1968 respectively in the two periods).[20] For the rest of the period our figures for both profits and sales would be independent of the investment undertaken in the period. By treating the problem in this way, although we do not remove completely the effects of investment over the period on profits and sales, its actual impact is restricted to only one year and the problem of a simultaneous equation bias in the model is to a large extent removed.

5.1.6   Results

The results of Model B.2 are given in table 5.2 for the years covered in the Second Plan and the period of the Third Plan. Because of the existence of multi-collinearity between the profit and sales variables during the Second Plan, the simple regression of each of these variables with investment is given separately.[21] Besides giving the results for our sample of all firms, we have also given separately the results for the cotton textile industry as well as for all firms besides textiles. The main points which emerge from the average data study are:

(i) Both profit and sales variables are now significant for our all

19 The gestation period is longer in Pakistan for two reasons. Firstly, all machinery has to be imported and is normally shown as an addition to fixed assets on the company's accounts, once the loan for it has been secured from the financial institutions and the order placed with the foreign manufacturer. Secondly, firms are given a six month 'trial period' after the machinery has been installed in order to remove any snags etc. in the production process. During this period the firms tend to show a minimum of output in order to avoid tax.

20 In order to check whether the inclusion of the profit figure and change in sales for that year were making any significant difference to our result we re-ran the model excluding the figures for that year. The overall results were in fact very similar.

21 Since we are testing the profit and accelerator hypothesis as two different explanations of investment behaviour, this will not change the interpretation of the Model B.2.

Table 5.2 *Results of regression analysis : Model B.2*

Industry	Firms (number)		Profit variable	Change in sales variable	Constant term	R^2
			1961–65			
All firms	36	(i)	0.14^b (1.939)	—	45.18	0.10
		(ii)	—	0.29^b (1.725)	51.86	0.08
		(iii)	0.11 (0.983)	0.18 (1.298)	42.39	0.13
Cotton textiles	11	(i)	0.10 (0.322)	—	50.62	0.01
		(ii)	—	1.27^a (2.792)	38.47	0.46
		(iii)	-0.28 (1.10)	1.56^a (2.999)	58.71	0.53
Other industries besides textiles★	16	(i)	0.17^b (2.191)	—	28.51	0.26
		(ii)	—	0.30 (1.073)	42.56	0.08
		(iii)	0.17^b (1.803)	0.09 (0.310)	25.16	0.26
			1965–70			
All firms	94		0.25^a (5.451)	0.32^a (3.379)	21.24	0.30
Cotton textiles	29		0.66^b (1.765)	0.15^a (5.248)	-6.51	0.54
Other industries besides textiles★	47		0.21^a (3.368)	0.41^a (2.523)	27.53	0.28

Note: Figures in parentheses are *t*-ratios.
— indicates that variable was not used in the regression analysis.

★ Excludes cotton textiles, jute textiles and other textiles.
^{a} significant at the 1 per cent level.
^{b} significant at the 5 per cent level.

firms sample during the two plan periods but both are *more significant* during the period of the Third Plan, as compared to the Second Plan period. Whereas both variables are significantly related with investment at the five per cent level for the Second Plan, during the Third Plan they are significant at the one per cent level.

(ii) The results for the firms belonging to the cotton textile industry are slightly different to the overall sample results. In this case, the profit variable is *not* significant at all during the Second Plan period whereas the sales variable is significant at the one per cent level. During the Third Plan, both the profit and sales variables are significant at the five per cent level.

(iii) In the case of the sample of firms belonging to other industries besides textiles for the Second Plan, the results are opposite to those of the textile industry. In this case the profit variable is significant at the five per cent level (as for our all firms sample) but the sales variable is not. For the Third Plan, both profits and sales are significant at the one per cent level.

The main conclusion that emerges from the average data study is that during the Third Plan period, whether we took the all firms sample, or that for cotton textiles, or for firms in other industries besides textiles, both profits and change in sales were significantly associated with investment behaviour of firms during this period. The results for the Second Plan are not only less significant but also display inter-industry variations.

5.2   Dependence on foreign exchange loans as a further explanation

5.2.1   The corporate environment

We now turn to the changing characteristics of the 'corporate environment' which have been discussed in detail in Chapter 2. From the viewpoint of the investor, these were:

(1) If he got the 'official' approval to undertake a particular investment project he could obtain the *foreign exchange component* of the investment as a loan from Pakistan Industrial Credit and Investment Corporation (P.I.C.I.C.) or Industrial Development Bank of Pakistan (I.D.B.P.) or from the Provincial governments (if the loan was small) at the *official exchange rate*. He could also apply in certain cases for a loan for the rupee component of the investment from these two financial institutions but this was a very small percentage of the total loans sanctioned by these institutions.[22]

22 During the period 1960–70 the rupee loans amounted to about 5 per cent of total loans sanctioned in the case of P.I.C.I.C. and about 22 per cent in the case of I.D.B.P. (Source: P.I.C.I.C., and I.D.B.P. Annual Reports.)

For a firm which was able to get these loans, there were two main advantages. Firstly, it could now import machinery at the 'official' exchange rate which was two to two and a half times below the market rate. Secondly, it would also have the added advantage of getting the loans at the very low rates of interest charged by these institutions.

(2) Without a loan, the firm could either import machinery on bonus vouchers at the market rate or buy machinery from commercial importers who had also imported it on bonus. The firm might do this if it felt that either the time taken for getting the loans from the institutions was too long,[23] or the chances of its getting the loan were bleak because it had already received its share of loans or because the financial institutions were themselves facing a shortage of foreign exchange to lend.

(3) There were also 'direct'[24] government controls regulating the industries in which one could invest, but the enforcement of these controls varied over the two plan periods. In the Second Plan, investors were, on the whole, free to invest in any industry, but during the Third Plan (except for the two years from mid 1966 to mid 1968) they could invest only in those industries which were export-oriented or saved foreign exchange or were based mainly on domestic raw materials.[25] This was because of the severe foreign exchange shortage felt by the government during this period.

The advantages accruing to a firm getting a loan from P.I.C.I.C. and I.D.B.P. to finance its investment must plainly have been very great both in reducing the costs of an investment project and reducing the importance of retained profits as a source of finance.

5.2.2 Availability of foreign exchange loans

A detailed exercise was therefore undertaken to establish the exact amount of borrowings by individual firms from P.I.C.I.C. and I.D.B.P. for our smaller sample of 39 firms for the period 1961–70. The information was collected from various agencies

23 As mentioned earlier, Durrani (1966, p. 18) estimated this as being between one and a half to two years.
24 By 'direct' controls is meant the government having the power of not giving permission to invest in a particular industry (see Section 2.1.1).
25 This is discussed in Section 7.1.

and official publications,[26] and the results of this investigation are given in table 5.3.

In the Second Plan for the years 1961–65, P.I.C.I.C. and I.D.B.P. financed 32.8 per cent of the total gross fixed investment undertaken by the 39 firms. If we include loans by Provincial governments and foreign investors (including direct foreign investment) the figures come to over 40 per cent. If we were to see the results only for the domestically owned companies (30 out of our firm sample of 39), the figure comes to about 38 per cent of total gross investment. In the case of foreign owned firms or those with a large share of foreign investment, there were no loans from P.I.C.I.C., or I.D.B.P., except for one firm (i.e. Packages Limited).

Our figures, however, refer only to the foreign exchange loans[27] which were made available to the firm. There is evidence[28] that

26 This information was collected from various agencies and official publications as follows:

(1) List of all loans disbursed by P.I.C.I.C. to individual firms during the period 1961–70 were collected by the author from the bank.

(2) Since I.D.B.P. would not disclose the amount of loans given to individual firms, an indirect method was used

(a) for the Second Plan period the list of loans sanctioned to firms by the I.D.B.P. was published by the Investment Promotion and Supplies Department (I.P.&S., 1966a)

(b) for the Third Plan period, figures for loans sanctioned by I.D.B.P. to firms in West Pakistan were collected from the I.P.&S. Department.

(c) since the I.P.&S. Department would not disclose investments in East Pakistan during the Third Plan, estimates were made from the balance sheets of companies, as published by the State Bank, which also summarise the annual reports of the company. Since these were only summary reports, our figures for I.D.B.P. loans could be a slight underestimate.

(3) For the Second Plan, figures for foreign investment and loans from the Provincial Governments were obtained from the same source as 2(a). However, these figures were not available for the Third Plan period but loans from the Provincial Governments were almost non-existent during this period. (See Section 2.3.)

27 We took only the foreign exchange loans because it was not possible to establish the amount of Rupee loans given to the firms by I.D.B.P., for either the Second or Third Plan. Although this was possible in the case of P.I.C.I.C., in order to maintain consistency they were therefore not included. However, as pointed out earlier they were only 5 per cent of total loans in the case of P.I.C.I.C., and about 20 per cent in the case of I.D.B.P., over the period.

28 The actual figure for the foreign exchange component of *all* investment projects actually implemented came out as 56.8 per cent and for cotton textiles and jute the figure is around 60 per cent. (Source: Calculated from I.P.&S., 1966b.) However, since this includes both new plants as well as those already in production we decided to take a slightly lower figure of 50 per cent as all our firms were already in production during this period.

Table 5.3 *Dependence on borrowed capital for financing investment (sample : 39 firms)*

1961–65 (Second Plan period)		
A. *All firms (39)*	*Amount* (Rs lacs)	*Per cent*
Total investment (rupee + foreign exchange component)	5090.0	100.0
Borrowing (foreign exchange only)		
1. P.I.C.I.C.	1258.1	24.7
2. I.D.B.P.	412.2	8.1
3. Provincial Government	9.1	0.2
4. Foreign investors	412.7	8.1
B. *Domestically owned firms (30)*		
Total investment (rupee + foreign exchange component)	4280	100.0
Borrowing (foreign exchange only)		
1. P.I.C.I.C.	1093.6	25.5
2. I.D.B.P.	412.2	9.6
3. Provincial Government	9.1	0.2
4. Foreign investors	96.9	2.3
C. *Foreign owned firms or with large share of foreign investment (9)*		
Total investment (rupee + foreign exchange component)	810.0	100.0
Borrowing (foreign exchange only)		
1. P.I.C.I.C. and I.D.B.P. (one firm only)	164.5	20.3
2. Foreign investors	315.8	39.0
1965–70 (Third Plan period)		
A. *All firms (39)*		
Total investment (rupee + foreign exchange component)	6056	100.0
Borrowing (foreign exchange only)		
1. P.I.C.I.C.	600.2	9.9
2. I.D.B.P.	223.6	3.7
B. *Domestically owned companies (30)*		
Total investment (rupee + foreign exchange component)	4492	100.0
Borrowing (foreign exchange only)		
1. P.I.C.I.C.	593.5	13.2
2. I.D.B.P.	217.0	4.8

Source: See n. 26, p. 124.

half the total investment typically consisted of imported plant and machinery. Thus, the loans from these financial institutions provided almost 70 per cent of the foreign exchange component of investment in our sample during the Second Plan.

For the Third Plan, figures were only available for P.I.C.I.C. and I.D.B.P. loans. The results showed that there was a substantial decline in the investment financed from loans from these institutions. It was only 13.6 per cent as compared to the figure of 32.8 per cent during the Second Plan period. In the case of domestically owned companies, 18.0 per cent of total investment was financed through loans from these institutions as compared to almost double this figure during the Second Plan.

Our study, therefore, clearly brings out the fall in loans made available to firms in the Third Plan as compared to the Second Plan period. The main reason for this was the slowing down in the Third Plan of foreign aid which was the source of funds for both P.I.C.I.C. and I.D.B.P.

5.2.3 Incorporating foreign exchange loans in a model of investment behaviour

In looking at external finance as a determinant of investment behaviour, two important considerations must be kept in mind. The first is that, given the system of multiple exchange rates and the fact that loans from the two financial institutions P.I.C.I.C. and I.D.B.P. were available at the official overvalued exchange rate, firms would in all cases have preferred to finance their investment from these funds rather than from any other source of borrowing, and rather than from their own internal funds so long as the risk involved in extra gearing were not too great.[29] The second point to be considered is the *extent of availability* of these loans from these financial institutions. Since the latter point, i.e. availability of funds, differed in the two plan periods, in trying to incorporate external finance in our model of investment behaviour at the firm level we must take into account these changed conditions and hence look at each of the plan periods separately.

During the period of the Second Plan, it could be convincingly

29 The advantages accruing from these loans have been discussed earlier (see Section 2.3).

argued that domestically controlled firms in our sample[30] in most cases were not constrained by the availability of foreign exchange loans from P.I.C.I.C. and I.D.B.P., since these were quite readily available. In the case of those firms, therefore, whose major investments were financed from funds from these institutions, it could be argued that, subject to a general shift in profitability, causation was from investment decision to external finance, i.e. firms took for granted that they could get foreign exchange loans on the prevailing advantageous terms; and, with this as common ground, individual firms responded to profits or changes in sales to determine their levels of investment. It was, therefore, decided to break up the sample of firms and to see whether causation ran this way for the domestically controlled firms who had financed the major portion of their foreign exchange component from loans from these two financial institutions.

During the period of the Third Plan, our study of the sample of firms had clearly shown that firms were able to get far less in loans to finance their investment from these financial institutions. In these conditions, foreign exchange loans available to firms could be incorporated into our model of investment behaviour as the *minimum* amount of investment that these firms would undertake. Moreover, since almost all the firms were in the same category, i.e. far less than 40 per cent of their industrial investment was financed from these loans, we did not have to break up our sample of firms into any sub-sample as had to be done for the earlier period.

For the period of the Third Plan, therefore, foreign exchange loans could be incorporated as an independent variable in our average data model as follows:

Model B.3

$$\sum_{1966}^{1970} I_i / K_{i(t-1)} = a_0 + a_1 \sum_{1965}^{1968} \frac{P_i}{K_{i(t-1)}} + a_2 \frac{\Delta S_i}{K_{i(t-1)}} \cdot \frac{\bar{K}_i}{\bar{S}_i}$$

$$+ a_3 \text{ F.E.L.} / K_{i(t-1)} + u_i$$

30 This is especially true here since these were amongst the largest firms as well as belonging in most cases to the monopoly houses. This is not to suggest, however, that *all* firms would have found no difficulty in getting loans. As we have pointed out earlier (Section 2.3), P.I.C.I.C., loans were only available for large projects and in the case of I.D.B.P. smaller firms would have had to compete with each other.

where

ΣI_i = sum of investment of the ith firm for the years 1966–70

ΣP_i = sum of profits of the ith firm for the years 1965–68

ΔS_i = change in sales of the ith firm between 1968 and 1965

$K_{i(t-1)}$ = gross fixed assets at cost of the ith firm in 1965

$\bar{K}/\bar{S}_i$ = four-year average of gross fixed assets and sales of the ith firm, i.e. 1965–68

$F.E.L.$ = increase in long-term liabilities (excluding debentures) of the ith firm during the period between 1965 and 1970. This was taken as a proxy for foreign exchange loans from these financial institutions during this period

u_i = error term

5.3   Empirical results

5.3.1   Second Five Year Plan

For the period of the Second Plan for the years for which data were available, we re-ran the model separately for two sub-samples. The first consisted of 29 domestically owned companies since these as we have seen were the principal receivers of loans from P.I.C.I.C. and I.D.B.P. We then further broke down this sample to those companies which were dependent on more than 40 per cent of their total investment on loans sanctioned from these two institutions. In each case we regressed the profit and sales variable separately on investment and got the following results.

(i) All domestically owned companies

(a) $$\sum_{1962}^{1965} I_{it}/K_{i(t-1)} = 32.4 + 0.30^a \sum_{1962}^{1964} P_{it}/K_{i(t-1)}$$
$$(3.202)$$

$$R^2 = 0.28$$

(b) $$\sum_{1962}^{1965} I_{it}/K_{i(t-1)} = 51.7 + 0.34^b (\Delta S_t/K_{i(t-1)} \cdot (\bar{K}/\bar{S}))$$ $R^2 = 0.14$
$$(2.063)$$

Number of observations = 29.

(ii) Firms with more than 40 per cent of investment financed from P.I.C.I.C. and I.D.B.P.

(a) $\sum_{1962}^{1965} I_{it}/K_{i(t-1)} = 28.4 + 0.30^a \sum_{1962}^{1964} P_{it}/K_{i(t-1)}$

$$(4.758) \qquad\qquad R^2 = 0.61$$

(b) $\sum_{1962}^{1965} I_{it}/K_{i(t-1)} = 52.2 + 0.38^b (\Delta S_{it}/K_{i(t-1)})(\bar{K}/\bar{S})$ $R^2 = 0.22$

Number of observations = 16.

Note: Figures in parentheses are *t*-ratios
[a] significant at the 1 per cent level.
[b] significant at the 5 per cent level.

Our results show that for domestically owned companies the profit variable is now significant at the 1 per cent level as compared to the earlier result, when it was significant at the 5 per cent level. However, the best results for the profit hypothesis are obtained from our smaller sample of companies which financed all their foreign exchange component of investment through foreign exchange loans from P.I.C.I.C. and I.D.B.P. For the sales variable the results are not significantly different as compared to the earlier result for the all firms sample.

For those firms, therefore, that were dependent on borrowings from financial institutions for the bulk of their foreign exchange component of investment, we do find that there is support for the profit hypothesis discussed earlier. It seems that in this case the relative amounts that the firms invested were influenced by the profits earned by the different firms. This influence of higher profits could have been both as a source of funds for the rupee component of the investment undertaken as well as an inducement to invest from the demand side, i.e. expectation of earning high profits in the future.

5.3.2 Third Plan

The results of incorporating external finance in our Model B.1 and Model B.3 for the period of the Third Plan are given in table 5.4. In all cases, external finance is significantly related with investment at the one per cent level and the inclusion of external finance greatly increases the explanatory power of Model B.1 as well as of Model B.3 (in comparison with Model B.2) for the same period.

Table 5.4 *Results of regression analysis incorporating external finance*

Model B.1 (number of firms = 94):

Year	Sales change $(t-1)$	Sales change $(t-2)$	Profits $(t-1)$	Profits $(t-2)$	External finance	Constant term	R^2
1966	n.a.	n.a.	0.05 (0.753)	—	1.00^a (9.042)	8.84	0.47
1967	0.03 (0.768)	n.a.	0.06 (1.193)	—	0.64^a (4.926)	7.26	0.23
1968	0.04 (1.21)	-0.02 (0.385)	$0.22\star^a$ (4.594)	—	0.36^a (2.398)	3.65	0.29
1969	-0.05 (1.002)	0.02 (0.305)	$0.23\star^a$ (3.480)	—	0.88^a (7.491)	3.99	0.45
1970	0.01 (0.433)	0.01 (0.403)	$0.21\star^a$ (4.373)	—	0.83^a (4.429)	3.19	0.33

Pooled data (number of observations = 376)

(i) $I_t/K_{t-1} = 5.34 - 1.1\alpha_2 - 0.9\alpha_3 - 1.74\alpha_4 + 0.08^c P_{t-1}/K_{t-1}$
$\qquad\qquad\quad (0.693)\,(0.551)\,(1.101)(1.609)$

$\qquad + 0.09^b P_{t-2}/K_{t-1} + 0.02(\Delta S_{t-2}/K_{t-1})\,(\bar{K}/\bar{S}) + 0.73^a F.E.L./K_{t-1}$
$\qquad\quad (2.039) \qquad\qquad (0.698) \qquad\qquad\qquad (10.86)$

$\qquad\qquad\qquad\qquad\qquad\qquad\qquad\qquad\qquad\qquad\qquad R^2 = 0.33$

(ii) $I_t/K_{t-1} = 5.0 - 0.83\alpha_2 - 0.71\alpha_3 - 1.4\alpha_4 + 0.19^a P\star/K_{t-1}$
$\qquad\qquad\qquad (0.521)\,(0.439)\,(0.903)(7.126)$

$\qquad\quad - 0.020\Delta S\star_t/K_{t-1} + 0.73^a F.E.L./K_{t-1} \qquad\qquad R^2 = 0.33$
$\qquad\qquad (0.876) \qquad\qquad (10.94)$

5.3.3 Investment behaviour of firms – an interpretation of our results

The major conclusions which emerge from our study at the firm level are as follows:

1. The influence of profits on investment by firms is difficult to pick up for the individual years (especially during the Second Plan period), but when we aggregate the figures for profits and investment over the plan period there is a significant relationship between them.

In the period of the Second Plan, profits appear to have influenced the inducement to invest mainly from the demand side whereas during the Third Plan it seems to have been influenced

Table 5.4 (*continued*)

Model B.3

Industry	Number of firms in sample	Profit variable	Changes in sales variable	Foreign exchange loans	Constant term	R^2
All	94	0.21[a] (6.030)	0.24[a] (3.212)	1.31[a] (7.931)	20.36	0.59
Cotton textiles	29	0.51[a] (3.898)	0.19[a] (2.482)	0.63[a] (2.474)	−0.21	0.63
Others besides textiles	47	0.20[a] (3.933)	0.20[b] (1.505)	1.36[a] (5.394)	28.12	0.57

Note: Figures in parentheses are *t*-ratios
— indicates that variable was not used in the regression analysis.
n.a. Data not available for that year.

[a] significant at the 1 per cent level
[b] significant at the 5 per cent level
[c] significant at the 10 per cent level
★ weighted profit and sales variable
Where $\alpha = 1$ for observation in year i,
$\quad i = 2, 3, 4$
$\quad = 0$, otherwise.

mainly through the supply side – as a source of funds to finance investment.

The reason for this lies in the peculiar institutional environment in which firms operated in Pakistan and the changing availability of loans at the official 'overvalued' exchange rate from the financial institutions. When these funds were readily available during the period of the Second Plan, the influence of profits on investment was diminished. However, for those firms for which finance was not a constraint during that period, we found that profits were significantly related to investment, indicating their importance from the demand side in influencing investment undertaken by these firms.

However, during the period of the Third Plan, profits were significantly related to investment when all firms are included in the analysis. The availability of loans from the financial institutions fell as foreign aid was cut and internal funds became the major source of funds for investment. This appears to explain why we find that profits were far more important in explaining investment than in the earlier period.

2. Our testing of the influence of the change in sales variable on investment was severely hampered because we could not adjust our sales figure for price changes and because the bonus on exports varied over the years, so that changes in sales values did not necessarily mean changes in sales volume.

The influence of year to year changes in prices would, however, be diminished but not eliminated when we look at changes in sales from beginning to end of a plan period. Here we find that changes in the sales variable were significantly related to investment although the relationship was more significant for the Third Plan period than the Second. This suggests that the more severe controls on investment by the government during the Third Plan did not significantly constrain investment of firms in our sample. In fact, our sample of firms mostly belonged to industries which were not subject to these restrictions.[31] Moreover, the firms quoted on the stock exchange were among the larger ones and would have found it easier to get permission to invest than smaller sized firms in the industry.

31 Since most of the firms in our sample belonged to either the cotton textile or jute manufacturing or other consumer good industries, they were not subject to 'direct' government controls. (See table 7.1 for the list of industries which were subject to controls during this period.)

6

INVESTMENT BEHAVIOUR OF MONOPOLY HOUSES

We now turn from the investment behaviour of the firm to the investment behaviour of monopoly houses in the large-scale manufacturing sector in the sixties. The manufacturing sector was dominated by a small number of monopoly houses, as we have seen in Chapter 2, and in these cases the investment decision is taken *not* at the level of the individual firm under its control but by the monopoly house for the group as a whole. The group, with its centralised family control, functions as a single coordinated organisation even though the corporate units under its control are separate legal entities.

This chapter starts with an explanation of why the monopoly house and not the individual firm is the unit of decision making in the corporate sector and looks at the way in which profits and the availability of cheap foreign exchange loans influenced investment decisions during the period of the sixties. A simple model of investment behaviour taking into account these factors is empirically tested for monopoly houses comprising firms which were quoted on the stock exchange and engaged predominantly in the manufacturing sector. The exercise was then enlarged to see to what extent the size of monopoly houses, with fixed assets taken as a measure of their economic power, influenced their growth and access to foreign exchange loans during this period.

6.1 Monopoly house as the decision-making unit

There are two main reasons why the monopoly house and not the individual firm is the unit for decision making in the corporate sector.

Firstly, in the corporate environment in which the monopoly house operates 'power, influence and connections' play a vital role in determining the amount of investment which it can undertake and these are exercised at the level of the monopoly house and not at the level of the firm. Secondly, the monopoly house can and does move its funds amongst the different firms under its control. The group is engaged in a range of activities from manufacturing to trading and banking and insurance, and in deciding its future investment policy it is guided not only by the 'expected' profits in a particular firm or sector but by the comparative expected profitability amongst the different firms under its control.[1] If the monopoly house is to be likened to the conventional profit maximiser then it is trying to maximise profit not for any individual firm but for all firms under its control.

This is done in various ways. Firms under the control of the monopoly house will invest in shares of other firms in the group or firms will make loans to or take loans from other firms in the control of the monopoly house.[2] Evidence of how this was done is now available from the Report of the Chemical Consultant (1972) on firms which were previously under the control of the monopoly houses and were nationalised by the government in February 1972. For example, Steel Corporation of Pakistan, a company belonging to Fancy Group, had given loans to three other companies of the group (namely, Pakistan Industries Limited, Steel Sales Limited and Industrial Investment Limited). At the same time, it had taken loans from four companies of the group (these being Industrial Cleaning and Services Limited, Management Corporation Limited, Share Trading Company and Pakistan Fisheries Limited). In the report, it was further stated that whereas the firm itself (i.e. Steel Corporation of Pakistan) was facing an 'acute cash shortage', it had a net sum of Rs 1.4 million owed to it by companies belonging to the Fancy Group.

Similarly, Hyeson Steel Mills, belonging to the Hyeson Group had made investments of the sum of Rs 12.4 million in shares of other companies in the group. Similarly it had given out as loans Rs 4.8 million to seven companies belonging to the Hyeson Group and had taken loans amounting to Rs 3.5 million from four companies of the group.[3]

1 The monopoly house or the ordinary firm may of course both look outside their existing field of activities when considering where to expand, though there is a presumption they will know best how to make profits in the field where they already have experience.

2 In some cases the groups had created a separate fund for this purpose for which loans were made to different firms under its control. (For example there was the Saigol Family Loan for the Saigol Group of companies. See Balance Sheets of companies controlled by the Saigol Group.)

3 The seven companies to which it had given loans were Hyesons Agriculture

The movement of funds amongst different companies (which are separate legal entities) brings out the importance of studying investment behaviour of the monopoly house *as a whole* rather than separately for its individual firms.

6.2 Factors influencing investment behaviour of monopoly houses[4]

6.2.1 Profit hypothesis

At the firm level, we tested the hypothesis that entrepreneurs' investment decisions were based on expectations of the future and that the factors determining these expectations could be represented by an index of the level of profits or changes in sales. One of the major shortcomings of this model[5] was that it would not pick up demand signals when a new field of profitable investment was opened up since these would not be reflected in either increases of profits or sales of the firm's products. Examples of developments which changed profitability in existing and new industries are shown in table 6.1.

Since import substitution induced by government measures was one of the major stimuli to industrial investment, especially in the early sixties, our inability to pick out this factor was a serious shortcoming in our study at the firm level.

At the monopoly house level we can try to take this factor into account. Our data for the different firms under the control of a

and Chemicals Ltd, Electric Lamp Manufacturing of Pakistan Ltd, Hyeson Commercial and Industrial Corporations Ltd, Tobacco International Ltd, Amalgamated Mines Ltd, General Investments Ltd, and National Steel of Pakistan. Companies from which it had taken loans were Hilal Tanneries Ltd, Union Cold Storage Ltd, Hyeson Sugar Mills and Mack Trucks of Pakistan.

4 Ghose (1974) has carried out a detailed study on the investment behaviour of monopoly houses in India. He has tried to show that the way in which the monopoly houses try to maximise their share of fixed assets in the economy is through the 'pre-emption of investment opportunities, i.e. the reservation of investment areas by the monopolist in excess of its own requirements' (op. cit., p. 1868). In our study we did not come across any instances of the non-utilisation of investment licences. This was principally because, given the large difference between the official and market rate of foreign exchange, it was far more profitable for them to carry out the investment.

5 This model is set out in Section 5.1.1.

Table 6.1 *Change in profitability in the manufacturing sector*

Industry	A. Result of government policy	B. Spontaneous economic changes (e.g. income, tastes, etc.)
A. Existing industry Ex. (i) Sugar	De-control of price of sugar in early sixties.	
(ii) Cotton textiles	Introduction of the export bonus scheme in 1959.	Large increase in agricultural incomes because of the 'green revolution' in the late sixties.
B. New industry Ex. (i) Chemical	Ban or very high tariffs on imports.	

monopoly house shows that in most cases[6] they reacted to the stimulus of demand for new products by setting up new companies, and we can find separate data on investment by the monopoly house in its existing and new companies.[7] We would, therefore, expect past profitability as an index of a monopoly house's investment decision to be extremely weak in a period of time when the monopoly house was diversifying into new products and this was forming the major part of its new investment.

This, however, is to see the impact of profits on investment only from the demand side. To the extent that the monopoly

6 The only exceptions we came across were the Saigol and Adamjee group who in certain cases expanded into new industries through their existing major companies, Kohinoor Industries (textiles, sugar, insecticides and engineering) and Adamjee Industries (textiles, paper and board and chemicals). However, for their major investment in the sixties, which was in the rayon industry, the Saigol group set up a separate company (Kohinoor Rayon Ltd) and when the Adamjee group went into a sugar industry it also set up a separate company (Adamjee Sugar Mills).

7 One reason why monopoly houses expanded in this manner could be because the new firms had a high gearing ratio, mainly because of the large dependence on external finance from the financial institutions. The monopoly house would not like to increase the risk to its existing firms by increasing the overall gearing ratio and therefore preferred to set up a new firm. (For a detailed discussion, see Patnaik, 1973, pp. 38-93.)

house's total retained profits influence its capacity to finance its investment plans, profits are also important from the supply side. However, the dependence of the monopoly house on its retained profits will be diminished if it can rely on external sources, principally the financial institutions, for loans to finance its investment. If these loans are readily available, the importance of retained profits will be reduced as the principal source of finance for investment.

6.2.2 Foreign exchange loans from financial institutions

The advantages which accrued from obtaining a foreign exchange loan from either P.I.C.I.C. or I.D.B.P. have been discussed in Chapter 2 and the conditions under which they could be incorporated in our model of investment behaviour at the firm level were discussed in Chapter 5.

In order to see the dependence of monopoly houses on foreign exchange loans to finance their investment, an exercise similar to the one carried out for our sample of continuous quoted companies, based on the same sources, was undertaken. Each monopoly house consists of all the quoted firms in the manufacturing sector under its control.[8]

The results of this exercise are given in table 6.2, where we have also given a breakdown by size[9] of the monopoly houses. There are two major differences between these results and the ones for the sample of quoted companies.

Firstly, the foreign exchange loan component of investment is higher for the monopoly houses (44.5%) as compared to the continuous firms sample (35.1%) during the period of the Second Plan. Also this dependence is far greater in the case of the smaller monopoly houses as compared to the larger and medium ones.[10]

8 The choice of monopoly houses and data limitations are discussed in Section 6.2.4.
9 The size of the monopoly house is represented by the total assets of *all* companies in the manufacturing sector (i.e. including non-quoted companies) under its control in 1970. (See Appendix B, table B.1 for a list of monopoly houses by size.)
10 There were two reasons for this. Firstly, the smaller groups mainly did not diversify into new industries and mostly expanded capacities of existing firms (normally in the same factory) and therefore the machinery component of investment (represented by the foreign exchange loan) was much higher in relation to construction costs etc. Secondly, for the only group which did

Table 6.2 *Dependence of monopoly houses on foreign exchange loans*

	Foreign exchange loans (Rs lacs)	Total investment (Rs lacs)	Percentage
1961–65			
All monopoly houses (26)	5511.8	12,295	44.8
(i) Large (11)	4270.0	9457	45.2
(ii) Medium (9)	904.8	2359	38.4
(iii) Small (6)	337.0	479	70.3
1965–70			
All monopoly houses (34)	7814.9	19,075	41.0
(i) Large (13)	6007.0	14,295	42.1
(ii) Medium (13)	1481.9	3985	37.2
(iii) Small (8)	326.0	805	40.5

Note: Large are those with assets of more than Rs 100 million in 1970; medium are those with assets of between Rs 50 and Rs 100 million; small are those with assets of less than Rs 50 million.
Sources: See Appendix F, tables F.1 and F.2.

Secondly, during the Third Five Year Plan, the dependence on foreign exchange loans decreased only slightly, to 41 per cent, for all monopoly houses, as compared to the very large decline in the case of our continuous companies sample, from 35 to about 18 per cent.[11] Only in the case of the smaller groups is there a sharp decline, from 70 to 40 per cent – but this figure is now much closer to that of the other groups.

In order to understand the reasons for this difference, we have to see the strategy which the monopoly houses adopted in order to obtain loans from these institutions and how this strategy changed during the period of the foreign exchange squeeze.

> diversify in our sample (in this case, the cement industry), its foreign exchange component was much higher as compared to the consumer goods industries. Since the larger and medium groups expanded both through new firms as well as their existing ones, their foreign exchange loan component of total investment was lower.

11 See Section 5.2.2.

(a) Second Five Year Plan

During the period of the Second Five Year Plan, there were two major kinds of projects for which foreign exchange loans were available. These were:

(i) Investments in new industries. These were mainly capital intensive intermediate goods industries (e.g. cement, chemicals and oil refining) which had a very large foreign exchange loan component in total investment.

(ii) Projects in existing industries – mainly cotton textiles, jute manufactures and sugar industry.

The different situations which the monopoly house could face regarding foreign exchange loans can be listed as follows:

(i) The monopoly house is able to get sufficient foreign exchange loans to satisfy its demand for investment in both new industries and its firms in existing industries. This situation will have been rare since projects in new industries (especially cement and chemicals) were limited and it would have had to compete for foreign exchange loans with a number of other groups. The deciding factor in most cases will have been the influence and connections which the group had with the government.

(ii) The monopoly house is able to get loans for investment in the new industry but this reduces the amount it can get for the existing firms in the group. In this case it will have to finance the import component of its investment in existing firms with imported machinery at the more expensive bonus rate of exchange.

(iii) The monopoly house is refused loans for setting up a firm in a new industry. In this case the monopoly group will *not* try to undertake this investment at the market rate, because the foreign exchange content of the investment (typically high) will make it unprofitable to do so. However, the fact that the monopoly group has not got permission to move into a new industry will improve its chances of getting loans sanctioned for its existing firms. We can take two situations (a) where the entire demand for loans is met and (b) where only part of this demand is satisfied.

For the typical monopoly group, the availability of foreign exchange loans will with rare exceptions have been a constraint to its overall investment plans even during the period of the Second Plan (i.e. situation (i) or (iiia). The basic strategy of the monopoly house was to apply for the maximum amount of loans it could hope to get and then decide its investment strategy on the basis of the loans that were sanctioned. Foreign exchange loans can therefore be incorporated as a factor influencing investment behaviour of the monopoly group even during the Second Plan period in that it would determine in most cases the minimum amount of investment that it would undertake.

(b) Third Plan period

During the period of the Third Plan − because of the foreign exchange squeeze − there was a change, noted earlier, in the government's industrial strategy and investment in new industries considerably curtailed.[12] We also saw that in our continuous firms sample there was a large drop in the foreign exchange loan component to finance investment.

How were the monopoly houses able to maintain their share of loans to finance their investment? The manner in which this was done is explained in detail in Section 6.4. Principally, monopoly groups got control of new firms in existing industries which had originally been sanctioned by P.I.C.I.C. and I.D.B.P. to other parties and in which the foreign exchange loan component was very high. In this way, the monopoly groups were able to counteract the decline in foreign exchange loans for their existing firms.

However, the fact that monopoly houses were considerably squeezed for foreign exchange loans for their existing firms and had to get loans through this indirect method suggests that the total investment they undertook in this period was more tightly constrained than before by the amount of foreign exchange loans they could acquire from the financial institutions directly and indirectly.

6.2.3   A model of monopoly houses' investment behaviour

Taking into account the factors mentioned above, we set up a simple model to explain the investment behaviour of monopoly

12 See Section 7.1 for details.

houses during the period of the Second and Third Five Year Plans.[13]

Model C.1

$$\Sigma I_i / K_{i(t-1)} = a_i + a_2 \Sigma P_i / K_{i(t-1)} + a_3 D + a_4 \Sigma F.E.L._i / K_{i(t-1)} + u_i$$

Model C.2

$$\Sigma I_i / K_{i(t-1)} = a_i + a_2 \Sigma P_i / K_{i(t-1)} + a_3 \Sigma F.E.L._i / K_{i(t-1)} + u_i$$

where

ΣI_i = total investment undertaken by all the quoted manufacturing firms (i.e. existing and newly established) of the ith monopoly house in the period 1962–65 (or 1966–70). Calculated by the increase in gross fixed assets (at cost) in the period

ΣP_i = sum of gross profits (i.e. net pre-tax profits + depreciation) of all quoted manufacturing firms for the ith monopoly house for the period 1961–64 (or 1965–68)

$K_{i(t-1)}$ = size of the monopoly house at the beginning of each period i.e. 1961 (or 1965) and is represented by the gross fixed assets (at cost) of all the quoted manufacturing firms of the monopoly house.

$\Sigma F.E.L._i$ = total foreign exchange loans obtained from P.I.C.I.C. and I.D.B.P. to finance this investment for the period 1962–65 (or 1966–70)

D = dummy variable for diversifying into a new industry by the monopoly house, i.e. moves out of the existing industries in which it is already established. $D = 1$ when the monopoly house diversifies into a new industry and $D = 0$ when it does not. (See Appendix F, table F.1.)

u_i = error term

According to Model C.1, the amount of investment undertaken by a monopoly house is related to three factors: the total amount

---

13 The model was not tested for the individual years for two reasons. Firstly, figures for foreign exchange loans were available only for the entire plan period. Secondly, since the study is based on both existing and new firms belonging to monopoly houses, the investment figure in individual years shows extreme variations depending on the year when the new firm was added. Over the plan period, this variation tends to even out.

of profits, the foreign exchange loans from financial institutions and whether it diversifies into new industries or not. Since, as we have discussed earlier, we would expect the importance of the profit variable to be diminished if the group diversifies into new industries, we try the same equation but without the dummy variable in Model C.2 for those monopoly groups which did not diversify so as to see how the coefficient on profits changes.

As in our study at the firm level, we normalise for size of the group by dividing across by the gross fixed assets at the beginning of each period, and, in order to take into account any simultaneous equation bias that might arise between investment undertaken and the profits generated, we only take the sum of profits and changes in sales for the years 1961–64 and 1965–68.[14]

6.2.4 Data: composition of the sample and problems with testing the model

There are two major shortcomings of this exercise on the investment behaviour of monopoly houses.

The first is that it is limited to firms in the manufacturing sector. Since monopoly houses also move funds from companies in the non-manufacturing to the manufacturing sector or vice versa, by limiting the exercise only to the manufacturing sector we understate the capacity of the monopoly house to finance its investments from retained profits in firms in the non-manufacturing sector. In order to minimise this problem we have included in our sample only those groups which were predominantly engaged in the manufacturing sector.

The second problem arises because data are not available for the non-quoted companies. The study is therefore limited only to the quoted companies controlled by the monopoly houses. This meant that those monopoly houses which had no quoted companies on the Karachi Stock Exchange (e.g. Monnoo or A. K. Khan) and those whose assets were mainly in non-quoted companies (e.g. the Hyeson Group) were left out.

A consolidated balance sheet of each of the remaining monopoly houses was prepared for the period 1961–70.[15] For the period of the Second Plan our sample consisted of 26 mono-

14 See Chapter 5, p. 120.
15 As pointed out earlier, State Bank data are not available for the earlier years.

poly houses and for the Third Plan we covered 34 monopoly houses.[16]

6.2.5 Results

Period: 1961–65

Model C.1: All 26 monopoly groups

$$\sum_{62}^{65} I_t / K_{61} = 43.1 - 0.11 \sum_{61}^{64} P/K_{61} + 62.2^a D$$
$$(0.510) \qquad (2.510)$$

$$+ 1.28^a \sum_{62}^{65} F.E.L. / K_{61}$$
$$(7.030)$$

$$R^2 = 0.79$$

Model C.2: 15 Monopoly groups that did not diversify

$$\sum_{62}^{65} I_t / K_{61} = 9.09 + 0.43^c \sum_{61}^{64} P/K_{61} + 1.32^a \sum_{62}^{65} F.E.L. / K_{61}$$
$$(1.569) \qquad (6.139)$$

$$R^2 = 0.78$$

Period: 1965–70

Model C.1: All 34 monopoly groups

$$\sum_{66}^{70} I_t / K_{65} = 25.8 + 0.25^c \sum_{65}^{68} P/K_{65} + 15.7 D + 1.30^a \sum_{66}^{70} F.E.L. / K_{65}$$
$$(1.675) \qquad (0.846) \qquad (14.971)$$
$$R^2 = 0.90$$

Notes: Figures in parentheses are *t*-ratios.
[a] significant at the 1 per cent level
[c] significant at the 10 per cent level

The results show that during the period of the Second Plan, for all monopoly groups, the profit variable was not significant at all and in fact has a negative sign. Both the diversification variable and foreign exchange loans are significant at the 1 per cent level. This would tend to confirm the hypothesis that during this

16 For a list of houses included in the sample, see Appendix F, tables F.1 and F.2.

period one of the major sources of growth of investment for the monopoly groups as a whole was through diversification into new industries. Since our profit variable is representative of the rate of return in the existing industries in which the monopoly house was engaged and the monopoly house was basing its decision on the expected profitability in the new industries, the importance of this variable is diminished from the demand side. From the supply side, its importance is also minimised for two reasons. Firstly, the foreign exchange loan component in these new industries was extremely high, especially in the more capital intensive industries. Secondly, since monopoly groups diversified in almost all cases by floating new firms, they were able to raise a large portion of the rupee component to finance this investment from the stock exchange.

For the monopoly groups which did not diversify into new industries, we ran Model C.2 for the same period. In this case, we find that the profit variable is significant at the 10 per cent level and is positively associated with investment. This would tend to strengthen what we have said earlier regarding the importance of the profit variable in this period. For groups which did not diversify the profit variable would have been more important from the demand as well as the supply side in influencing investment behaviour. However, the results show that its overall influence was still weak during the period of the Second Plan.

For the period of the Third Plan, we find that the profit variable is significant (at almost the 5 per cent level) and positively associated with the growth of investment. The foreign exchange loan variable is again significant at the 1 per cent level but the diversification variable is no longer significant.

During the period of the Third Plan, as we have pointed out, the government severely curtailed investment in new industry because of the foreign exchange constraint and allowed investment mainly in the traditional textile and jute industries – both of which were export oriented. Only in a few cases did monopoly houses diversify into new industries during this period. This would tend to suggest that, during the period of the Third Plan, when there was a greater squeeze on the availability of foreign exchange loans, profits were more important in explaining investment behaviour.

6.3 Relationship between size of monopoly houses, growth and foreign exchange loans

We have remarked more than once that, in the corporate environment which existed in the sixties, 'power, influence and connections' played an extremely important part in determining whether one would get permission from the government to undertake a particular investment or be able to get a foreign exchange loan from the financial institutions. It is extremely difficult to quantify these factors but one measure of this power and influence could be the size of the monopoly group.[17] Were there important differences in the rates of growth of investment and in getting foreign exchange loans for different size classes of monopoly groups over the two plan periods?

The monopoly houses are divided into three different size classes according to the size of assets in the manufacturing sector in 1970. The rate of growth of gross fixed assets and the value of foreign exchange loans in relation to fixed assets are given for the different size classes in the two plan periods in table 6.3.

(a) Second Plan period

During the period of the Second Plan, we find that the rate of growth of fixed assets was highest for the larger groups and lowest for the small groups. The relationship of foreign exchange loans from the financial institutions to assets was lowest for the medium sized groups but almost the same for the large and small groups.

In order to see whether these averages for the three groups were significantly different from each other, we carried out simple statistical tests for differences in means amongst different samples. The results, given in table 6.3, show that there were no significant differences between either investment or foreign exchange loans amongst the different size classes of monopoly houses.

This result would tend to show that, during the boom period of the Second Plan, when foreign exchange loans were more readily available and there were few government restrictions on invest-

---

17 A monopoly house of course was in a much more advantageous position to get government permission as well as foreign exchange loans as compared to firms belonging to non-monopoly houses. In this section we are only looking at differences *between* monopoly houses.

Table 6.3 *Size, growth and foreign exchange loans*

	1961–65	
Size	$\sum_{62}^{65} I_t / K_{61}$	$\sum_{62}^{65} F.E.L. / K_{61}$
Large (11)	181.6	85.9
Medium (9)	141.6	55.7
Small (6)	123.9	87.3

Separate variance estimates (*t*-values)		
Comparison	$\sum_{62}^{65} I_t / K_{61}$	$\sum_{62}^{65} F.E.L. / K_{61}$
(i) Large and medium	0.78	1.10
(ii) Medium and small	0.27	0.86
(iii) Large and small	0.91	−0.04

	1965–70	
Size	$\sum_{66}^{70} I_t / K_{65}$	$\sum_{66}^{70} F.E.L.: / K_{65}$
Large (13)	170.0	86.5
Medium (13)	118.7	53.5
Small (8)	65.6	25.7

Separate variance estimates (*t*-values)		
Comparison	$\sum_{66}^{70} I_t / K_{65}$	$\sum_{66}^{70} F.E.L. / K_{65}$
(i) Large and medium	0.89	0.79
(ii) Medium and small	1.36	0.98
(iii) Large and small	2.16^b	1.86^c

Note: Large groups are those with total gross fixed assets in manufacturing of more than Rs 100 million in 1970; medium groups are those with total gross fixed assets in manufacturing of between Rs 50 and Rs 100 million, in 1970, small groups are those with total gross fixed assets in manufacturing of less than Rs 50 million in 1970.

[b] significant at the 5 per cent level
[c] significant at the 10 per cent level
Source: Appendix F, tables F.1 and F.2.

ment, size differences between monopoly groups were not a significant factor in explaining differences in either the rate of growth of gross fixed assets or the amount of foreign exchange loans in relation to their assets they could get from the financial institutions.

(b)   Third Plan period

During the Third Plan period the growth of gross fixed assets was again the highest for the large groups and lowest for the small groups. But whereas the rate of growth had fallen only slightly for the large groups as compared to the Second Plan period, there was a marked decline for the medium groups and a still larger one for the small groups. Moreover, whereas the relationship of foreign exchange loans to assets had remained almost the same for the large and medium groups in the Second Plan period, there was a very large decline for the small groups.

A statistical test for differences in means showed that there were significant differences between the large and small groups both for the rate of growth of gross fixed assets (at the 5 per cent level) and for foreign exchange loans (at the 10 per cent level). However, the means were not significantly different between the large and medium and medium and small groups.

Thus, during the Third Plan the smaller groups did not do as well as the large and medium groups. In a period of foreign exchange squeeze and one of greater restrictions on industrial investments, the smaller groups seem to have been affected more.

How the larger groups were able to maintain their rates of growth of gross fixed assets and the amount of foreign exchange loans in relation to their assets from financial institutions will become clearer in the next section when we see how they were able to get their loans during this period.

6.4   Political licensing

One of the interesting findings of our investigation into the foreign exchange loans given by P.I.C.I.C. and I.D.B.P. was that the monopoly houses were able to maintain their share of these loans as a proportion of total investment undertaken even during the Third Plan. This was surprising because our study of a sample of continuous firms for the same period had shown that there was a large fall in foreign exchange loans to finance their investment and a large proportion of these firms were also controlled by the monopoly groups.

We also found that, whereas during the Second Plan period the monopoly houses had expanded through existing firms in industries in which they were already engaged, during the Third Plan they had done so by setting up *new* firms. While collecting information on loans sanctioned by P.I.C.I.C. and I.D.B.P. for these new firms, the author was told that in a number of cases these had, in fact, *not* been originally sanctioned to the monopoly groups, but they had gained control by 'buying' them from the people to whom the original sanctions had been made.

In order to find out the extent to which this had taken place, we undertook an exercise for cotton textiles, the largest industry in West Pakistan, which accounted for almost 50 per cent of private industrial investment in the Third Plan. The idea was to see to which firms loans from P.I.C.I.C. and I.D.B.P. were originally given and whether these firms remained under the control of the same people or were subsequently acquired by the monopoly houses.

In table 6.4 we have given a list of the firms (together with the background of their owners) to which these loans were originally given and the name of the monopoly house (and in some cases other industrialists) which they subsequently passed to during the Third Plan period. In most cases, the loans were originally given to politicians and in some cases to ex-military officers and, in one case, to an ex-bureaucrat.

Our evidence is limited to the cotton textile industry. We found one case in the sugar industry,[18] but it was not possible to pursue this exercise for the other industries.[19]

The nature of the squeeze in foreign exchange loans felt by the monopoly houses for their existing firms in the second half of the sixties was the result not only of the decline in foreign aid available to the industrial sector through P.I.C.I.C. and I.D.B.P. but also of two other factors.

Firstly, there had been considerable criticism of the govern-

18 For example, Shakarganj sugar mill was originally sanctioned to an East Pakistan politician and is now under the effective control of the Crescent Group.

19 From the little information we were able to gather for the other industries, it appears that political licensing was relatively rare outside the cotton textile industry.

Table 6.4 *List of 'political' licences in the cotton textile industry*

Project	Original sanction	Sold to or effectively controlled by
I.D.B.P.		
1. Anwar Textiles	Politician[a]	Baksh Group
2. Noor Textiles	Politician[b]	Anwar Industries
3. Anoor Textiles	Politician	Bawany Group
4. Kotri Textiles	Politician	Olympia Group
5. Yousaf Textiles	Politician	Habib Group
6. Mir Textiles	Politician[b]	Bawany Group
7. Madina Textiles	Politician	Bawany Group
8. Sapphire Textiles	Politician	Gulistan Industries
9. Ahmed Spinning	Politician	Baksh Group
10. Zaman Textiles	Politician[a]	Elahi Industries
11. Nafees Textiles	Ex-Bureaucrat	Colony (N) Group
P.I.C.I.C.		
1. Rachna Textiles	Politician	Saigol Group
2. Babri Textiles	Ex-Military	Ghandara Group
3. Globe Textiles	Politician	Gul Ahmed Group
4. Shams Textiles	Politician[a]	Crescent Group
5. Sally Textiles	Politician	Saigol Group
6. United Textiles	Politician	Muggoo Industries
7. Hidayutallh Textiles	Politician	Makaty Industries
8. Karim Textiles	Politician	Karim Group
9. Baksh Textiles	Politician[b]	Baksh Group

Note: [a] East Pakistani based politician.
[b] Feudal based politician.
Source: Information collected by the author.

ment in the last few years of the Second Plan to the effect that most of the loans from P.I.C.I.C. and I.D.B.P. had gone to the monopoly houses. It had figured as an important political issue during the presidential elections in 1965. The government was under pressure to take action and it had instructed P.I.C.I.C. and I.D.B.P. that there should be a cut back in loans to the monopoly groups and these should be given to new entrants in the industry. Secondly, the monopoly houses had to compete with other groups, especially the military and the bureaucracy, which were extremely powerful in the government, having gained in power after the 1965 war with India. These groups also wanted a share in the large profits being generated in the industrial sector.

Table 6.5 *Background of monopoly houses (amongst top thirty) which emerged in the sixties*

Name of group	Background
1. Ghandara	Ex-military
2. A Khaleeli	Ex-bureaucracy
3. Z. Ahsan	Ex-bureaucracy
4. G. Faruque	Ex-bureaucracy
5. Noon	Feudal landlord
6. Monnoo	Traders

In table 6.5 we give the names of the six new monopoly houses amongst the top thirty (in terms of control of manufacturing sector assets) which emerged in the sixties, together with their backgrounds.[20] As we can see, four of these groups had close connections with the military and the bureaucracy.

Another way in which the military competed with the monopoly houses was through the setting up of its own industrial complex (called 'Fauji Foundation') with investments in cotton textiles, sugar, tobacco and the cereal industry. By 1970, it was twelfth amongst the monopoly houses with assets of more than Rs 150 million.[21] This complex achieved its highest growth rate during the Third Plan and many projects were sanctioned to it in which the monopoly houses were themselves very keen to invest.[22]

The manner in which the monopoly houses responded to the more 'competitive' environment in the second half of the sixties as compared to the first half was by 'buying' licences which were sanctioned to the so-called 'new entrants' into the industrial sector. This they were able to do principally because the licences had been issued in a number of cases to politicians and other groups who were mainly interested in making a quick profit and who in most cases

20 For a detailed study of the backgrounds of the leading industrial families which had emerged by the end of the fifties, see Papanek, G. (1967, p. 42) and Papanek, H. (1972, pp. 1–32).
21 See Annual Reports of the Fauji Foundation.
22 This was, for example, true of the largest sugar mill sanctioned to the Fauji Foundation during the last years of the Third Plan and set up by it. This was the project most often mentioned by the family members of the larger monopoly houses in their interviews with the author.

had neither the know-how nor the rupee resources to successfully run these projects. However, to the extent that there were also new entrants who wished to set up firms in these industries and who did so successfully – as some indeed did[23] – the monopoly groups did face increased competition especially in the getting of foreign exchange loans. However, our earlier study for different size classes of monopoly groups indicates that this was felt far more severely by the smaller sized groups than by the large and medium sized ones.

6.5 Conclusions

Our conclusions about the monopoly houses are:

(1) During the period of the Second Plan, the influence of profits on industrial investment by the monopoly house was severely diminished for two reasons. The first was that the major stimulus to investment from the demand side came through diversification into new products, principally in the intermediate and capital goods industries, and here investment was more in response to the expected higher profitability of the new industry than the realised profits of the existing industries. Secondly, since foreign exchange loans from the financial institutions were the major source of funds with which this investment was financed, it considerably reduced the monopoly house's dependence on its own internally generated funds.

For those monopoly houses which did not diversify into new industries, we found that profits were related to investment, but that the level of significance was quite low. This would tend to suggest that although profits of the existing firms influenced investment behaviour to some extent, from the demand side, even in these cases foreign exchange loan availability was the more important factor in determining its overall investment behaviour.

(2) During the Third Plan, the influence of profits on investment was marginally more significant. One reason for this was that diversification into new industries was no longer possible, mainly as a result of government policy, and realised profits of existing firms did influence investment undertaken. Also monopoly houses were more dependent on internally generated

---

23 The Ghandara group was generally acknowledged to be amongst the most efficiently run in the country, both in terms of management and of high profits earned on its total assets.

funds to finance investment, at least for their existing firms, and this increased the importance of profits.

However, the fact that, even during this period, the influence of profits in investment was not strong (being significant at almost the 5 per cent level) and that monopoly houses were still able to get foreign exchange loans by getting control of licences issued to new firms, suggests that foreign exchange loans were still the dominant factor explaining investment behaviour at the monopoly house level during this period.

7

INVESTMENT BEHAVIOUR AT THE INDUSTRY LEVEL

When we move to the industry level, the main new question, which we examine in much greater detail in conjunction with our basic hypothesis, is the extent to which government controls succeeded in influencing the inter-industry pattern of investment, and we try to bring out the differences during the period of the Third Five Year Plan when the government enforced its 'direct' controls over private investment as compared to the Second Plan period when government controls were almost non-existent.

The chapter starts by describing the criteria for the pattern of industrial investment which the government outlined in plan documents and compares investments sanctioned with allocations over the two plan periods. It then goes on to test empirically the extent to which profits and changes in sales together with the varying degree of government controls influenced the pattern of industrial investment which emerged in the sixties. Because of the limits of the census data which are used, the study has been confined mostly to West Pakistan.

7.1 Criteria for the pattern of industrial investment

7.1.1 Second Five Year Plan (1960/61 to 1964/65)

In the outline of the Second Five Year Plan the government had stated that its broad strategy for industrial development over the plan period would be based on whether new capacity earned or saved foreign exchange substantially or was biased in favour of the use of indigenous raw materials. To quote: 'improvement in the balance of payments position has been the principal consideration in determining various production targets set in the Plan' (Planning Commission, 1960, p. 6).

The planners, however, did not commit themselves on how they would choose amongst different industries based on the above criteria and pointed out that 'the complexity of industrial

153

development does not permit the application of any simple criteria such as preference for heavy or producer good industries over light or consumer good industries' (Ibid., p. 222). However, in setting their investment targets, they provided for both consumer and capital goods industries. In the case of the former, preference was given to those industries with a low capital–output ratio,[1] with a bias towards earning foreign exchange and which used indigenous raw materials. Provisions for producer goods industries were made on the basis that they were expected to become important in the future, even though 'their immediate contribution to income and employment per unit of investment may not be large' (Ibid., p. 222).

7.1.2 Third Five Year Plan (1965/66 to 1969/70)

The plan document clearly stated that 'the first important element in the strategy of industrialisation for the Third Plan is a shift in emphasis from consumer to capital goods industries, to maintain the contribution to the savings effort and to extend the import substitution programme over a much wider front' (Planning Commission, 1965, p. 447). It went on to add, however, that 'the second important element of the strategy for industrialisation is the policy of setting up industries primarily for exports to achieve the country's export target for the Third Plan' (Ibid., p. 448).

As noted in Chapter 2, because of the suspension of foreign aid and the war with India in September 1965, the industrial investment schedule for the Third Plan was not published until April 1966 and was only in operation for two years before it was suspended in June 1968 and replaced by the Priority List of Industries (P.L.I.) Schedule. According to this schedule, emphasis was shifted away from capital goods industries. Priority was once again to be given to those industries which improved the balance of payments position but greater emphasis was laid on export oriented as distinct from import saving industries (I.P. & S., 1968, p. ii).

7.2 Implementation of government industrial policy

As was shown in Chapter 2 the government enforced the in-

1 To quote from the plan, 'industries have been favoured which are expected to

dustrial investment schedules far more vigorously in the Third Plan period than in the Second, when indeed the schedules were barely enforced at all. This change in government policy is well illustrated if we see the progress of the implementation of the investment schedules over the two plan periods. In table 7.1 we have given both the 'allocations' made in the investment schedules published over the plan periods and the 'sanctions' given by the different government agencies and financial institutions (i.e. P.I.C.I.C., I.D.B.P., I.P. & S., and the Provincial governments). For the Third Plan, figures for 'sanctions' have not been officially released and were obtained from the I.P. & S. Department. Unfortunately, they are available for West Pakistan only.

In West Pakistan during the Second Plan period, total sanctions exceeded allocations by 130 per cent. In the case of all but a few industries sanctions far exceeded allocations and where there were shortfalls they were not substantial. For East Pakistan this 'boom' situation was not repeated to the same extent. Sanctions were only 77 per cent of total allocations and in the case of only five industries, i.e. jute, tobacco, footwear, printing and publishing and basic metals, did the sanctions exceed allocations.

For the Third Plan period, figures for West Pakistan show that there was a shortfall in total 'sanctions' as against the 'allocations' made in the original industrial investment schedule. But in the case of those industries for which large provisions were made in the Priority List of Industries Schedule and for which no 'special' permission was required (marked A in the last column of Table 7.1), the investment targets were either exceeded (e.g. Food manufacturing and textiles) or fairly closely fulfilled. In the case of those industries (especially intermediate and capital goods) where smaller provisions were made in the Priority List Schedule and stringent conditions were laid out for getting permission (marked B), actual sanctions were generally far below the original plan targets.[2] There is considerable variation in the fulfilment ratio in both categories A and B, but a strong re-

make the largest net contribution to national income per unit of investment' (Planning Commission, 1960, p. 222).

2 The only exception to this is the Chemical industry (including Fertilisers), which is explained mainly by the large amount of foreign investment sanctioned in the fertiliser industry during the Third Plan period.

Table 7.1 *Investment sanctions as percentage of total allocations: Second and Third Plan periods*

| | Second Plan period[a] | | Third Plan period | |
| | | | | Sanctioning procedure (during period of P.L.I. Schedule) |
Industry	West (Durrani)	East (Durrani)	West (Amjad)	
1. Food manufacturing	397.2	66.0	196.0	A
2. Beverages	261.4	60.0	12.0	B
3. Tobacco	138.2	192.5	96.8	A
4. Textiles	163.2	89.7	121.6	A
(a) Jute	715.6	115.0	—	—
(b) Others	152.9	56.1	—	—
5. Footwear	241.7	120.0	56.6	A
6. Mfg of wood & cork	106.2	80.7	33.3	B
7. Mfg of furniture and fixtures	—	—	22.5	B
8. Pulp & paper products	3264.0	20.4	63.6	A
9. Printing and publishing	82.9	114.2	121.8	A

lationship between sanctions in relation to original allocations and the existence of direct government controls over industrial investment stands out.[3]

3 In order to test this relationship for the Third Plan period, we ran some simple regressions between sanctions, allocation and government controls (in the form of a dummy variable), first for all industries and then excluding the chemical industry.

The results for all 22 industries were:

$$S = -165.4 + 1.18A^{a} + 190.6D^{b}$$
$$(9.371) \quad (2.039) \qquad R^2 = 0.83$$

$$S/A = 33.7 + 0.75D^{a}$$
$$(3.332) \qquad R^2 = 0.36$$

The results excluding Chemical industry from the sample were:

$$S = -165.4 + 1.18A^{a} + 245.3D^{a}$$
$$(10.219) \quad (3.308) \qquad R^2 = 0.87$$

(cont. p. 158)

Industry	Second Plan period[a]		Third Plan period	
	West (Durrani)	East (Durrani)	West (Amjad)	Sanctioning procedure (during period of P.L.I. Schedule)
10. Leather and leather goods	78.7	22.1	42.6	A
11. Rubber products	228.1	27.0	45.6	A
12. Chemical products incl. fertilisers	284.0	58.1	168.1	B
13. Petro-chemical	64.4	—	15.8	B
14. Non-metallic minerals	128.7	85.1	12.0	B
15. Basic metals	504.8	190.2	13.3	B
16. Metal products	248.2	77.6	20.6	B
17. Machinery	101.6	34.8	16.8	B
18. Electrical machinery	239.6	70.7	43.6	B
19. Transport & equip.	288.5	28.7	25.2	B
20. Misc.	163.2	79.5	21.5	B
21. Service industries	—	—	117.5	A
22. Special industries	—	—	222.6	A
Total	229.7	77.3	87.1	

Notes: A = easy, i.e. no permission required from any government agency.

      B = difficult, i.e. situation where either no provision was made in the P.L.I. schedule (i.e. industry Nos. 2, 6, 7, 13) or permission was granted by the Investment Promotion and Supplies Department (No. 14) or permission was granted by the Economic Coordination Committee of the Cabinet (Nos. 12, 14 to 20).

[a]   For the Second Plan period the *total allocation* figure is that made in the Industrial Investment Schedule (1960) together with those made in the Revised Industrial Investment Schedule (1962).

      Total sanctions are those against which allocations were made in the I.I.S. and R.I.I.S., *but also* include sanctions against industries for which no provisions were made and which were termed as 'specific' industries in the R.I.I.S. (See Chapter 2, p. 49.)

Source: (i)   See Appendix G, tables G.1 to G.3.

      (ii)   For sanctioning procedure during period of Priority List of Industries Schedule, see I. P. & S. (1968).

7.3 Analysis of investment behaviour at the industry level

The basic model tested is similar to the one for our study at the firm and monopoly house level and tries to see to what extent the profit and accelerator theories of investment behaviour help explain the pattern of industrial investment.

In testing these hypotheses across industries, we must, however, take into account the following factors.

(i) During the period of the Third Plan when the government enforced its 'direct' controls over private industrial investment, we would expect both the profit and accelerator hypotheses to work less effectively than in the Second Plan period when government 'direct' controls were almost non-existent.

(ii) We would expect the accelerator hypothesis to work less effectively for those industries in the Second Plan for which demand was 'newly' created, i.e. because of the introduction of import restrictions or tariffs, investment took place in response to expected increase in sales of products which were previously imported.

The model was tested in two forms:

Model D.1

Because of the existence of strong multicollinearity between profits in preceeding years, as well as in the case of change in preceeding years, a weighted[4] profits and sales variable was used in

$$S/A = 21.5 + 0.87D^a$$
$$(4.624) \qquad R^2 = 0.53$$

where

S = total sanctions; A = total allocations; D = dummy variable
for government
controls
= 1 (denoted by A
in table 7.1)
otherwise = 0 (denoted by B
in table 7.1)

Note: [a] significant at the 1 per cent level
[b] significant at the 5 per cent level

4 The lag pattern for the profit and sales variables is based on our institutional knowledge of the time taken to get investment sanctioned from financial institutions and the government (see Chapter 5, p. 113).

the model:

$$I_{it}/K_{i(t-1)} = a + a_1 (0.25\, P_{i(t-1)}/K_{i(t-1)} + 0.50 P_{i(t-2)}/K_{i(t-1)}$$
$$+ 0.25\, P_{i(t-3)}/K_{i(t-1)}) + a_2 (0.25\, (S_{i(t-1)}/K_{i(t-1)})(\bar{K}_i/\bar{S}_i)$$
$$+ 0.5\, (S_{i(t-2)}/K_{i(t-1)})(\bar{K}_i/\bar{S}_i) + 0.25\, (S_{i(t-3)}/K_{i(t-1)})(\bar{K}/\bar{S}) + u_{it}$$

where

I_{it}	= gross investment in the ith industry in year t
$K_{i(t-1)}$	= book value of fixed assets at the end of the year $t-1$
$S_{i(t-1)}$	= change in sale value of output (at constant prices) of the ith industry in the year $t-1$
$P_{i(t-1)}$	= gross profits of the ith industry in the year $t-1$ (gross profits = sale value of output less indirect taxes minus (material costs + other costs + wages)
$\bar{K}_i/S_i$	= three year average of the ratio of fixed assets to sale value of output of the ith industry
u_{it}	= error term.

Model D.2[5]

$$\Sigma I_{it}/K_{i(t-1)} = \alpha + a_1 \Sigma P_i + a_2 (\Delta S_{it}/K_{i(t-1)})(\bar{K}/\bar{S}) + u_{it}$$

where

ΣI_{it}	= sum of gross investments of the ith industry for the years 1960/61 to 1964/65 (or 1965/66 to 1969/70)
ΣP_i	= sum of gross profits of the ith industry for the years 1959/60 to 1962/63 (or 1964/65 to 1967/68)
ΔS_{it}	= Change in sale value of output (at constant prices) of the ith industry between 1962/63 and 1959/60 (or 1967/68 and 1964/65).
$K_{i(t-1)}$	= book value of fixed assets of the ith industry in 1959/60 (or 1964/65)

5 As in our study at the firm and monopoly house level, in order to minimise the simultaneous equation bias which might arise in this aggregate model of investment behaviour, the last two years figures for profits and change in sales were dropped, i.e. 1963/64 and 1964/65 (or 1968/69 and 1969/70). In its present form our figures for profits and change in sales would be affected for only one year, i.e. 1962/63 and 1967/68 by the investment undertaken in the period covered, if, as postulated, there is a two-year gestation lag. However, in order to check whether our results were being significantly influenced because of the inclusion of these years, the model was re-run dropping the figure for profits and change in sales for 1962/63 and 1967/68. The overall results were not significantly different.

$\bar{K}_i/\bar{S}_i$ = four year average of the ratio of book value of fixed assets to sale value of output from 1959/60 to 1962/63 (or 1964/65 to 1967/68)

u_{it} = error term

The data used to test the model are based on Kemal (1976) who published consistent time series data for the large-scale manufacturing sector for the years 1959/60 to 1969/70 for West Pakistan, based on the Census of Manufacturing Industries. The data are reported at a two digit level of industrial classification and cover 16 industries. The only three industries which are excluded are the wood, cork and allied industries, the furniture industry and the petroleum products industry. However, these account for only 8.2 per cent of value added in West Pakistan in 1969/70. The gross value of output series was given at current prices and was converted to constant 1959/60 prices.[6]

Results: Model D.1

The results (table 7.2) clearly show that the growth of investment amongst industries was not significantly related to the weighted previous year's profit and change in sales variables. The profit variable was significant at the 5 per cent level only for one year (i.e. 1968/69) and at the 10 per cent level for three years (i.e. 1962/63, 1966/67 and 1969/70). The sales variable although significant in three years had the opposite sign to that predicted by the model.

Pooled data study

In order to increase the number of observations in our sample and to obtain more stable estimates of the coefficients for the profit and sales variable, we pooled the cross-sectional data for the nine years 1961/62 to 1969/70. Using dummy variables for the changes in intercepts in the different years, we got the

---

6 The price indices were taken in most cases from (C.S.O., 1972) but in the cases of food manufacturing, textiles, chemicals and chemical products, non-metallic minerals and metal products they were constructed by the author, using the index for the major products (given in the same source) and weighting them by the value of production in each industry group according to the 1964/65 Census of Manufacturing Industries.

Table 7.2 *Results of regression analysis: Model D.1 (16 industries)*

Year	Sales change (weighted)	Profits (weighted)	Intercept	R^2
1960/61	n.a.	0.46* (0.701)	0.87	0.03
1961/62	0.25** (1.087)	0.08 (0.389)	17.4	0.09
1962/63	−1.07[b] (2.205)	0.51[c] (1.608)	23.4	0.34
1963/64	−1.38[b] (2.385)	0.12 (0.625)	30.4	0.32
1964/65	0.13 (0.65)	−0.33 (0.906)	75.6	0.06
1965/66	−0.008 (0.12)	not significant	36.6	0.001
1966/67	−0.26 (1.146)	0.09[c] (1.349)	21.1	0.18
1967/68	−0.30 (0.449)	0.08 (0.16)	15.7	0.05
1968/69 (i)	—	0.17[b] (2.172)	8.6	0.25
(ii)	−0.42[a] (3.222)	—	20.4	0.43
1969/70	−0.62[a] (3.528)	0.09[c] (1.395)	18.3	0.49

Notes: *Profits in year $t-1$ only
** Change in sales in year $t-1$ only
[a] significant at the 1 per cent level
[b] significant at the 5 per cent level
[c] significant at the 10 per cent level.

following results:

$$I_t/K_{t-1} = \quad 0.24 + 0.11\alpha_2 - 0.02\alpha_3 + 0.44\alpha_4{}^a + 0.14\alpha_5 - 0.05\alpha_6$$
$$\quad\quad\quad (1.072)\ (0.219)\ (4.083)\quad (1.272)\ (0.435)$$

$$- 0.08\alpha_7 - 0.1\alpha_8 - 0.1\alpha_9 + 0.04\ P^*/K_{t-1} - 0.05\frac{\Delta S_t^\star}{K_{t-1}} \cdot \frac{\bar{K}}{\bar{S}}$$
$$(0.762)\ \ (0.954)\,(1.209)\,(0.501)\quad\quad\quad (0.927)$$

$$R^2 = 0.24$$

Number of observations = 144
significant at the 1 per cent level
* weighted profit and sales variable

The results tend to show that both the profit and change in sales variable is not significant. The intercepts for the different years are not significantly different from each other except for 1964/65, where it is significantly different at the 1 per cent level.

Results: Model D.2

The results of Model D.2, i.e. of aggregate data for investment, profits and change in sales are given in tables 7.3 and 7.4. Because of the existence of multicollinearity between the profit and sales variable they were run separately.

Table 7.3 *Results of regression analysis: Model D.2 (Second Plan period)*

Dependent variable	Number of observations (industries)	Profit variable	Sales variable	Intercept	R^2
1960/61 to 1964/65	16	0.63^a (2.899)	—	145.3	0.38
	16	—	0.85^c (1.737)	287.5	0.18
	8★	0.73^b (2.236)	—	63.5	0.46
	8★	—	2.61^b (1.937)	202.0	0.39
	8★★	0.74^c (1.649)	—	155.7	0.31
	8★★	—	0.52 (1.268)	290.4	0.21

★ (Consists of food manufacturing, beverages, tobacco, textiles, footwear, printing, leather and rubber products).
★★ (Consists of paper and paper products, chemical, non-metallic minerals, basic metals, metal products, machinery (except electrical machinery), electrical machinery and transport.
Note: Figures in parentheses are t-ratios.
[a] significant at the 1 per cent level
[b] significant at the 5 per cent level
[c] significant at the 10 per cent level.

ble 7.4 *Results of regression analysis: Model D.2 (Third Plan period)*

pendent iable ne iods)	Number of observations (industries)	Profit variable	Sales variable	Profit X dummy variable[*]	Sales X dummy variable[*]	Intercept	R^2
5/66 o 9/70	16	0.18[b] (2.019)	—	—	—	85.4	0.23
	16	—	1.03[b] (2.507)	—	—	66.3	0.31
	13[**]	0.16 (0.992)	—	—	—	77.9	0.8
	13[**]	—	0.39[c] (1.710)	—	—	90.5	0.21
	16	—	—	0.17[b] (2.426)	—	108.1	0.30
	16	—	—	—	0.93[a] (2.902)	97.5	0.38
	13[**]	—	—	0.14[b] (1.909)	—	100.7	0.25
	13[**]	—	—	—	0.36[c] (1.762)	103.1	0.20

e: [*]$D = 0$, in the case of beverages, chemicals, non-metallic minerals, basic
als, metal products, machinery, electrical machinery and transport equip-
$t = 1$ in the case of others (see table 7.1)
Excluding leather, tobacco, paper and board
ignificant at the 1 per cent level
ignificant at the 5 per cent level
ignificant at the 10 per cent level

(i) *Second Five Year Plan*

Our results show that the profit variable was significantly related
o investment at the 1 per cent level. The sales variable was,
however, only significant at the 10 per cent level.

To take into account those industries where increases in investment were mostly the result of starting production of products
which had previously been imported, we divided our samples so as
o exclude such industries and put them in a separate category.

Although the number of observations in each of the two subsamples is extremely small, the results do confirm that the profit and sales variable is more significant for existing industries than for new industries. Whereas for the former group of industries both the profit and sales variables are significant at the 5 per cent level, in the case of the latter it is only significant at the 10 per cent level for the profit variable and not significant at all for the sales variable.

(ii) *Third Five Year Plan*

Our results for the period of the Third Plan were considerably influenced by the performance of three industries, namely paper and board, tobacco and the leather industry. The paper and board industry had a rate of growth of gross fixed assets almost three times higher than the average for all the others and this was mainly the result of a large expansion from a very small base. The other two industries had very high profits (in relation to their size) as compared to the other industries. It was, therefore, decided to report results for the Third Plan first for all 16 industries and then excluding three industries.

The results (table 7.4) for all 16 industries showed that both the profit and sales variables were significant at the 5 per cent level. If, however, we drop the three industries mentioned above the profit variable is no longer significant but the sales variable is still significant at the 10 per cent level.

In order to take into account the existence of 'direct' controls by the government in certain industries in this period, we re-ran the model using a dummy variable as an interaction term with the profit and sales variables in the following forms:

(i) $\Sigma I_{it}/K_{i(t-1)} = a + b\Sigma P_{it}/K_{i(t-1)}D + u_{it}$

(ii) $I_{it}/K_{i(t-1)} = a + b\dfrac{\Delta S_{it}}{K_{i(t-1)}} \cdot \dfrac{\bar{K}}{\bar{S}} \cdot D + u_{it}$

where $D = 0$ for those industries with 'direct' controls on investment (shown in table 7.1 by 'B')

$= 1$ in the case of others (shown in table 7.1 by 'A')

In the case of the all industries sample, the results for both the sales and profit variables are improved with the sales variable now being significant at the 1 per cent level. In the case of the 1?

industries sample, the profit variable is now significant at the 5 per cent level (whereas earlier it had not been significant) but the significance of the sales variable remains unchanged at the 10 per cent level.

7.4 Conclusions

The main conclusions of our study at the industry level are:

(i) Investment in individual years amongst industries is not significantly related to changes in profits or sales in the previous years.

(ii) When we aggregate data over the plan period, gross investment is significantly related to profits, except when government direct controls as in the Third Plan period acted as a constraint on investment in certain industries.

(iii) The change in sales variable (again in our aggregate data study) works best when we exclude investment in new industries and introduce a dummy variable for 'direct' government controls. During the Second Plan period, investment in a number of industries took place not so much in response to increases in sales but in anticipation of increased sales because of the creation of a market as a result of tariffs or import controls.

(iv) Government 'direct' controls were important in determining the pattern of industrial investment during the Third Plan period when they were exercised by the government as compared to the Second Plan period when they were not used at all.

8

CONCLUSIONS:
AN INTERPRETATION OF THE
BEHAVIOUR OF PRIVATE INDUSTRIAL
INVESTMENTS IN THE SIXTIES

Our analysis of private industrial investment, which covers th
entire period of the sixties, i.e. the boom as well as the sub
sequent slowing down, provides us with substantial evidenc
of the factors which influenced it in this period. We hav
analysed the factors which induced the growth and pattern o
industrial investment and identified the importance of in
stitutional and supply factors, especially foreign aid, which
emerge as playing a crucial role in explaining industria
investment in this period.

Our analysis suggests that the economic system which operated
in Pakistan in the sixties was quite different from that suggested
by earlier writers. It bore little resemblance to classica
nineteenth-century capitalism (portrayed by writers lik
Papanek). On the other hand, the system did not fail because th
capitalist class were no longer prepared to 'play the game' or ha
lost the desire to invest (as, for example, Nulty would make u
believe). The system which operated in Pakistan came very clos
to being what we can term a 'Foreign Aid Dependent Regime' i
which the mechanics of industrial growth were in one way o
another made dependent on foreign aid inflows. Once these ai
flows slowed down, the system, not being able to replace foreig
aid with other forms of external finance like direct foreig
investment, and without the peculiar boost to profitability asso
ciated with the local system for dispensing aid, found it difficul
to sustain the earlier growth it had generated.

Behaviour of private industrial investment – an
explanation

We now offer an explanation of the behaviour of privat
industrial investment in the sixties based on the factors we hav

investigated in detail, together with other wider considerations where relevant. We look briefly back to the fifties, and to bring out the different stages of industrial growth through which the economy passed find it useful to adopt the following sub-division of the period examined.

Stage	Period covered	
I	1947–52	Establishment of merchant capital.
II	1952–56	Import substitution led industrial growth – the transformation of merchant capital into industrial capital.
III	1956–59	Limits to import-substitution-based growth.
IV	1959–65	Foreign aid based industrial growth.
V	1965–70	Slowing down of foreign aid inflows and private industrial investment.
(a)	1968–71	Political unrest – contradictions and collapse of the system.

Stage I: Establishment of merchant capital 1947–52

At the time of partition, the areas which became Pakistan had hardly any established industries at all and most of the trade was in the hands of the Hindu community. It is generally believed that the rise of an indigenous merchant class took place after partition with the large-scale emigration of the Hindu trading community, but the fact that there were Muslim communities with strong trading traditions in different parts of India is overlooked.[1] The most important of these were the Memons (cf. Kathiawar origin), Khoja Ismailis, Khoja Isnasheries and the Dawoodi Bohras (all from Bombay) and the Chinioti[2] traders from the Punjab. There is little evidence that members of these communities were directly associated with the Muslim League in the struggle for independence,[3] but they saw with partition the

---

1 For a detailed account, especially the backgrounds of these business communities, see Papanek, H. (1972).

2 They were called 'Chinioti' because they originally came from the small town of Chiniot in the West Punjab. The 'Chiniotis' mostly specialised in the trade of hides and skins.

3 There were some exceptions. Members of the Adamjee, Isphani, Habib and Rahimtoola Group S were associated with Mr. M. A. Jinnah and the Muslim League activities (see Papanek, H. (1972), p. 11).

opening up of considerable opportunities in the new state.[4]

Most of these traders (together with the large bulk of Muslim refugees who came from India into West Pakistan) settled in Karachi, which was not only West Pakistan's sole port but also the seat of the Federal government. Here they took over most of the trade left behind by the Hindu traders and operated it successfully. Some of these groups had been able to transfer capital from India, but it was during the period of the Korean boom, when prices of raw cotton and raw jute increased considerably in the world market, that they made large profits (mostly through speculation). This was to provide the initial capital for the early stages of the industrialisation process that was to unfold in the next period.

Stage II: Import substitution led industrial growth – the transformation of merchant capital into industrial capital 1952–56

The collapse of the Korean boom in 1952 and the resulting balance of payment crisis (as prices of raw jute and cotton fell drastically in the world market), to which the government responded by imposing import controls, has been looked upon by most economists as the 'historical accident' which led to the start of the industrialisation process in the country.[5]

There is little doubt that the impact of this policy of import controls was to lead to a sharp increase in the prices of manufactured consumer goods, making investment in the manufacturing sector a very profitable venture and changing the terms of trade in favour of industry and against the agricultural sector.[6] Also the collapse of the Korean boom meant that profits in trade declined, hence reinforcing the attraction of investing trade surpluses into manufacturing rather than trade. These high

4 To quote Papanek, H. (1972), 'There is certainly no question that these businessmen understood the potential offered by an independent Pakistan in terms of economic opportunities' (Ibid., p. 16).
5 A large amount of industrial machinery (especially for cotton textiles) had been imported during the period of the boom (see Islam, 1967b, pp. 87–8). It is quite possible that pressure by those who were going to set up these industries played a part in the government's decision to impose such severe import controls.
6 For agriculture's domestic terms of trade relative to world price standards for the period 1951/1952 to 1963/64 see Lewis (1970a, p. 65). For terms of trade faced by the agricultural sector at domestic prices see Lewis and Hussian (1966) and Lewis (1970b).

Table 8.1 *Sources of manufacturing growth[a]: percentage of increased output All Pakistan 1951–54*

Sector	Domestic demand	Export expansion	Import substitution
Consumer goods	3	1	96
Intermediate goods	7	5	87
Investment goods	7	1	106

[a] Import-substitution is defined as the amount of domestic output increase that can be 'explained' by a reduction in import shares, holding total domestic supplies (production + imports) constant. Demand growth is the increase in supplies, holding the import share constant. It is further divided into its domestic and foreign components (See Lewis (1969), pp. 20–2, for further details).
Source: Lewis (1969), p. 45.

profits (the rate of return was between 50 and 100 per cent[7]) acted as a major inducement to re-investing internally generated profits and was perhaps the most important factor responsible for the extremely high rate of growth of the manufacturing sector in this period. The government, too, played an important role in early industrialisation – setting up industries where the private sector was initially shy (e.g. the jute and paper industry in East Pakistan) and then selling them to the private sector at nominal prices.[8]

Thus, the major source of growth in the manufacturing sector during the period of the early fifties was import substitution; and the growth in the consumer good industries was confined to the cotton textile industry and mainly to the jute processing industry in the intermediate good industries.

Stage III: Limits to import-substitution-led growth 1956–59

Private industrial investment reached a peak in 1954/55 after

7 To quote Papanek, 'with high prices for consumer goods and low prices for the capital goods needed to produce them, annual profits of 50–100 per cent were possible' Papanek (1967), p. 33.
8 For details of disinvestment of projects by the government sponsored corporation, Pakistan Industrial Development Corporation, see Amjad (1974), p. 19.

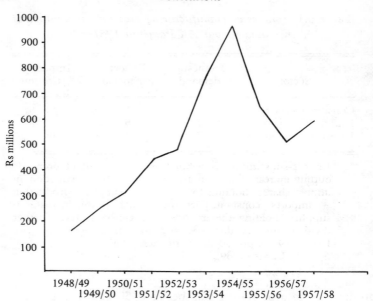

Figure 8.1   Estimates of Private Industrial Investment in the Fifties
Source: Papanek, 1964, p. 474.

which it began to decline, showing the inverted U-shaped path predicted by most models of import-substitution-led growth (see Bagchi, 1972, pp. 13–19).

There were a number of factors which were responsible for this slowing down. The first was a gradual exhaustion of easy import-substitution possibilities of growth in most consumer good industries and a continued lack of growth of total home demand, mainly the result of stagnation in agriculture,[9] which was the dominant sector in the economy. Also the lack of growth of industrial exports between 1955/56 and 1958/59 meant that there was no compensation for the stagnation in domestic demand. Then there was a decline in profitability in the manufacturing sector attributed by Papanek[10] mainly to an

9 This was the result of adverse policies followed by the government towards the agricultural sector – a combination of import controls and consequently higher prices of industrial products, export taxes and price controls on agricultural produce. For details of these policies see Falcon and Gotsch (1968) and I.B.R.D. (1968).

10 See Papanek (1967), pp. 37–9.

increase in competition amongst domestic producers but clearly partly due to the earlier mentioned factors. In those industries where demand opportunities still existed, the situation was made worse by the emergence of a foreign exchange constraint, which meant that investors could not import industrial machinery to realise investment plans. This was the result both of a lack of growth of export earnings and the exhaustion of the foreign exchange balances accumulated in the Korean boom.

To add to these there were two other factors which had a direct bearing on business confidence. Firstly, general elections were to be held in 1959 and the indications were that the political parties dominated by the rural landlord interests would be returned to power. It was generally believed that there would be a backlash against the highly discriminatory policies followed in the fifties which favoured the industrial sector and ignored agriculture. Secondly, there were growing signs of unrest amongst the industrial labour class, mainly as a result of stagnant, if not declining, real wages in the fifties.[11]

Stage IV: Foreign aid led industrial growth 1959–65

The military coup of October 1958 was to provide solutions to a number of the problems which the industrial sector faced in the late fifties. On the domestic front, general elections were shelved and the fears of an agricultural backlash against the industrial sector (as a political party dominated by the landlords came to power), if not completely removed, were at least greatly reduced. Labour strikes as well as trade-union activity were banned.[12] Both measures did much to improve and restore business confidence.

The real inducement to private industrial investment, however, was the result of three factors, each one of which, directly or indirectly, influenced the rate of return in the manufacturing sector. These were, firstly, the foreign exchange regime; secondly, the abandonment of 'direct' controls, to be replaced by a reliance on market forces both in the regulation of foreign trade

11 For the behaviour of wages in Pakistan see Khan (1967), Hamid, N. (1974) and Lewis (1971, p. 43).
12 Although trade unions themselves were not banned trade union activity was stopped. The government also imposed a ban on all strikes and inflicted heavy punishments on those who participated in them.

as well as in the sanctioning of industrial investment; and, thirdly, the large increase in foreign aid inflows.

The main feature of the foreign exchange regime was the over-valued exchange rate, which resulted in cheap foreign exchange to import industrial machinery and low prices of agricultural inputs, and subsidies on manufactured exports in the form of the export bonus scheme. The high rates of return in the manufacturing sector as a result of these measures were further supplemented by a combination of fiscal incentives (mainly tax holidays and capital allowances) and the very favourable lending terms of the financial institutions. But, besides these factors, there were others, which were investigated by us, which influenced the rate of return in particular industries. The existence of a high degree of concentration in markets for industrial products and quantitative restrictions on imports appear to have raised price–cost margins of manufactured goods as compared to what they would have been under more competitive conditions. And the increase in capacity utilisation, mainly the result of easier availability of imported inputs, led to an increase in profitability.

If high profitability acted as an important inducement to investment, it was the large increases in foreign aid which mainly made it possible to undertake this investment and it is the crucial role played by foreign aid in the industrial boom which stands out from our study of the corporate environment and of investment behaviour at the firm and monopoly house level. Foreign aid to the industrial sector (which many envisage as a simple government to government transaction) was linked into the financial institutions of the economy, in such a way that it had a direct bearing on investment behaviour in this period.

To start off with, the large increase in foreign aid removed the foreign exchange constraint which the industrial sector had faced in the late fifties and made available the foreign exchange needed to obtain industrial machinery in an economy where there was a negligible domestic plant and machinery sector. But, besides this, there were three other important aspects of the foreign aid boom which our study reveals.

Firstly, the government policy of reducing direct controls, even if not made by the donors an explicit condition for the receipt of aid (as some economists[13] have argued) would have been almost impossible without aid. Indeed, the government had to abandon import liberalisation policies and re-introduce direct controls for the major part of the Third Plan, once foreign aid inflows were reduced.

Secondly, the manner in which foreign exchange loans were distributed to the industrial sector acted not only to increase the profitability of those who received the loans, as noted above, but reduced the dependence on internal funds for the financing of investment. This emerges as one of the major differences from our study at the micro level with most studies of corporate investment behaviour for the advanced industrial countries, which show that firms are dependent mainly on internal funds for financing industrial investment. Our analysis shows that during the Second Plan about 40 per cent of total investment (and more than 70 per cent of the foreign exchange component of this investment) was financed through loans from the financial institutions. In fact, it was this reliance on external finance which resulted in profits being very weakly associated with investment during the Second Plan period, as our analysis both for firm and monopoly house investment behaviour shows.

Thirdly, representatives of foreign donors and of the large monopoly houses were directly associated in the running of the financial institutions which distributed these loans, and these loans went mainly to monopoly houses, which already dominated the manufacturing sector and financial intermediaries.

The market for manufactured goods was provided for not by import-substitution as had been the case in the early fifties but mainly as a result of increases in domestic demand. This increase resulted partly from agricultural expansion (after a period of stagnation in the fifties) and from a movement into new industries, especially in the intermediate and capital goods sector. An analysis of the sources of growth (although not available for the entire period) as compared with that of the early fifties shows how great the change was.

The investment boom of the first half of the sixties was, therefore, a combination of increased business confidence, high profitability, the expansion of the domestic market and, most important of all, the receipt of foreign aid. With this went the

13 See for example, Hamid, N. (1970).

Table 8.2 *Sources of manufacturing growth (All Pakistan) 1959–63 (percentages)*

	Domestic demand	Export expansion	Import substitution
Consumer goods	110	− 1	− 9
Intermediate goods	48	22	30
Investment goods	109	1	− 10

Source: Lewis (1969), p. 45.

oligarchic system of distribution of that aid, which must have served to reinforce profitability and confidence amongst the community of monopoly houses. That the Ayub government embraced or condoned this oligarchy can be seen as a consequence of its pursuit of industrialisation and hence its implicit coalition with the urban industrial and merchant elites rather than with the landlord rural elite. Having once begun to rely institutionally on the monopoly houses, it allowed the stronger members of that group to acquire increasing power at the expense of weaker members and potential newcomers. One can never be sure how many rivals there were or how effective they would have been as entrepreneurs had their chances of entering been better. All we know is that a few newcomers did emerge successfully, mainly from the military and bureaucracy, and that, given the extremely favourable conditions in which licence holders operated, the chances of failure must have been small, at least in industries where technology was not very sophisticated.

Stage V: Slowing down of foreign aid inflows and private industrial investment 1965–70

The effect of the decline in foreign aid during the period of the Third Plan was made worse by the increase in military imports after the 1965 war with India, the need to import foodgrains because of bad harvests during the first two years of the Third Plan and by the mounting burden of debt repayment which by the end of the plan period was over 18 per cent of total export earnings.[14] Consequently a foreign exchange constraint similar to that of the late 1950s re-emerged, and government policy changed in three ways. Firstly, measures taken to liberalise import policy gave way to government controls and this led to a fall in the availability of imported inputs as well as a slightly higher price for them. Secondly, the government abandoned its Third Plan strategy of a planned shift from growth of consumer goods to growth of capital goods industries. Thirdly, partly as a result of this change in industrial strategy, 'direct' controls on industrial investment were now quite strictly enforced.

This change in economic conditions had a direct influence on the growth of the industrial sector and on private industrial investment. The decline in foreign exchange loans from the financial institutions[15] meant a reduction in imported industrial machinery while the domestic plant and machinery sector was still extremely small. Also capacity utilisation declined in certain existing industries because of a reduction in imported raw material inputs and there was less availability of these inputs for new investment projects.

However, despite the existence of these supply constraints, there still remained a considerable desire to undertake new investment in the industrial sector, with the exception of those industries where capacity utilisation was extremely low. There were two main reasons for this. Firstly, an expansion in demand for manufactured goods and, secondly, because the rate of return on industrial investment was still very attractive.

The increase in demand during this period was the result of a very high rate of growth of exports and the expansion of the domestic market.[16] Manufactured exports in this period

14 Debt servicing as a percentage of total foreign exchange receipts was:

1965/66	1966/67	1967/68	1968/69	1969/70
12.0	14.8	15.6	16.9	18.5

Source: Planning Commission (1971, p. 184).

15 Foreign Exchange Loans disbursed by P.I.C.I.C. and I.D.B.P. during this period were as follows (Rs million):

1964/65	1965/66	1966/67	1967/68	1968/69	1969/70
422.0	368.3	255.9	288.0	300.9	335.8

Source: P.I.C.I.C. and I.D.B.P. Annual Reports.

16 That domestic demand and export expansion were the major source of growth of the manufacturing sector in this period can be seen from Guisinger's study

increased by almost 20 per cent per annum. The agricultural
sector saw a large increase in output in the last three years of the
plan period because of the introduction of the new high yielding
varieties of seed, and output of the major crop, wheat, almost
doubled. The resulting increases in agricultural income meant
that the absorption capacity of the major sector of the economy
for manufactured goods was considerably enlarged.

Profitability in the manufacturing sector was still very
attractive, mainly because the government continued its policy of
allowing the import of industrial machinery, where sanctioned
by the financial institutions, at the over-valued official exchange
rate. Although the rate of return on net assets was on the average
lower in the second half of the sixties as compared to the first
half, the decline in profit on net worth, which is what is
important from the shareholder's point of view, was much
smaller,[17] because of the rise in the gearing ratio combined with
the continuing low rate of interest and long repayment period on
loans. Finally, during the second half of the sixties, despite
pressure of increasing costs of imported inputs (which was placed
on the cash-cum-bonus exchange rate) and higher prices of
domestic agricultural inputs, the manufacturing sector was able
to pass on higher costs in the form of higher prices of
manufactured goods and maintain price–cost margins.

Given the demand to undertake industrial investment, the
major constraint came from the shortage of foreign exchange
loans made available by the financial institutions. The alternative
for the private sector was to import machinery at either the bonus
rate, which was more than double the official rate, or through the
'Pay As You Earn Scheme' (P.A.Y.E.) which implicitly involved
the same premium as the bonus, as one could sell the foreign

for West Pakistan between 1963–70, which is an extension of Lewis's (1969)
analysis for the earlier years.

Sources of manufacturing growth, West Pakistan 1963–70 (percentages)

Sector	Domestic demand	Export expansion	Import substitution
Consumer goods	59	26	15
Intermediate goods	77	23	0
Capital goods	71	3	26

Source: Guisinger (1976, p. 13).

17 Excluding one extraordinary bad year for the jute and sugar industry.

exchange earned for bonus if not retained for P.A.Y.E. At this higher rate of exchange, it was worthwhile to import only spare parts, replacements and machinery for new projects of exceptional profitability.

Our analysis of the factors which now influenced investment behaviour reflects these changes in economic conditions. There is a closer association between profits and investment behaviour mainly because retentions as a source of funds became more important as loans diminished. However, this evidence is stronger for our study at the firm level, where internal funds were used more to finance investment at the premium foreign exchange for replacement and expansion, and was lower at the monopoly house level. There appear to be two reasons for this. In the first place, variations in profitability and investment are evened out by aggregation across firms. Secondly, and more important, access to licences (and loans) for new projects was still crucial as it was not feasible to undertake large investments at the unfavourable exchange rate.

If the constraint on private industrial investment came not from the demand side, but mainly from a shortage of foreign exchange, the question which arises is why did not increased exports or inward foreign investment help out, as it appears to have done in some other Asian countries, e.g. Taiwan and South Korea? With active support and aid from the Americans, these countries followed policies rather similar to those of Pakistan in the period up to 1965 and apparently went on to a period of sustained growth, highly dependent on exports and direct foreign investment. We have not studied the other countries in detail, but one can see reasons why the Pakistan economy did not 'take off' like that.

First and foremost was the fact that Pakistan experienced a breach in relations with the United States and had aid severely curtailed for the rest of the Third Plan period after a temporary total interruption in the first year of the Plan.

As regards exports, the performance of the manufacturing sector, as noted above, was extremely impressive, with a growth rate of 20 per cent per annum during this period. However, exports of non-manufactures did not do as well and this brought down the growth rate of total export earnings in the period to about 6.5 per cent.[18] This increase in exports certainly played an

18 See Planning Commission (1971, p. 34).

important part in sustaining the overall foreign exchange position and avoided any significant decline in imports of raw material inputs (which would certainly have resulted if exports had not increased) but was not sufficient to offset the decline in aid, the rise in debt payment and in military imports and still provide a large and rising amount for the import of industrial machinery.

If the country's export performance (in the manufacturing sector) was impressive during this period, that of private foreign investment was certainly not so. Whereas one would have imagined that because general political and economic conditions were so favourable, direct foreign investment would have been quite substantial, even at its peak in the late sixties it was only 6 per cent of total private industrial investment.[19] What were the reasons for this very low inflow of direct foreign investment, despite the fact that foreign firms could repatriate capital and transfer profits at the official exchange rate?

Certain reasons were given by private foreign investors which could provide some explanation. Firstly, foreign investment was restricted to certain industries – mainly in the capital goods sector.[20] This created the strong impression that the government was inclined to restrict operations in activities where there was a substantial Pakistani interest and foreign investors feared that if they were to invest in the capital intensive technologically advanced industries they might at a later date find long-term growth restricted if Pakistani firms also moved into these industries. Secondly, in all large investments (in excess of Rs 2 million), they had to form public limited companies and offer shares to the Pakistani public, which they, in certain cases, objected to as they would prefer to retain complete ownership. Thirdly, there were restrictions on foreign firms' ability to borrow from domestic banks, which acted as a disadvantage. Finally, and perhaps most important of all, foreign investors found it very difficult to adjust to, or operate in, an economic system where costs, prices and import regulations – especially the rate of bonus and items included in the list of imports – were subject to frequent changes of a kind which to a foreign investor would appear unpredictable and avoidable if he invested in another country.

19 See Appendix A, table A.7.
20 Foreign investment was restricted to heavy engineering, heavy chemicals, mining, oil refining, pharmaceuticals, and manufactures of producer goods and spare parts.

During the end of the Third Plan period, the government was successful to a limited extent in getting foreign investment in the manufacturing sector (mainly the fertiliser industry) and P.I.C.I.C., too, arranged for foreign investors to invest directly with Pakistani firms. But any hopes of this process continuing suffered a serious set-back as large-scale political agitation broke out throughout the country in the winter of 1968.

The concentration of industrial economic power

The political unrest which broke out in the winter of 1968 was not the result of economic factors alone. But what cannot be denied is that the economic policies followed by the Ayub government and the inequalities in the distribution of income, wealth and power which they generated, were a very important contributory factor. Haq (1973), who had been Chief Economist of the Planning Commission in the sixties, described the situation as follows:

> What gave us real anxiety was the collusion between the industrial and financial interests, so that a few family groups had come to acquire control over basic economic decision-making. For all practical purposes, the 22 families had become by 1968, both the Planning Commission and the Ministry of Finance for the private sector. They pre-empted most investment permits, import licences, foreign credits and government patronage because they controlled or influenced most of the decision-making forums handing out such permissions. They had virtually established a stranglehold on the system and were in a position to keep out new entrepreneurs.

Our analysis provides evidence on a number of these points. Our study shows clearly the monopoly houses' dominating position in the economy, especially regarding their control over assets in the manufacturing sector. In 1970, 44 monopoly houses controlled 80 per cent of assets of private domestic companies listed on the Karachi Stock Exchange (K.S.E.) and 48 per cent of total domestic assets of the large-scale manufacturing sector. The 18 largest of these monopoly houses controlled 60 per cent of assets of all private domestic companies quoted on the K.S.E. and 35 per cent of the domestic assets of the entire large-scale manufacturing sector.

The close linkage between industrial and finance capital was illustrated by the control of monopoly houses of banks, which in 1970 accounted for about 60 per cent of total deposits and 50 per cent of all loans and advances made by banks operating in Pakistan. In terms of private domestic banks (i.e. excluding foreign owned and state controlled) this came to over 86 per cent of deposits and 84 per cent of all loans and advances made in 1970.

Our study also shows that the monopoly houses sat on the board of directors of financial institutions which channelled aid as foreign exchange loans to the private sector or were set up to raise domestic resources for the industrial sector (i.e. N.I.T. and I.C.P.). For example, of the total loans disbursed by P.I.C.I.C. between its inception in 1958 and 1970, almost 65 per cent went to 37 monopoly houses with 13 of the largest getting about 70 per cent of this amount.

Our analysis of monopoly house investment behaviour shows that not only did they get most of the loans directly sanctioned to them from the financial institutions, but, during the period of the Third Plan, when the government did make some attempt to broaden the ownership in the industrial sector by sanctioning licences to those not belonging to the monopoly houses, these licences were traded and mostly ended up in the control of the monopoly houses.

The high degree of concentration of ownership in manufactures did not find expression only in the exercise of power in investment licensing and loans but also manifested itself in market power and access to imports. Our statistical analysis shows a strong and significant association between industrial concentration and price–cost margins across industries, and also that the check on monopoly power through competitive imports was weakened by the linkage between the manufacturers and traders, who in many cases turned out to be the same people.

Finally, one can speculate whether the economic system which existed in Pakistan could have sustained itself if foreign aid inflows had continued. Or would the contradictions which the system developed within itself – the concentration of economic power, the stagnation of real wages, the growth of inter-regional disparity – have spelled out its end anyway? The answer is impossible to provide.

APPENDICES

Appendix A–Table A.1 *Gross national expenditure: All Pakistan (current prices) (Rs. million)*

Flows	1959/60	1960/61	1961/62	1962/63	1963/64	1964/65	1965/66	1966/67	1967/68	1968/69	1969/70
1. Private consumption expenditure	27,706.5	31,550.7	32,367.9	33,832.5	36,197.7	40,535.2	41,654.7	49,778.6	53,608	57,974.9	62,325.6
2. Government consumption expenditure	2,291.5	2,467.9	2,580.0	2,563.1	3,150.5	3,372.8	5,519.3	4,656.9	4,933.9	5,394.6	6,202.4
(a) Defence	(1,043.5)	(1,112.4)	(1,108.6)	(954.3)	(1,156.5)	(1,262.3)	(2,855.0)	(2,293.5)	(2,486.5)	(2,426.8)	(2,749.2)
3. Gross domestic fixed capital formation	3,040	4,315	5,350	6,330	7,233	8,332	7,674	8,449	9,180	9,304	10,313
(i) Private	1,430	2,625	3,135	3,180	3,662	4,198	3,979	4,203	4,292	4,206	4,663
(ii) Public	1,610	1,690	2,215	3,150	3,571	4,134	3,695	4,246	4,888	5,098	5,650
4. Changes in stocks	800	290	360	380	240	558	575	1,335	518	915	1,000
5. Exports (goods and services) (G & S)	2,157.0	2,208.0	2,262.9	2,737.1	2,803.0	3,019.8	3,379.9	3,585.9	4,111.3	4,204.6	4,331.0
6. Less imports (G & S)	3,161.0	4,114.6	4,290.8	4,831.7	5,463.2	6,501.1	5,760.9	6,487.4	7,094.2	6,455.1	6,777.0
Balance on G & S	(−1,004)	(−1,906.6)	(−2,027.9)	(−2,094.6)	(−2,660.2)	(−3,481.3)	(−2,381.0)	(−2,901.5)	(−2,982.9)	(−2,250.5)	(−2,446.0)
7. Gross domestic expenditure	32,834	36,717	38,630	41,011	44,161	49,317	53,042	61,318	65,257	71,338	77,395
8. Net factor income from abroad	(−) 33	(−) 32	(−) 37	(−) 78	(−) 115	(−)109	(−)100	(−) 95	(−) 46	(−) 59	(+) 6
9. Gross national expenditure	32,801	36,685	38,593	40,933	44,046	49,208	52,942	61,223	65,211	71,279	77,401

Notes on table A.1–All Pakistan

Line (1): *Private consumption expenditure*
Residual

Line (2): *Government consumption expenditure*
Sum of (i)   Central government expenditure
       (ii) Provincial government expenditure
      (iii) Local bodies' expenditure

(i)   Ministry of Finance, *Budget in Brief, 1971/72*, Islamabad, pp. 198–201

(ii) Sum of West Pakistan (see notes to table A.2) and East Pakistan (see notes to table A.3) provincial government expenditure

(iii) This was worked out at roughly 8.5% of total government expenditure[1]

Line (2a): *Defence expenditure*
Ministry of Finance, *Budget in Brief, 1971/72*, Islamabad, pp. 198–201

Line (3): *Gross domestic fixed capital formation (G.D.F.C.F.)*
(i)   1959/60 to 1962/63 (Planning Commission, 1966, p. 181)
(ii) 1963/64 to 1969/70 (C.S.O., unpublished mimeo)

Line (3) (i): *G.D.F.C.F. (private)*
(i)   1959/60 (Planning Commission, 1966, p. 143).
(ii) 1960/61 to 1962/63 (Ibid., p. 8)
(iii) 1963/64 to 1969/70 (C.S.O., unpublished mimeo)

Line (3) (ii): *G.D.F.C.F. (public)*
(i)   1959/60 to 1962/63 residual (line 3 – line 3(i))
(ii) 1963/64 to 1969/70 (C.S.O., unpublished mimeo).

Line (4): *Change in stocks*
(i)   C.S.O., 1972, p. 304.

Line (5): *Exports*
(a) Visible exports from:
     (i)   1959/60 to 1968/69,
           Planning Commission, 1970a, Vol. I, p. 143.
     (ii) 1969/70, C.S.O., 1972, p. 304.
(b) Invisible exports from Planning Commission, 1970a, Vol. I, pp. 145–49.

Line (6): *Imports*
The same as for line (5).

Line (7): *Gross domestic expenditure*
Residual (line (9) – line (8))

Line (8): *Net factor income from abroad*
C.S.O., 1972, p. 304.

Line (9): *Gross national expenditure*
C.S.O., 1972, p. 304.

---

1 This figure is used by the C.S.O. in its calculations of total government expenditure. Although this figure is not as such given it was calculated by us as a residual from different sources which gave breakdowns of total government expenditure between the central and provincial governments. (See C.S.O., *Monthly Statistical Bulletins*, September 1968, January 1970, February 1971, and October 1972).

Table A.2 Gross provincial expenditure: West Pakistan (current prices) (Rs million)

Flows	1959/60	1960/61	1961/62	1962/63	1963/64	1964/65	1965/66	1966/67	1967/68	1968/69	1969/70
1. Private consumption expenditure	14,431.8	16,089.3	16,610.4	17,215.3	19,612.6	22,400.2	21,543.7	26,268.2	29,228.1	31,717.6	32,957.1
2. Government consumption expenditure	1,635.1	1,749.6	1,829.5	1,785.4	2,151.1	2,238.7	3,996.7	3,384.3	3,488.1	3,744.2	4,338.5
3. Gross domestic fixed capital formation	2,014	3,053	3,590	4,495	5,027	6,010	5,468	5,840	5,781	3,031	6,746
(i) Private	781	1,901	2,099	2,337	2,868	3,228	3,014	3,155	3,163	3,631	3,489
(ii) Public	1,233	1,152	1,491	2,158	2,159	2,782	2,454	2,685	2,618	2,185	3,257
4. Changes in stocks	630	222	271	284	172	416	428	963	339	586	614
5. Exports (goods and services) (G & S)	1,563.1	1,657.8	1,654.0	2,281.4	2,250.9	2,368.9	2,782.4	3,045.0	3,525.2	3,639.0	3,886.4
6. Imports (G & S)	2,525.0	3,087.7	3,334.9	3,888.1	4,114.6	4,899.8	4,435.8	5,132.5	5,646.4	4,846.8	5,233.0
Balance on G & S	−961.9	−1,429.9	−1,680.9	−1,606.7	−1,863.7	−2,530.9	−1,653.4	−2,087.5	−2,121.2	−1,207.8	−1,346.6
7. Gross domestic provincial expenditure	17,749	19,684	20,620	22,173	25,099	28,534	29,783	34,368	36,715	40,656	43,309
8. Net factor income from abroad	(−) 16	(−) 16	(−) 18	(−) 39	(−) 57	(−) 55	(−) 50	(−) 47	(−) 23	(−) 29	(+) 3
9. Gross provincial expenditure	17,733	19,668	20,602	22,134	25,042	28,479	29,733	34,321	36,692	40,627	43,312

Notes on table A.2 – West Pakistan

Line (1): *Private consumption expenditure*
Residual.

Line (2): *Government consumption expenditure*
 Sum of (i)   Central government expenditure
       (ii) Provincial government expenditure
       (iii) Local bodies' expenditure

(i) All Pakistan (see note to table A.1) minus allocation to East Pakistan (see note to table A.3).

(ii) Ministry of Finance, *Budget in Brief, 1971/72*, Islamabad, pp. 276–93.

(iii) 60 per cent of All Pakistan figure (see note to table A.1).

Line (3): *Gross domestic fixed capital formation*

(i) 1959/60 to 1962/63 (Planning Commission, 1966, p. 181).

(ii) 1963/64 to 1969/70, (C.S.O., unpublished mimeo). The C.S.O. estimates excluded certain items from the provincial estimates. In the case of private G.D.F.C.F. the figures for banking, insurance and other institutions were not allocated to the provinces. They, however, accounted for only 1 per cent of total private G.D.F.C.F. for All Pakistan and were allocated by us between West and East in the ratios of 60 per cent to the former and 40 per cent to the latter. For public G.D.F.C.F. the unallocated items accounted for almost 10 per cent of the total during the first half of the sixties and about 15 per cent during the second half. These were allocated to East and West on the basis of sector-wise public sector development expenditures in the two provinces during the Second and Third Plan period based on detailed breakdowns availabe in Planning Commission, (1966) and (1971).

Line (3) (i) Private G.D.F.C.F.

(i) 1959/60 to 1962/63 – residual All Pakistan (see note to table A.1) minus East Pakistan (see note to table A.3).

(ii) 1963/64 to 1969/70 – C.S.O., unpublished mimeo plus unallocated items. See note 3(ii).

Line (3) (ii) Public G.D.F.C.F.

(i) 1959/60 to 1962/63, same as for line 3(i).

(ii) 1963/64 to 1969/70, C.S.O., unpublished mimeo plus unallocated items. See note 3(ii).

Line (4): *Change in stocks*
Residual between All Pakistan (see note to table A.1) and East Pakistan (see note to table A.3).

Line (5): *Exports*

(i) Visible exports – Planning Commission, 1970a, Vol. I, p. 143.

(ii) Invisible exports – Ibid., p. 154.

(iii) Inter-wing trade – Ibid., p. 144 (excludes invisibles for which separate data are not available).

Line (6): *Imports*
The same as for line (5).

Line (7): *Gross domestic expenditure*
Residual – line (9) minus line (8).

Line (8): *Net factor income from abroad*
Taken as 50% of All Pakistan figure (see note to table A.1).

Line (9): *Gross provincial expenditure*
Residual All Pakistan (see note to table A.1) minus East Pakistan (see note to table A.3).

Table A.3 Gross provincial expenditure: East Pakistan (current prices) (Rs million)

Flows	1959/60	1960/61	1961/62	1962/63	1963/64	1964/65	1965/66	1966/67	1967/68	1968/69	1969/70
1. Private consumption expenditure	13,277	15,461	15,755.2	16,617.5	16,585.1	18,135.3	20,111	23,510.4	24,379.9	26,257.3	29,368.6
2. Government consumption expenditure	656.4	718.3	750.5	777.7	999.4	1,134.1	1,522.6	1,272.6	1,445.8	1,650.4	1,863.9
3. Gross domestic fixed capital formation	1,023.7	1,262.4	1,762.3	1,834.7	2,206	2,322	2,206	2,609	3,399	3,488	3,567
(i) Private	548.7	724.4	1,038.3	842.7	794	970	965	1,048	1,129	1,175	1,174
(ii) Public	475.0	538	724	992.0	1,412	1,352	1,241	1,561	2,270	2,313	2,393
4. Changes in stocks	170	68	89	96	68	142	147	372	179	329	386
5. Exports (goods and services) (G & S)	1,525.7	1,739.2	1,886.0	1,884.1	1,958.5	2,062.5	2,457.9	2,604.6	2,604.2	2,821.3	3,034.9
6. Imports (G & S)	1,567.8	2,215.9	2,233.0	2,372.0	2,755.0	3,012.9	3,185.5	3,418.6	3,465.9	3,864.0	4,134.4
Balance on G & S	−42.1	−476.7	−347.0	−487.9	−796.5	−950.4	−727.6	−814.0	−861.7	−1,042.7	−1,099.5
7. Gross domestic provincial expenditure	15,085	17,033	18,010	18,838	19,062	20,783	23,259	26,950	28,542	30,682	34,086
8. Net factor income from abroad	(−) 17	(−) 16	(−) 19	(−) 39	(−) 58	(−) 54	(−) 50	(−) 48	(−) 23	(−) 30	(+) 3
9. Gross provincial expenditure	15,068	17,017	17,991	18,799	19,004	20,729	23,209	26,902	28,519	30,652	34,089

Notes on Table A.3 – East Pakistan

Line (1): *Private consumption expenditure*
Residual
Line (2): *Government consumption expenditure*
Sum of (i)   Central government expenditure in East Pakistan (A − B)
(see below)
(ii)   Provincial government expenditure
(iii)   Local bodies' expenditure
(i)   A. Amount allocated to East Pakistan out of total central government
expenditure was as follows:
(a) Direct demands on revenue (40%); (b) civil administration
(excluding frontier region) 40%; (c) currency and mint (10%); (d)
civil works and central road funds (50%); (e) misc. (5%); (f) defence
(15%); (g) development expenditure (25%); (h) other heads (15%).
B. (Sales revenue) Amount allocated to East Pakistan was as follows:
(a) administrative (40%); (b) defence (15%); (c) misc. (30%);
(d) other heads (5%).
(ii)   Ministry of Finance, *Budget in Brief, 1971/72*, pp. 292–3.
(iii)   40% of All Pakistan figure.
Line (3): *Gross domestic fixed capital formation*
(i) 1959/60 to 1962/63 (Planning Commission, 1966, p. 181).
(ii) 1963/64 to 1969/70, C.S.O., unpublished mimeo plus unallocated
items. See note 3 (ii) p. 185.
Line (3) (i)   Private G.D.F.C.F.
1959/60 to 1962/63 – residual line (3) minus line 3 (ii).
1963/64 to 1969/70 – C.S.O., unpublished mimeo plus unallocated
items.
Line 3   (ii)   Public G.D.F.C.F.
1959/60 to 1962/63 – Alamgir and Berlage (1974, p. 209).
1963/64 to 1969/70 – C.S.O., unpublished mimeo plus unallocated items.
Line (4): *Changes in stocks*
Alamgir and Berlage (1974, p. 211).
Line (5): *Exports*
(i)   Visibles. Planning Commission (1970a, Vol. I, p. 143).
(ii)   Invisibles (Ibid., p. 154).
(iii)   Inter-wing exports (Ibid., p. 144) (Excludes invisibles for
which separate data is not available).
Line (6): *Imports*
The same as for line (5)
Line (7): *Gross domestic expenditure*
Residual (line (9) minus line (8)).
Line (8): *Net factor income from abroad*
Taken as 50% of All Pakistan figure (see note to table A.1)
Line (9): *Gross provincial expenditure*
Alamgir and Berlage (1974, p. 159). Taken as sum of G.D.P. (at current
factor cost) as prepared by C.S.O. plus unallocated items plus indirect
taxes less subsidies plus net factor income from abroad.

Table A.4 Estimates of private industrial investment by quoted companies[1] (Rs million)

	1960	1961	1962	1963	1964	1965	1966	1967	1968	1969	1970
Increase in gross fixed assets	343.1	641	440	400	880	890	773	875	683	943	948
Adjustments (i)	−40	−30	−51	−59	−37	−162	−59	−34	−105	−24	−151
(ii)	×2.1	×2.1	×2.1	×2.1	×2.1	×2.1	×2.1	×2.1	×2.1	×2.1	×2.1
	636.5	1283.1	816.9	716.1	1770.3	1528.8	1499.4	1766.1	1213.8	1929.9	1673.7

Source: State Bank of Pakistan, *Balance Sheet Analysis of Joint Stock Companies* (Karachi, various issues)

Adjustments: (i) Increase in gross fixed assets because of newly listed companies which were known to represent take-overs of assets of other firms or the going public of established firms is deducted.

(ii) Tax provision for companies covered above have been compared with total corporate tax collections to give an estimate of the percentage of industrial activity represented by companies listed on the Karachi Stock Exchange. This assumes that other companies receive roughly the same tax holiday status as quoted companies and earn the same return on fixed assets.

These figures for taxes were obtained from I.B.R.D. (1970, Vol. III, p. 10) and, based on them, an expansion factor of 2.1 was applied to investment by companies adjusted for (i).

1 This method was originally used by the I.B.R.D. (op.cit., p.9) but their estimates were only for the years 1962–66. For 1967 and 1968 their estimates were based on a smaller sub-sample of companies quoted on the K.S.E.

Table A.5 Price index for industrial investment

West Pakistan (1959/60 = 100)

1960/61	1961/62	1962/63	1963/64	1964/65	1965/66	1966/67	1967/68	1968/69	1969/70
100.4	99.9	99.9	101.8	107.4	111.2	114.9	117.3	119.9	126.4

Note: Based on price index for machinery and construction (cement, steel and wages). Weights were assigned as follows: machinery 75%, cement 5%, steel 5% and wages 15%. Breakdown between machinery and construction, Planning Division (1973, p. 31). Breakdown of construction, i.e. cement, steel & wages, Planning Commission (1966, pp. 179–80).

Sources: (i) Price index for machinery, cement and steel (C.S.O., 1972, pp. 318–20).
 (ii) Price index for wages (Hamid, N., 1974, p. 52).

East Pakistan (1959/60 = 100)

1960/61	1961/62	1962/63	1963/64	1964/65	1965/66	1966/67	1967/68	1968/69	1969/70
108.4	112.7	117.3	118.9	124.3	127.7	130.0	129.0	132.3	131.8

Note: Based on price index for machinery and construction (cement, steel and wages). Weights were assigned as follows: machinery 70%, cement 5%, steel 5%, wages 20%. Breakdown between machinery and construction, C.S.O. (unpublished mimeo). Breakdown of construction, i.e. cement, steel & wages, Planning Commission (1966, pp. 179–80).

Sources: (i) Price index for machinery, cement and steel (C.S.O., 1972, pp. 318–20)
 (ii) Price index for wages (Alamgir & Berlage, 1974, p. 212).

Table A.6 Estimates of private industrial investment (current prices) (Rs million)

	1960/61	1961/62	1962/63	1963/64	1964/65	1965/66	1966/67	1967/68	1968/69	1969/70
All Pakistan	983.6	1254.3	913.2	1381.5	1613.5	1456.8	1478.0	1536.0	1522.6	1667.4
West Pakistan	808.3	809.2	639.9	1044.1	1188.1	1084.0	1011.2	1050.8	1003.3	1165.7
East Pakistan	175.3	445.1	273.3	337.4	425.3	372.8	466.8	485.2	519.3	501.7

Sources: (i) For 1960/61 to 1962/63, Planning Commission, 1966, p. 189.
(ii) For 1963/64 to 1969/70, figures obtained from the Central Statistical Office, Karachi (unpublished mimeo).

Table A.7 *Private foreign investment in the manufacturing sector[a] – All Pakistan (at constant 1959/60 prices) (Rs million)*

	1959/60	1960/61	1961/62	1962/63	1963/64	1964/65	1965/66	1966/67	1967/68	1968/69	1969/70
Total	17.0	32.6	37.3	36.7	39.2	34.0	26.8	29.9	58.4	75.6	60.2
As % of private industrial investment	n.a.	2.8	3.1	4.2	3.0	2.4	2.1	2.4	4.6	6.2	5.9

Source: Syed (1974), p. 93 and Chaudhry (1970)

Estimates from the above sources were at current prices. They were converted into constant prices using the indices given in table A.5.

[a] These figures include re-invested earnings which are considered as direct private investment since these amounts are fully repatriable. However, they do not finance either the import of capital equipment or the service of technicians in foreign exchange. Re-invested earnings amounted to about 38 per cent of total private foreign investment in the Second Plan period and 27 per cent in the Third Plan period. Separate figures for the manufacturing sector are not available. See Syed (1974), pp. 88–9.

Table A.8 Sectoral breakdown of private investment[1] – major sectors (percentages)

Sector		1963/64	1964/65	1965/66	1966/67	1967/68	1968/69	1969/70
Agriculture	All Pakistan	14.1	13.1	11.7	12.3	13.1	13.9	15.7
	West Pakistan	12.0	11.3	10.7	10.8	10.3	11.4	13.8
	East Pakistan	22.5	19.7	15.5	17.4	21.5	21.4	22.3
Manufacturing[a]	All Pakistan	36.3	37.0	34.8	33.9	34.7	35.1	36.4
(large scale)	West Pakistan	35.6	35.9	34.5	31.4	33.0	33.2	35.1
	East Pakistan	40.6	42.4	37.6	42.7	40.8	42.8	43.0
Ownership of	All Pakistan	14.6	14.6	17.8	16.9	17.6	17.0	13.7
dwellings	West Pakistan	14.3	14.9	18.0	17.5	18.3	18.9	14.6
	East Pakistan	16.3	14.0	18.2	15.5	16.3	13.5	11.8
Electricity	All Pakistan	4.2	4.9	3.8	4.7	5.4	4.1	2.4
and gas	West Pakistan	5.4	6.4	5.0	6.3	7.4	5.7	3.1
	East Pakistan[2]							
Transport and	All Pakistan	12.7	14.9	13.7	13.8	11.2	9.1	12.3
communication	West Pakistan	15.4	17.1	14.7	15.9	13.3	11.1	15.0
	East Pakistan	3.2	8.4	11.2	8.1	5.8	4.5	5.0
Services	All Pakistan	9.1	8.4	9.8	10.1	10.2	10.6	10.0
	West Pakistan	9.0	8.5	10.3	10.7	10.9	11.7	10.6

Note:

[a] This figure will not tally with that shown in table A.6 as it excludes investment in residential building and also the price of land which is shown under ownership of dwellings.

Source: C.S.O., unpublished mimeo.

1. Total private investment in all sectors was as follows (Rs million):

	1963/64	1964/65	1965/66	1966/67	1967/68	1968/69	1969/70
All Pakistan	3,661.8	4,197.6	3,979.3	4,202.9	4,291.8	4,206.3	4,662.6
West Pakistan[a]	2,845.4	3,200.2	2,984.7	3,133.0	3,136.7	2,981.4	3,441.8
East Pakistan[a]	778.3	951.3	945.6	1,033.3	1,111.2	1,141.4	1,141.6

Note: [a] Estimates of West and East Pakistan exclude estimates of banking, insurance and other institutions included in the All Pakistan figure. Investment in this sector was not allocated between East and West in the C.S.O. estimates.

Source: C.S.O., unpublished mimeo.

2. In East Pakistan it was less than 1 per cent.

Table A.9 *Estimates of public industrial investment (constant prices) (Rs million)*

	1960/61	1961/62	1962/63	1963/64	1964/65	1965/66	1966/67	1967/68	1968/69	1969/70
West Pakistan	43.5 (5.1)	33.0 (3.9)	118.1 (15.6)	34.0 (3.2)	119.7 (9.8)	117.5 (10.8)	107.6 (10.9)	117.6 (11.6)	76.1 (8.3)	140.1 (13.2)
East Pakistan	44.7 (21.7)	63.4 (13.8)	99.0 (29.8)	92.9 (24.3)	109.4 (24.3)	97.5 (25.0)	118.3 (24.8)	423.9 (53.0)	404.0 (50.7)	320.3 (45.7)

Note: Figures in parentheses are percentages of total industrial investment (i.e. private plus public).

Source: (i) For 1960/61 to 1962/63, Planning Commission (1966, pp. 191–3).

(ii) For 1963/64 to 1969/70, C.S.O., unpublished mimeo.

Estimates from the above sources were at current prices. They were converted into constant prices using the indices given in table A.5.

Appendix B—Table B.1 *Monopoly houses' assets in Pakistan in 1970* (Gross fixed assets at cost) (Rs million)

No. House	Non-financial quoted companies	Manu-facturing quoted companies	All manu-facturing companies (including) non-quoted)
	West Pakistan		
1. Saigol	460.6	460.6	536.5
2. Crescent	237.8	237.8	270.1
3. Colony (N)	235.9	213.1	240.4
4. Valika	312.0	228.3	228.3
5. Dawood	220.0	197.9	219.7
6. Adamjee	166.5	166.5	186.5
7. Hoti	166.8	166.8	168.3
8. Wazir Ali	119.3	119.3	161.0
9. Habib	139.8	138.5	143.5
10. Amins	221.8	130.4	130.4
11. Bawany	125.3	125.3	125.3
12. Nishat	77.0	77.0	121.3
13. Colony (F)	96.6	96.6	96.6
14. Ghandara	69.5	69.5	93.9
15. Zafar-ul-Ahsan	80.2	80.2	90.2
16. Husein	89.4	89.4	89.4
17. Gul Ahmed	66.3	66.3	87.4
18. Hyesons	50.7	50.7	80.9
19. Premier	70.4	70.4	79.5
20. B.E.C.O.	64.0	64.0	64.0
21. Monnoo	—	—	60.0
22. Rahimtoola	52.7	52.7	52.7
23. Maula Bux	32.1	32.1	52.1
24. Shahnawaz	37.1	37.1	52.1
25. Reyaz-o-Khalid	50.9	50.9	50.9
26. Noon	48.8	48.8	48.8
27. Fateh	46.5	46.5	46.5
28. Fancy	107.8	36.3	44.3
29. Karim	38.6	38.6	38.6
30. G. Faruque	38.1	38.1	38.1
31. Dada	37.4	37.4	37.4
32. Hafiz	35.5	35.5	35.5
33. Arag	24.1	24.1	33.8
34. Dadabhoy	29.7	29.7	29.7
35. Khanzada	28.7	28.7	28.7
36. Haji Dost	26.7	26.7	28.7
37. Millwala	—	—	20.0
38. Rangoonwala	18.3	18.3	18.3
39. Haroon	7.5	7.5	11.6

Table B.1 (cont.)

No. House	Non-financial quoted companies	Manu-facturing quoted companies	All manu-facturing companies (including non-quoted)
40. A. Khaleeli	10.4	10.4	10.4
41. Isphani	—	—	10.0
42. Ferozesons	9.8	9.8	9.8
East Pakistan			
1. Dawood	311.8	311.8	311.8
2. Adamjee	213.3	209.6	221.2
3. A. Khaleeli	146.0	146.0	146.0
4. Isphani	81.4	81.4	138.4
5. Fancy	120.0	120.0	120.0
6. Bawany	111.2	111.2	119.2
7. Amins	64.8	64.8	64.8
8. Karim	63.5	63.5	63.5
9. Maula Bux	59.0	59.0	59.0
10. A. K. Khan	—	—	50.0
11. Gul Ahmed	41.9	41.9	41.9
12. Hafiz	35.0	35.0	35.0
13. Bawa	28.9	28.9	28.9
14. Monnoo	25.0	25.0	25.0
15. Habib	—	—	5.0
16. Rahimtoola	1.0	1.0	1.0

Notes on table B. 1

Lists of firms under the control of monopoly houses are available from the author and can be obtained on request.

Estimates of fixed assets of quoted companies were obtained from the balance sheets. In the case of non-quoted companies, assets were estimated as follows:

(a) For firms mainly in the cotton textiles, jute manufacturing and sugar industries, after finding their production capacity, the value of their fixed assets was found from equivalent sized firms which had come into production about the same time.

(b) Where equivalent companies on the K.S.E. were not available the value of fixed assets was obtained through indirect enquiries. Estimates in these cases were therefore not very reliable but since these normally were the smaller companies controlled by the monopoly houses, this would not significantly affect the overall size of the monopoly house.

Sources:

(1)   Government of Pakistan, 1965, 'Report of the Anti-Cartel Law Study Group' (unpublished; made available to the author).

(2)   State Bank of Pakistan, *Balance Sheet Analysis of Joint Stock Companies, 1965–70* (Karachi).

(3)   Tareen, A. K. (ed.), *Directory of Pakistan Cotton Textile Industry* (Karachi, 1970).

(4)   Haidari, I. and Khan, A. H., 1968, *Stock Exchange Guide to Pakistan* (Economic and Industrial Publications, Karachi, various issues).

(5)   Haidari (1969).

(6)   Haidari (1970).

(7)   I.P. and S. (1966a).

(8)   I.P. and S. (1972).

(9)   Information collected by the author from the I.P. and S. Department, Karachi, for sanctions made during the Third Plan period.

(10)   Direct enquiries in Karachi including interviews with members of the major monopoly houses.

Table B.2 *Estimates of gross fixed assets (at cost) 1970* (Rs million)

	All non-financial companies quoted on the K.S.E.			All manufacturing companies quoted on the K.S.E.			Total large-scale manufacturing sector (1969/70)		
	All	Private[a]	Private domestic[b]	All	Private	Private domestic	All	Private	Private domestic
All Pakistan	9580.0	6944.1	6140.6	6555.7	6337.2	5633.0	15992.1	12755.5	11668.7
West Pakistan	7974.7	5338.8	4572.1	5063.8	4845.3	4141.0	10686.6	9631.6	8811.1
East Pakistan	1605.3	1605.3	1568.5	1491.9	1491.9	1491.9	5305.5	3123.9	2857.6

Note: [a]Excluding government controlled companies
[b]Excluding government and foreign controlled companies.

Sources: (i) For companies on the K.S.E. compiled from the State Bank of Pakistan, *Balance Sheet Analysis of Joint Stock Companies, 1965–70* (Karachi).

(ii) For total large-scale manufacturing sector, see notes on next page.

Notes to table B.2: Estimating fixed assets (at cost) in the large-scale manufacturing sector 1969/70

(A) PRIVATE FIXED ASSETS

(i) *West Pakistan*

Kemal (1976) gives a figure of Rs 5564.8 million for total net assets in 1969/70. To this was added the net assets of the three industries which he excludes, namely petroleum, furniture and wood, cork and allied industry (obtained from C.S.O., *Census of Manufacturing Industries 1969/70*, Karachi, hereafter C.M.I.) which was Rs 173.2 million. The figure for accumulated depreciation (which is not given in Kemal) was available until 1966/67 in the C.M.I. 1966/67 and came to Rs 1508.9 million. Since the coverage of C.M.I. 1966/67 underestimates the actual assets in the large-scale manufacturing sector this was increased by the proportion of net assets as given in Kemal (1976) for 1966/67 and the C.M.I. for the same year. This increased the figure of accumulated depreciation to Rs 2296.6 million. The figures for actual depreciation in the three years 1967/68, 1968/69 and 1969/70 were calculated from Kemal and these came to Rs 1541.5 million. To this was added Rs 55.5 million as depreciation for the three excluded industries (i.e. petroleum, furniture and wood, cork and allied industry) based on a ratio of the net assets of these three industries to the rest in 1969/70 as given in the C.M.I. 1969/70. This gave us a total of Rs 9631.6 million.

One major shortcoming of total assets calculated in this way is that we were not able to take into account retirements of fixed assets between 1966/67 and 1969/70. This was not possible as it would have meant getting a series of investment estimates for about 30 years giving breakdowns of different types of assets and this is not available. Our estimates of gross fixed assets, therefore, overestimate the actual figure by the amount of the retirement. However, there are two major reasons why this amount will not be large. Firstly, life of industrial buildings is normally assumed to be 50 years and the average life of most plant and machinery in manufacturing is normally above 34 years. Since there was an almost non-existent manufacturing sector in Pakistan at the time of independence in 1947, a large portion of the fixed assets investment made after 1947 would still be in operation. Secondly, the amount of investment in manufacturing in the early fifties, which would be due for retirement in the late sixties, was not very large in relation to the investment made in the sixties.

(ii) *East Pakistan*

The figure for net assets in 1969/70 in the large-scale manufacturing sector is given as Rs 1874 million in the Bangladesh Bureau of Statistics (1972) based on the C.M.I. of that year. Alamgir and Berlage (1974,

p. 189) suggest that this underestimates actual assets by about 10 per cent. The figure was therefore increased to Rs 2061.4 million. The figure for accumulated depreciation until 1964/65 (in the C.M.I. 1964/65) was given as Rs 155.8 million and this was increased by 10 per cent to take into account under-coverage.

Depreciation between the years 1965/66 and 1969/70 was obtained as follows. For the investment undertaken between 1960/61 and 1969/70, we used our series (table A.6) and then calculated depreciation, on the same lines as used by Kemal (1976) for West Pakistan. This came to Rs 751.0 million. Since a series on industrial investment in the fifties was not available, an indirect method was used to obtain that series. Gross fixed assets in 1959/60 as given in the C.M.I. for that year were Rs 622.3 million. These were then distributed between the years 1951/52 and 1959/60 on the basis of an index constructed for the import of industrial machinery during these years based on Islam (1967b). Depreciation of these investments was then calculated using the same method as had been done for the sixties (i.e. Kemal, 1976). This came to Rs 140.4 million.

Adding accumulated depreciation for these years to net assets in 1969/70 gives us a figure of Rs. 3123.9 million for gross fixed assets at cost in East Pakistan in 1969/70.

(B) ESTIMATES OF FOREIGN CONTROLLED ASSETS 1970

There were three different categories of foreign firms engaged in manufacturing and their *net worths* are given separately.

(i) For firms and companies registered or incorporated outside Pakistan it is Rs 22.9 million.

(ii) For firms in partnership with foreign capital, it is Rs 3.4 million.

(iii) For manufacturing firms incorporated in Pakistan with foreign liabilities it is Rs 967.1 million.

This gives a total figure of Rs 993.4 million for net worth of foreign controlled assets in the large-scale manufacturing sector. In order to blow up this figure to net assets we had to use the ratio of net worth to net assets for *all* foreign quoted firms as it was not available separately for the manufacturing sector. This gives us a figure of total net assets controlled by foreigners in 1970 as Rs 1086.8 million.

Separate figures for the two provinces were not available and these were obtained by dividing the total on the basis of the ratio of private fixed assets in the two provinces.

(C) ESTIMATES OF GOVERNMENT CONTROLLED ASSETS

(a) West Pakistan

This was obtained as follows:

(i) For West Pakistan Industrial Development Corporation the figure of fixed assets at cost is Rs 833.22 million (based on West Pakistan Industrial Development Corporation, *Annual Report*, 1970, Karachi).

(ii) For Fauji Foundation it came to Rs 151.5 million (based on Annual Report).

(iii) For Associated Cement Company it was Rs 20.3 million (based on Annual Report).

(iv) For other assets controlled by the provincial government a rough estimate of Rs 50 million was used based on direct enquiries.

This gives a total figure of Rs 1055 million.

(b) East Pakistan

Based on the East Pakistan Industrial Development Corporation, *Annual Reports*, (Dacca, various issues) we obtained an estimate of Rs 2181.6 million.

Table B.3 *Total foreign exchange loans obtained by monopoly houses from P.I.C.I.C. and I.D.B.P (from 1958 to 1970 in the case of P.I.C.I.C. and from 1961 to 1970 in the case of I.D.B.P.) (Rs million)*

Monopoly house	I.D.B.P.	P.I.C.I.C.
1. Dawood	3.37	123.58
2. Saigol	100.56	46.62
3. Adamjee	19.95	50.69
4. Valika	21.93	27.1
5. Crescent	0.68	117.76
6. Bawany	14.8	42.91
7. Amins	6.92	16.27
8. Habib	9.8	46.17
9. Gul Ahmed	5.4	48.1
10. Karim	1.3	27.92
11. Hoti	—	38.39
12. Wazir Ali	3.56	23.64
13. A. Khaleeli	1.54	—
14. Isphani	8.08	8.82
15. Colony (N)	25.34	37.12
16. Maula Bux	2.70	34.62
17. Ghandara	33.1	16.07
18. Husein	—	22.45
19. Colony (F)	10.64	18.0
20. Reyaz-o-Khalid	30.95	—
21. Hyesons	1.5	13.38
22. Zafar-ul-Ahsan	28.4	2.74
23. Nishat	9.66	15.88
24. B.E.C.O.	—	7.57
25. Rangoonwala	0.37	6.87

Table B.3 (*continued*)

Monopoly house	I.D.B.P.	P.I.C.I.C.
26. Premier	—	5.72
27. Dada	—	1.49
28. G. Faruque	—	13.84
29. Fateh	2.95	8.71
30. Ferozesons	2.05	1.94
31. Haroon	—	0.67
32. Bawa	—	6.94
33. Noons	9.3	23.24
34. Arag	—	4.61
35. Shahnawaz	1.19	27.0
36. A. K. Khan	9.26	1.17
37. Dadabhoy	0.20	7.3
38. Hafiz	—	9.12
39. Khanzada	—	6.96
40. Monnoo	9.05	—
Total	374.55	911.43

Sources: (i) Information on loans given by P.I.C.I.C. obtained by the author from their Karachi office.

(ii) For I.D.B.P. loans

(a) Directory of Industrial Units sanctioned during Second Plan period (I.P. & S., 1966a).

(b) Investments sanctioned by I.D.B.P. during Third Plan. (Information collected from I.P. & S. Department, Karachi.)

(c) Balance sheets of quoted companies of firms controlled by the monopoly house.

Table B.4 *Share of monopoly houses' companies in total N.I.T. investments 1970 (percentages)*

Monopoly house	%	Monopoly house	%	Monopoly house	%
1. Dawood	6.95	14. Faruque	1.43	27. Rahimtoola	0.35
2. Saigol	5.82	15. Husein	1.45	28. Hoti	0.24
3. Adamjee	5.02	16. A. Khaleeli	1.29	29. Bawa	0.19
4. Bawany	4.42	17. Arag	1.26	30. A. K. Khan	0.12
5. Ghandara	3.67	18. Fateh	1.11	31. Frontier	0.13
6. Fancy	2.84	19. Noon	1.04	32. Shahnawaz	0.22
7. Colony (N)	2.67	20. Valika	0.81	33. Dada	0.26
8. Gul Ahmed	2.80	21. Wazir Ali	0.96	34. Colony (F)	0.17
9. Nishat	2.2	22. Isphani	0.80	35. Haroons	0.31
10. B.E.C.O.	2.74	23. Hafiz	0.42	36. Ferozesons	0.04
11. Karim	1.94	24. Zafar-ul- Ahsan	0.36	37. Rangoonwala	0.18
12. Crescent	1.81	25. Millwala	0.34	38. Premier	0.01
13. Habib	1.64	26. Hyesons	0.35	39. Reyaz-o-Khalid	0.01
				40. Amin	2.51

(1) As % of all companies = 60.88%.
(2) As % of domestic companies (i.e. excluding foreign companies) = 64.8%.
(3) As % of private domestic companies (i.e. excluding foreign and government controlled companies) = 73.9%.

Source: National Investment (Unit) Trust, *Director's Report and Statement of Accounts, 1st July 1969 – 30 June 1970* (Karachi, 1970).

Table B.5 *Investment corporation of Pakistan: investment in shares of companies controlled by monopoly houses (percentages)*

Monopoly house	First I.C.P. fund	Second I.C.P. fund	Third I.C.P. fund	Fourth I.C.P. fund
B.E.C.O.	2.6	—	—	9.3
Habib	14.0	—	—	0.6
Husein	6.2	6.8	1.0	1.6
Ghandara	2.7	—	0.6	1.0
Karim	3.8	—	—	—
Dawood	12.8	12.4	1.1	—
Noon	9.3	—	—	—
Colony	—	2.8	0.7	1.2
Crescent	—	0.6	—	—
Wazir Ali	2.2	14.3	—	6.2
Amin	—	2.0	—	6.7
Fancy	—	—	9.9	—
Saigol	—	—	4.6	—
Premier	—	—	14.7	3.4
Isphani	—	—	—	3.1
Bawany	—	—	0.7	2.8
As % of all companies	53.6	38.9	33.3	35.9

Note to Table B.5

	First I.C.P. fund	Second I.C.P. fund	Third I.C.P. fund	Fourth I.C.P. fund
(a) As % of domestic companies only (i.e. excluding foreign)	70.8	47.2	33.3	35.9
(b) As % of private domestic companies only (i.e. excluding foreign and government owned companies).	95.6	100.0	82.4	90.1

Source: Investment Corporation of Pakistan, *Annual Report 1970* (Karachi 1970).

Table B.6 *Direct foreign loans arranged
by P.I.C.I.C. (Rs million)*

Country/agency	Amount
Japan	295.35
France	78.95
International Finance Corporation	59.77
West Germany	41.62
Saudi Arabia	40.05
U.K.	29.79
Rumania	19.05
Belgium	9.75
	574.33

Source: P.I.C.I.C., *13th Annual Report*,
Karachi, December 1970.

Appendix C — Table C.1 *Previous results on behaviour of profitability*

Study	Period covered	Sample	Indicators used	Results	Reasons given
1. Papanek (1967)	1947–58	Direct survey of large firms with capital of Rs 1 million or more.	Gross pre-tax profits[a]/net assets	On the average profits *declined* 30% between 1947/55 and 1956/58.	(i) Increase in domestic competition
2. Safiullah (1967)	1955–63	65 firms quoted on the Karachi Stock Exchange (K.S.E.) covering jute, cotton textiles, tea, food and cement industry.	—	No decline between 1955 and 1963.	—
3. Haq and Baqai (1967)	1959–63	All *non-financial companies* quoted on the K.S.E.	Gross pre-tax profits[b] as a proportion of share-capital, net worth, total capital employed[c] and sales.	*Decline* in price-cost margin (7.6% in the period) as well as in the rate of return on net worth and gross capital employed (about 7%).	(i) Liberalisation of import policy leading to increase in capacity utilisation. (ii) Greater degree of competition.
4. Alamgir and Rahman (1974)	1961–62 to 1968–69	East Pakistan only. *Non-financial companies* quoted on K.S.E., Dacca Stock Exchange and Companies belonging to E.P.I.D.C.[d] (Their study therefore *includes* some *public sector* firms).	Some as above except for total capital employed they used net assets.	Considerable fluctuation but *overall decline* of about 50% in all measures of profitability.	Not given.

[a] Includes profits, interest, management fees, taxes and depreciation.
[b] Net pre-tax profits plus depreciation but excludes interest payments.
[c] Net assets and stocks.

Sources: (1) Papanek (1967, p. 37).
(2) Safiullah (1967, pp. 42–3, 59).
(3) Haq and Baqai (1967, pp. 290–6).

Table C.2 *List of companies included in continuous
companies sample*

1961–65

Cotton textiles
1. Burewala Textiles
2. Colony Textiles
3. Colony (Thal)
4. A. Bawany Textiles
5. Hussein Industries
6. Fateh Textiles
7. Bahawalpur Textiles
8. Dost Mohammad Cotton
9. Khairpur Textiles
10. F. P. Textiles
11. Hafiz Textiles

Other textiles

12. Harnai Woolen
13. National Silk & Rayon

Jute

14. Adamjee Jute Mill
15. Latif Bawany Jute
16. Amin Jute Mills
17. Karim Jute Mills
18. Victory Jute Mfg.

19. Chittagong Jute Mfg.
20. Platinum Jubilee

Others

21. Charsaddah Sugar Mills
22. Premium Sugar Mills
23. Frontier Sugar Mills
24. Souvenier Tobacco
25. Asbestos Cement
26. Brooke Bond
27. Lipton (Pak.)
28. Karnaphully Paper Mills
29. Packages
30. Pakistan Oxygen
31. I.C.I.
32. Glaxo Laboratories
33. Steel Corporation of
    Pakistan
34. Pakistan Cables
35. Kohinoor Industries
36. Adamjee Industries
37. Wazir Ali Industries
38. Hashim Can
39. Murree Brewery

1965–70
(Above 39 firms were also in the sample)

Cotton Textiles

40. Dawood Cotton Mills
41. Valika Textiles
42. Colony (Sarhad)
43. Nishat Mills
44. Crescent Textiles
45. Gulberg Textiles
46. Olympia Textiles
47. Bawany Industries
48. Nishat Industries
49. Tangail Cotton Mills
50. Amin Textiles
51. Janana de Malucho
52. Khyber Textiles

53. Satrang Textiles
54. Feroze Sultan Industries
55. Indus Dyeing & Mfg
56. M.F.M.Y. Industries
57. Arag Industries

Other textiles

58. Valika Woolen Mills
59. Valika Art Fabrics
60. Lawerencepur Woolen &
    Textiles Mills.
61. H.M. Silk Mill
62. Fulbrite

Jute

63. United Jute Mills
64. Bawa Jute Mills
65. Pak Jute Mills
66. Amin Fabrics
67. Pakistan Tobacco

Others

68. Premier Tobacco
69. Crescent Sugar Mills
70. Habib Sugar Mills
71. Hyeson Sugar Mills
72. Thal Industries
73. Pakistan Paper Products
74. Chittagong Board Mill
75. Pakistan Industrial Gases
76. Sandoz (Pak)
77. Ferozesons Laboratories
78. B.E.C.O.

79. Mack Trucks of Pakistan
80. Ghandara Industries
81. Rana Tractors
82. Shaigan Electric & Engineering
83. Johnsons & Phillips
84. Haji E. Dossa & Sons
85. Burmah Oil Mill
86. Maqbool Co.
87. Associated Industries
88. East Pakistan Lubricants Blenders
89. Haroon Oils
90. Pakistan Refinery
91. Pakistan Rope Works
92. Usmania Glass Sheet Factory
93. Hilal Tanneries
94. Valika Cement
95. Ismail Cement
96. Zeal Pak Cement

Problems with data

It should be pointed out that for the earlier years 1961–65, the basic source for the data used, i.e. State Bank of Pakistan, *Balance Sheet Analysis of Joint Stock Companies 1961–66* (Karachi), had serious shortcomings. The major problem was that for a large number of companies where the data for one year was missing, they were substituted by the figures for earlier or later years, and this was *not* subsequently corrected. Also figures for sales, gross fixed assets, net profits before tax and other fixed liabilities in a number of cases were either misprinted or not correctly copied from the balance sheets. The data for each of the companies were therefore re-checked wherever possible from the actual balance sheet of companies or from Haidari and Khan (1968), and corrections made or the missing year substituted. Where the figures for the missing years could not be obtained the company was dropped from the sample.

The data published by the State Bank for the period 1965–70 are fortunately far more reliable. Cross-checking with the actual company accounts or Haidari and Khan (1968) showed many fewer mistakes.

However, the major problem for this series is that in 1969 (because of a directive by the Central Board of Revenue that all companies should change over to the accounting year beginning October to end September) a number of companies drew up their accounts for a period ranging from 9 to 14 months. For these companies, their accounts had to be re-adjusted to a one year period so as to make the series consistent. All figures for sales, profits, dividends and retentions were therefore proportionately changed.

Table C.3 *Sales of sample companies in relation to sales of whole large-scale manufacturing sector* (percentages)

	1962/63			1964/65			1969/70		
	All Pakistan	West Pakistan	East Pakistan	All Pakistan	West Pakistan	East Pakistan	All Pakistan	West Pakistan	East Pakistan
All quoted companies									
(i) 39 continuous companies	25.4	34.4	22.2	32.0	35.8	19.5	41.9	44.8	31.8
(ii) 96 continuous companies	18.8	18.1	20.5	16.4	15.7	17.2	15.0	14.7	18.9
All quoted companies	—	—	—	—	—	—	31.8	36.3	22.7
Important industries									
1. Cotton textiles	36.0	40.2	7.2	37.8	41.2	12.0	49.0	51.7	29.1
2. Jute	84.3	—	84.3	80.6	—	80.4	84.5	47.5	87.9
3. Sugar	23.5	32.4	—	66.0	100.0	—	58.8	71.7	—
4. Chemicals	11.5	16.0	—	10.4	14.3	—	27.2	34.9	1.9
5. Cement	36.9	n.a.	—	42.8	n.a.	—	n.a.	68.5	—
6. Paper and board	39.1	100.0	59.6	39.2	100.0	50.8	95.0	100.0	90.0
7. Tea	n.a.	n.a.	—	43.7	—	—	n.a.	—	—
8. Tobacco	77.1	97.2	—	72.6	99.0	—	n.a.	100.0	—
9. Engineering[a]	19.6	41.6	—	16.2	21.6	—	15.8	26.5	2.0

Note: n.a. data not available.

— No coverage by sample firms of that industry.

[a] Includes basic metals, metal products, electrical machinery, machinery (except electrical) and transport equipment industries.

Source: (i) C.S.O., *Census of Manufacturing Industries* (Karachi, various issues)
(ii) For East Pakistan 1969/70, Bangladesh Bureau of Statistics (1972)
(iii) State Bank of Pakistan, *Balance Sheet Analysis of Joint Stock Companies* (Karachi, various issues).

Table C.4 *Behaviour of profitability: All Pakistan*

	1961	1962	1963	1964	1965	1966	1967	1968	1969	1970	Average 1961–65	Average 1966–70 (excluding 1967)
All quoted companies												
(1) Gross profits★/ net worth	25.0	24.1	26.0	22.1	18.4	20.4	15.6	20.8	22.1	21.4	23.1	21.2
(2) Gross profits/ net assets	23.8	22.9	23.9	19.0	15.8	17.0	13.4	16.9	17.9	17.4	21.1	17.3
(3) Price–cost margin	17.4	18.7	19.4	17.8	16.1	16.8	12.4	15.6	15.7	14.9	17.9	15.8
(4) Gearing ratio	7.3	7.4	14.4	22.4	25.7	26.7	28.7	30.7	30.6	30.6	15.4	29.7
39 continuous firms												
(1) Gross profits★/ net worth	23.0	26.4	28.3	26.2	22.7	23.4	17.9	24.8	24.3	25.1	25.3	24.4
(2) Gross profits/net assets	21.8	24.6	25.8	23.6	20.2	20.5	16.1	21.7	21.5	21.7	23.2	21.4
(3) Price–cost margin	14.5	18.2	19.3	17.9	16.0	15.0	12.4	15.4	14.9	14.5	17.2	15.0
(4) Gearing ratio	7.9	9.9	12.6	14.5	17.1	18.7	18.6	17.9	19.4	19.9	12.4	19.0
96 continuous companies												
(1) Gross profits★/net worth					21.5	21.6	19.7	23.6	24.3	22.8	—	23.1
(2) Gross profits/net assets					19.0	19.0	17.4	20.8	21.2	20.0	—	20.3
(3) Price–cost margin					15.4	14.6	13.2	15.0	15.1	13.5	—	14.6
(4) Gearing ratio					18.7	19.4	19.0	18.1	19.2	18.9	—	18.9

★Excluding interest.

Source: Compield from State Bank of Pakistan, *Balance Sheet Analysis of Joint Stock Companies* (Karachi, various

Table C.5 *Profitability: by provinces*

	1961	1962	1963	1964	1965	1966	1967	1968	1969	1970	Average 1961–65	Average 1965–70	Per cent change
West Pakistan													
(1) Gross profit★/ net work	28.2	22.5	25.8	22.6	18.4	19.5	16.7	21.3	22.7	22.2	23.5	20.5	− 12.8
(2) Gross profit/ net assets	27.1	21.6	23.6	19.2	20.5	16.3	14.2	17.3	18.3	18.1	22.4	16.8	− 25.0
(3) Gross profit/ sales	20.3	17.7	19.1	17.8	16.0	16.5	12.4	15.1	16.0	14.6	18.2	14.9	− 18.1
(4) Gearing	5.5	6.2	12.3	23.3	27.1	27.9	27.9	29.3	30.1	28.8	14.9	28.8	+ 93.3
East Pakistan													
(1) Gross profit★/ net worth	14.4	30.2	26.7	19.9	18.3	23.9	11.3	18.0	19.6	18.2	21.9	19.9	− 9.1
(2) Gross profit/net assets	13.6	27.5	24.1	17.8	16.3	20.7	10.3	18.0	15.8	14.7	19.9	17.3	− 13.1
(3) Gross profit/sales	9.4	22.2	19.9	17.5	16.4	17.6	8.1	19.1	14.1	15.8	17.1	16.7	− 2.3
(4) Gearing	12.9	11.8	13.8	17.8	18.8	21.1	31.5	37.4	32.6	37.2	15.0	32.1	+ 113.3

★ Excluding interest charges

Note: Average for 1965–70 for East Pakistan for (1) to (3) excludes 1967.

Source: Complied from State Bank of Pakistan, *Balance Sheet Analyses of Joint Stock Companies* (Karachi, various issues).

Table C.6 *Profitability: cotton textile industry (province-wise)*

	1961	1962	1963	1964	1965	1966	1967	1968	1969	1970
(i) Gross profits (excluding interest)/net worth										
(a) West Pakistan	31.8	24.8	23.3	23.0	20.1	19.2	19.6	21.0	26.1	23.1
(b) East Pakistan	24.5	12.9	7.9	12.4	10.4	11.8	11.4	20.8	21.7	20.6
(ii) Gross profits/net assets										
(a) West Pakistan	30.5	23.3	21.1	20.5	18.0	17.4	17.7	18.3	21.9	19.2
(b) East Pakistan	21.7	11.9	7.9	11.6	9.7	11.0	10.5	16.5	19.1	19.2

Sources: (i) For West Pakistan, compiled from State Bank of Pakistan, *Balance Sheet Analysis of Joint Stock Companies* (Karachi, various issues).

(ii) For East Pakistan, Alamgir and Rahman (1974, pp. 191–2) except for 1970 which is based on (i). Their figures were used because of their much wider coverage of the cotton textile industry in East Pakistan. Interest charges were calculated by the same method as used by us.

Table D.7 *Other industries' profitability (gross profits[a]/net worth)*

Industry	1961	1962	1963	1964	1965	1966	1967	1968	1969	1970
1. Other textiles	33.3	14.3	11.1	13.2	13.3	12.9	12.3	18.6	15.5	13.5
2. Paper and board	23.7	23.9	23.2	22.0	21.4	22.6	19.6	21.6	18.5	18.9
3. Engineering	21.7	14.9	21.4	27.6	20.9	25.5	21.7	24.7	23.7	18.3
4. Chemicals										
(i) All	16.7	14.3	12.5	13.9	15.8	14.2	15.4	7.0	14.8	16.1
(ii) 8 continuous firms	—	—	—	—	19.4	19.3	21.8	22.4	22.1	20.4

[a]Excluding interest.
Source: State Bank of Pakistan, *Balance Sheet Analysis of Joint Stock Companies* (Karachi, various issues).

Appendix D—Table D.1 *Results of regression analysis: price–cost. margins, concentration and capital–output ratios (25 industries)*

Price-cost margin (PC_1) (dependent variable)	Concentration ratio (CR_4)	Capital–output ratio (K/O)	Concentration ratio (log CR_4)	Capital–output ratio (log K/O)	Constant term	R^2
1965/66★						
(1) PC_1	0.16[b] (2.091)	−1.94 (0.6663)			12.85	0.17
(2) PC_2	0.20[b] (2.473)	2.48 (0.8031)			16.68	0.30
(3) Log PC_1			0.44[a] (2.815)	0.09 (0.6261)	1.23	0.36
1966/67						
(1) PC_1	0.18[b] (2.502)	−0.63 (0.217)			11.24	0.27
(2) PC_2	0.15[b] (1.847)	6.89[b] (2.078)			15.10	0.43
(3) Log PC_1			0.28[b] (2.151)	0.14 (1.155)	1.94	0.35
1967/68						
(1) PC_1	0.21[a] (3.087)	−4.04 (0.882)			11.94	0.31
(2) PC_2	0.26[a] (4.589)	5.33[c] (1.424)			12.51	0.63
(3) Log PC_1			0.41[a] (2.943)	0.06 (0.398)	1.42	0.36
1969/70						
(1) PC_1	0.33[a] (4.414)	−1.32 (0.346)			7.82	0.50
(2) PC_2	0.37[a] (4.652)	−1.64 (0.3)			12.25	0.52
(3) Log PC_1			0.52[a] (4.216)	0.07 (0.6387)	1.19	0.51

Note: Figures in parentheses are *t*-ratios.
★ 24 industries (excludes products of petroleum and coal).
[a] significant at the 1 per cent level.
[b] significant at the 5 per cent level.
[c] significant at the 10 per cent level.

Table D.2 *Results of regression analysis: impact of imports on domestic profitability*

Price-cost margin (PC_1) (dependent variable)	Concentration ratio (CR_4)	Capital–output ratio (K/O)	Competing imports (M)	Dummy for imports (M_D)	Constant term	R^2
1965/66						
	0.20[a]	− 3.67	− 0.23[b]	—	11.53	0.35
	(3.237)	(1.327)	(2.298)			
	0.24[a]	− 2.97	—	− 7.58[c]	12.11	0.26
	(2.605)	(1.018)		(1.483)		
1966/67						
	0.21[a]	− 0.76	− 0.08	—	10.89	0.29
	(2.591)	(0.259)	(0.876)			
	0.23[a]	− 0.69	—	− 6.31[c]	10.46	0.33
	(2.946)	(0.243)		(1.450)		
1967/68						
	0.21[a]	− 4.23	0.03	—	12.10	0.31
	(2.580)	(0.895)	(0.122)			
	0.22[a]	− 3.84	—	− 1.48	11.65	0.31
	(2.780)	(0.815)		(0.514)		
1969/70						
	0.37[a]	− 1.36	− 0.11	—	7.04	0.52
	(4.226)	(0.308)	(0.973)			
	0.40[a]	− 1.18	—	− 7.79[c]	6.47	0.55
	(4.639)	(0.274)		(1.501)		

Note: Figures in parentheses are *t*-ratios.
[a] significant at the 1 per cent level.
[b] significant at the 5 per cent level.
[c] significant at the 10 per cent level.

Table D.3 *Results of regression analysis: price–cost margins, concen-*
tration and other variables

Price–cost margin (PC_1) (dependent variable)	Concentration ratio (CR_4)	Capital–output ratio (K/O)	Capacity utilisation (CU)	Exports (X)	Advertising (A)	Constant term	R^2
1965/66							
	0.18[b]	−2.99	0.07	—	—	7.21	0.20
	(2.205)	(0.920)	(0.762)				
	0.17[b]	−2.40	0.08	−0.40	0.34	6.34	0.24
	(2.029)	(0.704)	(0.762)	(0.818)	(0.715)		
1966/67							
	0.21[b]	−1.27	0.14[b]	—	—	−0.61	0.35
	(2.732)	(0.409)	(1.759)				
	0.19[a]	−0.56	0.09	−0.58[c]	0.13	5.10	0.40
	(2.684)	(0.184)	(1.140)	(1.558)	(0.321)		
1967/68							
	0.22[a]	−4.76	0.05	—	—	8.30	0.32
	(4.375)	(0.998)	(0.598)				
	0.22[a]	−4.08	0.07	−0.41[c]	0.44	6.28	0.41
	(3.022)	(0.862)	(0.825)	(1.373)	(1.041)		
1969/70							
	0.37[a]	−4.14	0.22[a]	—	—	−8.73	0.64
	(5.605)	(1.054)	(2.894)				
	0.37[a]	−4.67	0.20[a]	0.48[c]	−0.28	−7.67	0.69
	(5.762)	(1.182)	(2.670)	(1.614)	(0.711)		

Note: Figures in parentheses are *t*-ratios.

[a] significant at the 1 per cent level.

[b] significant at the 5 per cent level.

[c] significant at the 10 per cent level.

Table D.4 *Results of regression analysis: impact of effective protection on profitability (number of industries: 18)*

Price–cost margin (PC_1) (dependent variable)	Per cent by which domestic price exceeds world price P_1	Protection		Constant	R^2
		Effective tariff protection P_2	Protection from all sources P_3		
1965/66*	—	—	− 0.02 (0.667)	20.2	0.03
	—	− 0.01 (0.222)	—	18.7	0.003
1966/67	—	—	− 0.09 (2.052)	27.7	0.21
	− 0.02 (0.924)	—	—	23.7	0.05
	—	− 0.15 (2.971)	—	24.5	0.36
1967/68	—	—	− 0.08 (1.60)	28.8	0.14
	− 0.01 (0.42)	—	—	24.3	0.01
	—	− 0.11 (1.680)	—	25.4	0.15
1969/70	—	—	− 0.12 (1.924)	36.7	0.19
	− 0.05 (1.395)	—	—	33.4	0.11
	—	− 0.12 (1.480)	—	30.6	0.12

Note: Figures in parentheses are *t*-ratios.
*Only 17 industries.

Table D.5 *Estimates of concentration ratios for selected industries in West Pakistan (1968)*

Industry	Four-firm-concentration ratio	Methodology	Source
1. Grain milling	11.0	Installed capacity	I.P.&S. (1972, Vol. III)
2. Sugar	33.7	Sales	State Bank of Pakistan, *Balance Sheet Analysis of Joint Stock Companies* (Karachi, various issues) and C.S.O., *Census of Manufacturing Industries*, (Karachi, various issues)
3. Edible oil	20.5	Production-weighted average of vegetable ghee and edible oil industry	I.P.&S. (1972, Vol. I)
4. Drinks and carbonated water	70.0	Production	I.P.&S. (1972, Vol. II)
5. Cigarettes	79.7	Production	I.P.&S. (1972, Vol. I)
6. Cotton spinning	30.0	Production-weighted averaged of spinning and weaving industry	I.P.&S. (1972, Vol. I)
7. Wool spinning	65.2	Sales	Jafri (1968)
8. Silk and art silk	10.0	Installed capacity	Government of West Pakistan (1969)
9. Dyeing and bleaching	7.4	Production	I.P.&S. (1972, Vol. I)
10. Rubber footwear	67.1	Production	I.P.&S. (1972, Vol. III)

			C.S.O., *Census of Manufacturing Industries* (Karachi, various issues)
11. Books and periodicals	30.0	Sales	
12. Tanning and leather	40.0	Production	I.P.&S. (1972, Vol. I)
13. Cotton ginning	7.0	Production	I.P.&S. (1972, Vol. I)
14. Cement	67.0	Production	I.P.&S. (1972, Vol. I)
15. Tyres and tubes	90.0	Production	I.P.&S. (1972, Vol. I)
16. Fertiliser	100.0	Production	I.P.&S. (1972, Vol. II)
17. Paints and varnishes	52.4	Production	I.P.&S. (1972, Vol. II)
18. Pharmaceuticals	44.8	Sales	Fazili (1969)
19. Products of petroleum and coal	100.0	Production	I.P.&S. (1972, Vol.II)
20. Acids, alkalis and salts	100.0	Production-weighted average	I.P.&S. (1972, Vol. I)
21. Iron and steel	45.9	Production-weighted average	I.P.&S. (1972, Vols. I, II and III)
22. Motors, generators and transformers	74.5	Production	I.P.&S. (1972, Vol. I)
23. Communication equipment	90.0	Production	I.P.&S. (1972, Vol. I)
24. Mechanical vehicles	80.0	Production-weighted average	I.P.&S. (1972, Vols. I and III)
25. Engines and turbines	62.3	Production	I.P.&S. (1972, Vol. I)

Methodology

We have measured the concentration ratio in terms of the share of the four largest firms in 1968 of total sales or output and in a few cases where these were not available in terms of production capacity of the industry. In the case of multi-product industries we have used the weighted average of four firm concentration ratios of the main products. In the case of an industry which has firms belonging to the same management or industrial house listed separately, the output of the different firms are taken together to represent one firm.

Table D.6(a) Estimates of price–cost margins (PC_1) for selected industries in West Pakistan

Industry	1965/66	1966/67	1967/68	1969/70	Average 4 years
1. Grain milling	1.8	7.0	2.4	3.8	3.8
2. Sugar	23.1	20.5	22.7	26.9	23.3
3. Edible oils	5.8	7.4	10.6	10.1	8.5
4. Drinks and carbonated water	24.9	18.7[b]	12.5	18.7[b]	18.7
5. Cigarettes	50.3	34.0	33.2	43.8	40.3
6. Cotton spinning	14.3	11.0	14.8	29.4	17.4
7. Wool spinning	33.6	16.3	28.1	14.5	23.1
8. Silk and art silk	14.9	14.4	16.2	15.2[a]	15.2
9. Dyeing and bleaching	11.2	19.0	11.4	15.1	14.2
10. Rubber footwear	10.7	9.5	10.7	45.5	19.1
11. Books and periodicals	27.7	25.6	24.6	28.6	26.6
12. Tanning and leather	27.5	20.3	18.2	19.0	21.3
13. Cotton ginning	6.9	6.2	11.0	7.1	7.8
14. Cement	20.3	32.8	32.2	23.7	27.3
15. Tyres and tubes	18.3	28.9	30.8	49.7	31.9
16. Fertiliser	17.5	36.6	25.0	47.5	31.7
17. Paints and varnishes	18.7	26.8	24.4	18.1	22.0
18. Pharmaceuticals	34.4	33.8	25.9	19.8	28.5
19. Products of petroleum and coal	—	43.1[a]	37.1	49.0	43.1

20. Acids, alkalis and salts	22.0[a]	12.2	11.6	42.1	22.0
21. Iron and steel	19.2	17.6	17.3	13.5	16.9
22. Motors, generators and trans-formers	14.1	18.4	52.3	30.0	28.7
23. Communication equipment	16.1	22.1	24.2	20.8[a]	20.8
24. Mechanical vehicle	24.8	13.0	23.5	12.9	18.6
25. Engines and turbines	17.9	16.9	17.3	22.4	18.6

[a]Based on average of three years
[b]Based on average of two years
Source: Calculated from C.S.O., *Census of Manufacturing Industries* (Karachi, various issues).

Table D.6(b) Estimates of price–cost margins (PC_2) for selected industries in West Pakistan

Industry	1965/66	1966/67	1967/68	1969/70	Average 4 years
1. Grain milling	3.2	8.1	3.4	4.9	4.9
2. Sugar	29.7	28.9	31.0	30.6	30.1
3. Edible oils	11.5	12.0	15.2	12.1	12.7
4. Drinks and carbonated water	34.7	24.7	23.6	27.7[a]	27.7
5. Cigarettes	54.5	39.4	38.5	47.1	44.9
6. Cotton spinning	24.6	20.2	24.1	35.3	26.1
7. Wool spinning	42.5	23.2	35.0	20.4	30.3
8. Silk and art silk	21.3	19.3	21.1	20.6[a]	20.6
9. Dyeing and bleaching	18.9	24.6	16.9	19.2	19.9
10. Rubber footwear	25.3	15.1	16.3	50.3	26.8
11. Books and periodicals	34.8	32.4	31.4	39.1	34.4
12. Tanning and leather	29.7	22.9	20.8	21.9	23.8
13. Cotton ginning	8.6	7.5	12.3	8.8	9.3
14. Cement	36.1	42.5	41.8	31.8	38.1
15. Tyres and tubes	32.8	39.7	41.7	58.4	43.2
16. Fertiliser	44.0	59.2	47.6	50.2	50.3
17. Paints and varnishes	28.6	37.5	35.2	32.2	33.4
18. Pharmaceuticals	50.5	51.2	43.3	36.4	45.4
19. Products of petroleum and coal	—	23.0	48.3	53.0	41.4
20. Acids, alkalis and salts	19.2	45.5	44.9	59.1	42.2
21. Iron and steel	25.5	24.4	24.2	19.2	23.3
22. Motors, generators and transformers	34.7	31.6	39.9	42.6	37.2
23. Communication equipment	25.9	30.4	32.5	29.6[a]	29.6

[a] Based on average of three previous years.

Source: Calculated from C.S.O., *Census of Manufacturing Industries* (Karachi, various issues).

Note: One major problem that we faced was in calculating the price – cost margin for 1967/68 since only the summary statistics are available for this year and these do not include figures for fixed costs and indirect taxes. This left us only with the option of calculating these based on the same proportion of fixed costs and indirect taxes to total sales as in 1966/67. (The only exception was the petroleum industry for which it was based on 1969/70.)

The Census of Manufacturing Industries, as in the case of most data on the industrial sector collected in developing countries like Pakistan, suffers from many weaknesses and it is generally acknowledged that firms tend to show lower profits than earned. There is, of course, no way of finding out whether this practice is more widespread in some industries as compared to others. We have, therefore, no other choice but to work on the assumption that the tendency of firms to underestimate their profits is somewhat uniform amongst different industries.

Given the fact that there is considerable scope for inaccuracy in both the collection and the computing of the data (see Hogan, 1968), the price–cost margins calculated by us seem to be fairly consistent and do not show extreme fluctuations. Only in the case of a very few industries did we have to drop an observation and replace it by the average figure for years for which the data seemed more consistent. This had to be done in the case of two years for the drinks and carbonated water industry and in the case of one year for acids, alkalis and salts, communication equipment, and products of the petroleum and coal industry. In each case, the figure obtained was very different from the other years and could not be justified on any economic grounds whatsoever. (For example, in the case of PC_2 the calculated value for drinks and carbonated water for 1969/70 was 0.2 as compared to the average of 27.7 for the previous 3 years and 2.3 for communication equipment compared to the average of 29.6 for the previous 3 years.) In the case of the silk and art silk industry for 1969/70, the average of the previous years had to be used since the Census of Manufacturing Industries for that year did not give separate figures for the industry and was included with other industries under the heading of rayon and synthetic industry.

Table D.7 *Estimates of capital–output ratios for selected industries West Pakistan*

Industry	1965/66	1966/67	1967/68	1969/70	Average 4 years
1. Grain milling	0.11	0.09	0.13	0.14	0.1
2. Sugar	0.56	0.95	1.16	0.55	0.8
3. Edible oil	0.23	0.25	0.20	0.16	0.2
4. Drinks	0.70	1.0	0.91	0.94	0.8
5. Cigarettes	0.25	0.30	0.19	0.15	0.2
6. Cotton spinning	0.88	0.92	0.64	0.51	0.7
7. Wool spinning	1.28	0.87	0.50	0.71	0.8
8. Silk and art silk	0.50	0.43	0.31	n.a.	0.
9. Dyeing and bleaching	0.72	0.68	0.52	0.54	0.6
10. Rubber footwear	0.49	0.40	0.20	0.16	0.
11. Books and periodicals	0.66	0.65	0.56	0.52	0.6
12. Tanning and leather	0.11	0.13	0.11	0.11	0.1
13. Cotton ginning	0.12	0.10	0.10	0.08	0.1
14. Cement	2.84	1.18	1.00	1.92	1.7
15. Tyres and tubes	0.69	0.73	0.67	0.32	0.6
16. Fertiliser	3.22	2.65	2.10	2.03	2.5
17. Paints and varnishes	0.42	0.31	0.22	0.13	0.2
18. Pharmaceuticals	0.32	0.34	0.25	0.27	0.
19. Products of petroleum and coal	—	1.16	0.37	0.26	0.
20. Acids, alkalis & salts	0.99	3.24	1.42	1.10	1.6
21. Iron and steel	0.31	0.32	0.22	0.34	0.
22. Motors, generators and transformers	0.52	0.34	0.50	0.17	0.3
23. Communication equipment	0.32	0.66	0.51	1.00	0.6
24. Mechanical vehicle	0.29	0.27	0.39	0.35	0.
25. Engines and turbines	0.65	0.68	0.59	0.45	0.5

Source: Calculated from C.S.O. *Census of Manufacturing Industries* (Karachi) various issues

able D.8 *Imports as a percentage of domestic supply of selected industries in West Pakistan*

dustry	1965/66	1966/67	1967/68	1969/70	Average 4 years
. Grain milling	—	—	—	—	—
. Sugar	4.8	0.2	0.8	0.1	1.5
. Edible oil	3.2	1.0	0.3	0.1	1.2
. Drinks	—	—	—	—	—
. Cigarettes	—	—	—	—	—
. Cotton spinning	4.7	4.9	2.4	0.8	3.2
. Wool spinning	—	—	—	—	—
. Silk and art silk	—	—	—	—	—
. Dyeing and bleaching	—	—	—	—	—
. Rubber and footwear	—	—	—	—	—
. Books and periodicals	—	—	—	—	—
. Tanning and leather	—	—	—	—	—
. Cotton ginning	—	—	—	—	—
. Cement	2.5	3.2	1.0	0.3	1.8
. Tyres and tubes	47.3	33.7	29.1	41.2	37.8
. Fertiliser	38.0	53.9	58.3	60.4	52.7
. Paints and varnishes	30.4	30.5	15.2	18.3	23.6
. Pharmaceuticals	19.9	18.8	15.5	17.2	17.9
. Products of petroleum and coal	—	17.9	11.3	4.5	8.4
. Acids, alkalis & salts	51.8	38.0	39.3	57.5	46.7
. Iron and steel	41.5	53.0	34.7	36.5	41.4
. Motors, generators and transformers	62.3	62.5	54.0	67.8	61.7
. Communication equipment	43.6	31.0	32.6	21.3	32.1
. Mechanical vehicle	54.6	53.7	45.5	50.0	51.0
. Engines and turbines	62.6	55.7	71.7	44.4	58.6

te: —indicates no imports

urce: Calculated from C.S.O. *Monthly Statistical Bulletins* (Karachi, various issues) and C.S.O., *Census of Manufacturing Industries* (Karachi, various issues).

Table D.9 *Estimates of capacity utilisation for selected industries in*
Pakistan

Industry	C.S.O. (for 1965)	I.B.R.D. (for 1967/68 except where specified differently)	Fig us
1. Grain milling	100.0	n.a.	100
2. Sugar	92.4	100.0(1968/69)	92
3. Edible oil	86.7	65.0 (average 1965–69)	65
4. Drinks	100.0	n.a.	100
5. Cigarettes	83.1	100.0	83
6. Cotton spinning	90.1	94.0	90
7. Wool spinning	100.0	n.a.	100
8. Silk and art silk	59.0	n.a.	59
9. Dyeing and bleaching	82.3	n.a.	82
10. Rubber footwear	79.6	n.a.	79
11. Books and periodicals	100.0	n.a.	100
12. Tanning and leather	56.9	n.a.	56
13. Cotton ginning	87.3	n.a.	87
14. Cement	100.0	80.0	100
15. Tyres and tubes	98.5	41.9	98
16. Fertiliser	77.6	n.a.	77
17. Paints and varnishes	n.a.	40.0	40
18. Pharmaceuticals	19.2	n.a.	53
19. Products of petroleum and coal	100.0	n.a.	100
20. Acids, alkalis and salts	n.a.	53.4	53
21. Iron and steel	42.5	44.1	42
22. Motors, generators and transformers	n.a.	55.0	55
23. Communication equipment	44.3	37.0	44
24. Mechanical vehicle	59.0	24.2	24
25. Engines and turbines	29.1	53.8	29

Note: The data we have used in the case of most of the industries are from
C.S.O. survey carried out in 1965 and which is still the only comprehensive sur
on capacity utilisation carried out during this period. In most cases, the result
the survey are about the same as those for the I.B.R.D. (1970) reported figures
capacity utilisation and we have therefore used the C.S.O. figures. The o
exception is the mechanical vehicle industry where we have opted for the I.B.R
(1970) figure as it seems to reflect better the situation in that industry as is kno
from other sources.[1] In the case of acids, alkalis and salts we used the I.B.R
(1970) figure as it was not available in the C.S.O. (1967) survey.

The only industry for which we have used an alternative source is
pharmaceutical industry. The C.S.O. survey seemed a gross under-estimation
Hogan 1968, p. 41) and therefore we have used the study on the pharmaceut
industry (Fazili, 1969) which was a very detailed investigation into the industry
also provides figures for capacity utilisation of most of the firms in the industr
Source: (1) C.S.O. (1967) (2) I.B.R.D. (1970) (3) Fazili (1969)

1. See, for example, Chemical Consultants (1972).

Pakistan

Industry	1965/66	1966/67	1967/68	1969/70	Average
1. Grain milling	—	—	—	—	—
2. Sugar	0.9	2.1	1.4	1.2	1.4
3. Edible oil	—	—	—	—	—
4. Drinks and carbonated water	—	—	1.9	4.0	3.0
5. Cigarettes	—	—	—	—	—
6. Cotton spinning	18.4	18.6	24.2	22.1	20.8
7. Wool spinning	—	—	—	—	—
8. Silk and art silk	—	—	—	—	—
9. Dyeing and bleaching	—	—	—	—	—
10. Rubber footwear	9.5	12.9	19.8	19.0	15.3
11. Books and periodicals	—	—	—	—	—
12. Tanning and leather	0.4	0.9	1.5	1.1	1.0
13. Cotton ginning	—	—	—	—	—
14. Cement	0.2	4.0	4.0	6.2	3.6
15. Tyres and tubes	—	—	—	—	—
16. Fertiliser	—	—	—	—	—
17. Paints and varnishes	7.6	5.5	11.9	11.1	7.2
18. Pharmaceuticals	2.7	2.0	1.9	2.0	2.2
19. Products of petroleum and coal	—	—	—	—	—
20. Acids, alkalis and salts	5.5	7.9	7.1	3.6	6.0
21. Iron and steel	—	—	—	—	—
22. Motors, generators and transformers	—	—	—	—	—
23. Communication equipment	3.0	6.8	0.9	1.8	3.1
24. Mechanical vehicles	0.5	3.2	0.7	2.1	1.6
25. Engines and turbines	6.4	10.8	4.1	2.4	5.9

Note: — indicates no exports.
Source: Calculated from C.S.O. *Census of Manufacturing Industries* (Karachi, various issues).

Table D.11 *Advertising as a percentage of value added of selected industries in West Pakistan.*

Industry	Advertising expenditure (1966/67)
1. Grain milling	0.3
2. Sugar	3.1
3. Edible oils	12.9
4. Drinks and carbonated water	13.7
5. Cigarettes	5.2
6. Cotton spinning	5.3
7. Wool spinning	1.9
8. Silk and art silk	1.5
9. Dyeing and bleaching	0.9
10. Rubber footwear	2.7
11. Books and periodicals	0.9
12. Tanning and leather	2.1
13. Cotton ginning	1.7
14. Cement	2.1
15. Tyres and tubes	1.4
16. Fertiliser	0.5
17. Paints and varnishes	5.5
18. Pharmaceuticals	17.8
19. Products of petroleum and coal	4.8
20. Acids, alkalis and salts	3.6
21. Iron and steel	4.6
22. Motors, generators and transformers	13.8
23. Communication equipment	2.3
24. Mechanical vehicles	7.3
25. Engines and turbines	4.5

Source: Calculated from C.S.O. *Census of Manufacturing Industries 1966/67* (Karachi).

Appendix E—Table E.1 *List of firms in sample[a] which financed more than 40% of investment with foreign exchange loans during the period 1962–65*

1. Burewala Textiles
2. Colony Textiles
3. A. Bawany Textiles
4. Husein Industries
5. Fateh Textiles
6. Bahawalpur Textiles
7. F.P. Textiles
8. Hafiz Textiles
9. Latif Bawany Jute
10. Amin Jute
11. Frontier Sugar Mills
12. Souvenier Tobacco
13. Steel Corporation of Pakistan
14. Adamjee Industries
15. Wazir Ali Industries
16. Muree Brewery

[a] For list of all 39 firms in sample, see table D.2.
Source: See text (Chapter 5, p. 129).

Appendix F—Table F.1 *Estimates of investment, profits and foreign change loans of monopoly houses (quoted companies in manufacturing se only): Second Plan period* (Rs lacs)

House	$\sum\limits_{62}^{65} I_t$	$\sum\limits_{61}^{64} P_t$	$\sum\limits_{62}^{65} F.E.L.$	$K \atop 61$	Diversification into new industry
1. Dawood	727	1926	394.5	1659	—
2. Saigol	2330	901	1181.2	1282	Rayon, sugar and engineering
3. Adamjee	1574	1768	402.5	1716	—
4. Valika	864	565	619.1	611	Cement & chemic:
5. Crescent	439	695	144.4	293	Sugar and jute
6. Bawany	920	398	169.6	337	Sugar
7. Amins	770	273	518.1	185	Oil refining
8. Wazir Ali	302	202	127.0	234	—
9. Colony (N)	1020	600	485.7	571	Cement
10. Karim	356	120	190.7	116	—
11. Hoti	155	195	37.2	183	—
12. Isphani	254	297	72.9	274	—
13. Ghandara	288	164	192.5	173	—
14. Husein	121	347	82.8	223	—
15. Colony (F)	663	44	218.3	162	Cement
16. Rahimtoola	98	273	58.4	188	Chemicals
17. Zafar-ul-Ahsan	149	26	50.0	118	Chemicals
18. Nishat	347	134	132.7	157	Chemicals
19. B.E.C.O.	294	246	63.7	259	
20. Premier	145	408	33.5	373	—
21. Fateh	113	140	75.7	306	—
22. Dada	152	69	94.9	40	Cement
23. Ferozesons	22	21	16.3	25	—
24. Hafiz	67	28	22.9	124	—
25. Khanzada	47	30	38.0	111	—
26. Bawa	78	40	69.4	55	—

Note: I_t = investment
P_t = profits
$F.E.L.$ = foreign exchange loans
K = gross fixed assets (at cost)

Sources: (i) State Bank of Pakistan, *Balance Sheet Analysis of Joint Stock C panies* (Karachi, various issues).

(ii) For foreign exchange loans, see text (Chapter 5, p. 124n).

able F.2 *Estimates of investment, profits and foreign exchange loans★ of
onopoly houses (quoted companies in manufacturing sector only) : Third Plan
period* (Rs lacs)

House	ΣI_t 70 66	ΣP_t 68 65	$\Sigma F.E.L.$ 70 66	K 65	Diversification into new industry
. Dawood	2711	2289	897.2	2386	Rayon and chemicals
. Saigol	437	915	195.1	3612	—
. Adamjee	650	1570	303.9	3290	Sugar
. Valika	1016	503	298.2	1335	—
. Crescent	1616	1336	703.2	732	Sugar
. Bawany	1138	563	336.2	1257	Chemicals
. Amins	997	770	376.1	1016	—
. Habib	1090	192	464.0	319	—
. Wazir Ali	657	430	284.0	536	—
. Colony (N)	768	893	201.2	1591	—
. Karim	549	297	231.5	472	—
. Hoti	1330	339	762.2	338	Paper
. A. Khaleeli	1326	93	964.3	238	Oil refining
. Isphani	286	376	64.0	528	—
. Ghandara	407	688	195.0	288	—
. Husein	550	404	141.7	344	Sugar
. Colony (F)	141	166	68.1	825	—
. Reyaz-o-Khalid	243	21	100.0	266	—
. Rahimtoola	251	404	22.5	286	—
. Zafar-ul-Ahsan	653	67	546.4	149	—
. Nishat	266	233	61.6	504	—
. B.E.C.O.	87	629	0	553	—
. Premier	186	665	16.3	518	
. Maula Bux	699	186	215.6	212	—
. Hyesons	133	152	19.0	374	—
. Rangoonwala	83	113	31.7	100	—
. Fateh	46	179	40.9	416	—
. Dada	182	91	—	192	—
. Ferozesons	51	93	23.6	47	—
. Hafiz	164	41	56.4	191	—
. Khanzada	129	58	86.0	158	—
. Bawa	156	58	50.0	133	—
. Arag	− 10	105	19.5	252	—
. Faruque	87	38	49.0	294	—

ncludes 'direct' foreign exchange loans arranged by P.I.C.I.C.

te: I_t = investment

      P_t = profits

      F.E.L. = foreign exchange loans

      K   = gross fixed assets (at cost)

urces: (i)   State Bank of Pakistan, *Balance Sheet Analysis of Joint Stock Companies* (Karachi, various issues).

      (ii) For foreign exchange loans, see text (Chapter 5, p. 124n).

Appendix G—Table G.1 *Investment schedule allocations and sanction.
during Second Plan: West Pakistan* (Rs million)

Industrial group	Allocation[1] (i)	Sanctions[1] (ii)	Sanctions[3] including 'specific' (iii)
1. Food manufacturing	140.0	250.46	556.1
2. Beverages	7.0	16.71	18.3
3. Tobacco	16.5	22.8	22.8
4. Textiles	490.5	760.9	800.6
5. (a) Jute	9.0	64.4	64.4
(b) Others	481.5	696.5	736.2
5. Footwear	6.0	14.5	14.5
6. Mfg wood and cork	6.5	6.9	6.9
7. Pulp & paper products	12.5	76.76	408.0
8. Printing & publishing	25.7	21.3	21.3
9. Leather & leather goods	15.0	11.8	11.8
10. Rubber products	19.2	43.4	43.8
11. Chemical products	294.8	799.12	837.2
12. Petro-chemicals	197.5	123.82	127.1
13. Non-metallic minerals	258.2	257.6	332.2
14. Basic metals	130.5	656.54	658.8
15. Metal products	35.3	58.04	87.6
16. Machinery	67.1	55.68	68.2
17. Electrical machinery	55.1	97.11	132.0
18. Transport equipment	36.5	32.26	105.3
19. Miscellaneous	120.5	184.96	190.4
Total	1934.4	3490.7	4442.9

Notes: 1 Total allocations made in the Industrial Investment Schedule (I.I.S.)
as well as in the Revised Industrial Investment Schedule (R.I.I.S.)
2 Total sanctions against allocations made in the I.I.S. and R.I.I.S.
3 Includes sanctions against industries for which no provisions were
made and were termed as 'specific' industries in the R.I.I.S.
Source: Compiled from Durrani (1966).

Table G.2 *Investment schedule allocations and sanctions during Second Plan: East Pakistan* (Rs million)

Industrial group	Allocation[1] (i)	Sanctions[2] (ii)	Sanctions[3] including 'Specific' (iii)
1. Food manufacturing	139.1	89.5	91.8
2. Beverages	7.0	4.1	4.2
3. Tobacco	24.0	46.2	46.2
4. Textiles	684.9	612.6	614.3
(a) Jute	391.0	449.5	449.5
(b) Others	293.9	163.1	164.8
5. Footwear	9.0	10.8	10.8
6. Mfg of wood and cork	15.5	12.5	12.5
7. Pulp & paper products	63.5	12.4	13.3
8. Printing & publishing	12.7	14.5	14.5
9. Leather & leather goods	24.0	5.3	5.3
10. Rubber products	13.7	3.7	3.7
11. Chemical products	100.5	58.4	58.4
12. Petro-chemicals	80.0	—	—
13. Non-metallic minerals	68.4	40.9	58.2
14. Basic metals	75.0	142.7	142.7
15. Metal products	41.5	30.1	32.2
16. Machinery	86.4	30.1	30.1
17. Electrical machinery	30.4	15.5	21.5
18. Transport equipment	42.2	12.1	12.1
19. Miscellaneous	88.6	70.4	70.4
Total	1606.4	1211.8	1242.2

Note: 1 Total allocations made in the I.I.S. and R.I.I.S.
      2 Total sanctions against allocations made in the I.I.S. and R.I.I.S.
      3 Includes sanctions against industries for which no provisions were made and were termed as 'specific' industries in the R.I.I.S.

Source: Compiled from Durrani (1966).

Table G.3 *Investment schedule allocations and sanctions during Third Plan West Pakistan.* (Rs. million)

Industrial group	Allocation[1]	Sanction
1. Food manufacturing	356.4	698.6
2. Beverages	5.0	0.6
3. Tobacco	15.6	15.1
4. Textiles	1636.3	1990.3
5. Footwear	24.4	13.8
6. Wood, cork & allied	9.0	3.0
7. Mfg of furniture and fixtures	8.0	1.8
8. Paper and paper products	170.0	108.1
9. Printing, publishing & allied	22.5	27.4
10. Mfg of leather and leather products	25.8	11.0
11. Mfg of rubber products	20.6	9.4
12. Mfg of chemicals including fertilisers	800.6	1345.7
13. Petro-chemicals	530.0	84.0
14. Non-metallic minerals	631.0	75.7
15. Basic metals	281.5	37.3
16. Metal products	211.5	43.6
17. Machinery except electrical	205.4	34.5
18. Electrical machinery	134.5	58.7
19. Transport equipment	153.0	38.5
20. Miscellaneous industries	199.5	42.8
21. Service industries	101.5	119.3
22. Special industries[2]	65.0	144.7
Total	5607.1	4903.9

Notes: 1 Total allocations made in the Comprehensive Industrial Investment Schedule for the Third Plan period.

2 Industries based principally on 100% indigenous raw materials with foreign exchange requirements of machinery and equipment not exceeding Rs 5 lacs.

Sources: (i) I.P. & S. (1966c)

(ii) Data for sanctions compiled by the author from the I.P. & S. Department, Karachi.

BIBLIOGRAPHY

Alamgir, Mohiuddin, 1968, 'The Domestic Prices of Imported Commodities in Pakistan: A Further Study', *Pakistan Development Review*, Vol. VIII, No. 1, Spring 1968.

Alamgir, M., and Berlage, L. J., 1974, *Bangladesh: National Income and Expenditure 1949/50–1969/70*, Research Monograph No. 1, Dacca: The Bangladesh Institute of Development Studies.

Alamgir, M., and Rahman, A., 1974, *Savings in Bangladesh 1959/60–1969/70*, Research Monograph No. 2, Dacca: The Bangladesh Institute of Development Studies.

Alfatah, 1971, *Baees Khandan-Kon Kaya Hai* (22 Families – Who's Who) 30 December 1971, Karachi (weekly) in Urdu.

Amjad, Rashid, 1972, 'A Critique of the "Green Revolution" in West Pakistan', *Pakistan Economic and Social Review*, Vol. X, No. 1, June 1972.

– 1973, 'Growth, Profitability and Savings of Quoted Public Limited Companies 1964–70', *Pakistan Economic and Social Review*, Vol. XI, No. 4, Winter 1973.

– 1974, Industrial Concentration and Economic Power in Pakistan, South Asian Institute, Lahore: Punjab University Press.

– 1975, 'Impact of Concentration on Profitability in Pakistan – An Alternative Test of White's Hypothesis', unpublished mimeo.

– 1976a, 'Impact of Concentration on Profitability in Pakistan', *Journal of Development Studies*, April, 1977. Also published as Research Paper No. .1, Faculty of Economics and Politics, University of Cambridge, Cambridge.

– 1976b, 'A Study of Investment Behaviour in Pakistan, 1962–70', *Pakistan Development Review*, Vol. XV, No. 2, Summer 1976.

– 1977, 'Private Industrial, Investment in Pakistan, 1960–70', Ph. D. thesis, Cambridge University.

Andrus, J. R., and Mohammed, A. F., 1958, *The Economy of Pakistan*, Stanford: Stanford University Press.

Anwar, Abdul, A., 1970, *Production of Sugar, Policies and Problems*, Research Paper No. 41, Planning and Development Department, Lahore, Government of West Pakistan.

Azfar Jawaid, 1973, 'The Distribution of Income in Pakistan, 1966–67', *Pakistan Economic and Social Review*, Volume XI, No. 1, Spring 1973.

Bagchi, Amiya, K., 1962a, 'Investment by Privately Owned Joint Stock Companies in India', *Arthaniti*, Vol. V, No. 2, July 1962.

– 1962b, 'Private Investment in a Partially Planned Economy', Ph. D. thesis (unpublished), Cambridge University.

235

– 1971, 'The Theory of Efficient Neo-Colonialism', *Economic and Political Weekly*, Vol. VI, Nos. 30, 31 and 32, special number July 1971.

– 1972, *Private Investment in India, 1900–1939*, South Asian Studies, Cambridge: Cambridge University Press.

Bangladesh Bureau of Statistics, 1972, *Census of Manufacturing Industries 1969/70*, Dacca: Government of Bangladesh.

– *Statistical Digest*, various issues, Dacca: Government of Bangladesh.

Benishay, M., 1967, 'Concentration and Price-Cost Margins: A Comment', *Journal of Industrial Economics*, Vol. XVI, No. 1, November 1967.

Bergan, Asbjorn, 1967, 'Personal Income Distribution and Personal Savings in Pakistan, 1963/64', *Pakistan Development Review*, Vol. VII, No. 2, Spring 1967.

Bergsman, Joel, 1970, *Brazil: Industrialization and Trade Policies*, London: Oxford University Press.

Bhagwati, J. N., and Desai, P., 1970, *India, Planning for Industrialisation: Industrialisation and Trade Policies Since 1951*, London: Oxford University Press.

Brecher, I., and Abbas, S. A., 1972, *Foreign Aid and Industrial Development in Pakistan*, Cambridge: Cambridge University Press.

Bruton, H. J., and Bose, S. R., 1963, 'The Pakistan Export Bonus Scheme', Monograph No. 11, Karachi: Pakistan Institute of Development Economics.

Chaudhry, Shahid Amjad, 1970, 'Private Foreign Investment in Pakistan', *Pakistan Development Review*, Vol. X, No. 1, Spring 1970.

Chemical Consultants and Other Associated Agencies, 1972, 'Survey of the First Group of Industrial Establishments controlled by the Government under the Economic Reforms Order 1972, Lahore: mimeo.

Chenery, Hollis B., 1952, 'Overcapacity and the Acceleration Principle', *Econometrica*, Vol. 20, No. 1, January 1952.

– 1960, 'Patterns of Industrial Growth', *American Economic Review*, Vol. 4, No. 4, September 1960.

Chenery, H. B., and Taylor, L., 1968, 'Development Patterns: Among Countries and Over Time', *The Review of Economics and Statistics*, Vol. 4, No. 4, November 1968.

Child, Frank C., 1968a, 'Liberalization of the Foreign exchange Market', *Pakistan Development Review*, Vol. VIII, No. 2, Summer 1968.

– 1968b, 'Reform of a Trade and Payments Control System: The Case of Pakistan', *Economic Development and Cultural Change*, Vol. 16, No. 4, July 1968.

Chowdhury, Nuruddin, A.H.M., 1969, 'Some Reflections on Income Redistribution Intermediation in Pakistan', *Pakistan Development Review*, Vol. 9, No. 2, Summer 1969.

Clark, J. H., 1917, 'Business Acceleration and the Law of Demand. A Technical Factor in Economic Cycles', *Journal of Political Economy*, Vol. XXV, No. 1, March 1917.

Collins, N. R., and Preston, L. E., 1968, *Concentration and Price–Cost Margins in Manufacturing Industries*, Berkeley, California: University of California Press.

Controller of Insurance, 1971, *The Pakistan Insurance Year Book, 1970*, Karachi: Printing Corporation of Pakistan Press.

C.S.O. (Central Statistical Office), *Census of Manufacturing Industries*, various issues, Karachi: Government of Pakistan

– *Monthly Statistical Bulletin*, various issues, Karachi: Government of Pakistan.

– *Foreign Trade Statistics of Pakistan*, monthly, Karachi: Government of Pakistan.

– 1967, *Report on Survey of Capacity Utilisation of Manufacturing Industries, 1965*, Karachi: Government of Pakistan.

– 1972, *Twenty-Five years of Pakistan in Statistics, 1947–72*, Karachi: Government of Pakistan.

Dawn, Karachi, English daily.

Dimsdale, N. H., and Glyn, A. J., 1971, 'Investment in British Industry: Cross-Sectional Approach', *Bulletin of the Oxford University Institute of Economics and Statistics*, Vol. 33, No. 3, August 1971.

Durrani, M. T., 1966, 'The Pattern of Private Industrial Investment in Pakistan During the Second Five Year Plan Period (1960–65), Research Report No. 54, Karachi: Pakistan Institute of Development Economics.

East Pakistan Industrial Development Corporation, *Annual Reports*, Dacca: various years.

Economist (pseud.) 1969, 'Monopolies in Pakistan. I. Monopoly with State Connivance', *Pakistan Times* (Lahore), 6 October 1969, pp. 6–7; II. 'Some Significant Facts', 7 October 1969, pp. 6–7; III. 'A Critical Look at the New Ordinance', 8 October 1969, pp. 6–7.

Eichner, A. S., 1973, 'A Theory of the Determination of the Mark-Up under Oligopoly', *Economic Journal*, Vol. 83, No. 332, December 1973.

Eisner, Robert, 1960, 'A Distributed Lag Investment Function', *Econometrica*, Vol. 25, No. 1, January 1960.

Eisner, R., and Strotz, R. H., 1963, 'Determinants of Business Investment', in Commission of Money and Credit, *Impact of Monetary Policy*, New Jersey, Prentice-Hall.

Falcon, Walter P., and Gotsch, Carl H., 1968, 'Lessons in Agricultural Development-Pakistan', in G. F. Papanek (ed.), *Development Policy – Theory and Practice*, Cambridge, Mass: Harvard University Press.

Fauji Foundation, *Annual Reports* and *Selected Reports*, Rawalpindi.

Fazili, M. A., 1969, *Pharmaceutical Industry in West Pakistan*, Directorate of Industries and Commerce, Lahore: Government of West Pakistan.

Galbraith, John K., 1967, *The New Industrial State*, Boston: Houghton Mofflin.

Gerakis, A. S., 1974, 'Pakistan's Export Bonus Scheme', *Finance and Development*, Vol. II, No. 2, June 1974.

Ghose, Aurobindo, 1972, 'Monopoly in Indian Industry', *Economic and*

  Political Weekly, Vol. VII, Nos. 5, 6 and 7, Annual Number,
  February 1972.
– 1974, 'Investment Behaviour of Monopoly House. I. Structure of
  Fixed Investment Decisions', *Economics and Political Weekly*, Vol.
  IX, No. 43; 'II. Economics of Pre-Emption', Vol. IX, No. 44; 'III.
  Time Profile of Fixed Investment and Other Implications of the
  Structure of the Investment Decision', Vol. IX, Nos. 45 and 46.
Glassburner, Bruce, 1968, 'Aspects of the Problem of Foreign Exchange
  Pricing in Pakistan', *Economic Development and Cultural Change*,
  Vol. 16, No. 4, July 1968.
Government of Pakistan, 1965, 'Report of the Anti-Cartel Study Group'.
  Islamabad.
– 1967, 'Report of the Working Group on Import Policy', Islamabad.
Government of West Pakistan, 1969, *Directory of Industrial
  Establishment in West Pakistan*, Lahore, Directorate of Industries
  and Commerce.
Griffin, Keith, 1965, 'Financing Development Plans in Pakistan',
  Pakistan Development Review, Vol. V, No. 4, Winter 1965.
Griffin, Keith and Khan, A. R. (eds.), 1972, *Growth and Inequality in
  Pakistan*, New York: St Martin's Press.
Guisinger, Stephen E., 1976, 'Patterns of Industrial Growth in
  Pakistan', *Pakistan Development Review*, Vol. XV, No. 2, Spring
  1976.
Haidari, Iqbal, *Corporate Companies at a Glance*, Karachi: Economic and
  Industrial Publications, various issues.
– 1969, *Jute Industry in Pakistan*, Karachi: Economic and Industrial
  Publications.
– 1970, *Cotton Textile Industry in Pakistan*, Karachi: Economic and
  Industrial Publications.
Haidari, Iqbal and Khan, Abdul Hafeez, 1968, *Stock Exchange Guide of
  Pakistan*, Karachi: Economic and Industrial Publications.
Hamid, Javed, 1970, 'A Review of the Agricultural Breakthrough in
  West Pakistan', *The Punjab University Economist*, Vol. VIII, No. I,
  June 1970.
Hamid, Naved, 1970, 'A Critical Appraisal of Foreign Aid Strategy',
  Punjab University Economist, Vol. VIII, No. 2, December 1970.
– 1974, 'The Burden of Capitalist Growth – A Study of Real Wages and
  Consumption in Pakistan', *Pakistan Economic and Social Review*,
  Vol. XII, No. 1, Spring 1974.
Haq, Khadija, and Baqai, M., 1967, 'Savings and Financial Flows in the
  Corporate Sector, 1959–63', *Pakistan Development Review*, Vol. VII,
  No. 3, Autumn 1967.
Haq, Mahbub ul, 1966, *The Strategy of Economic Planning*, Karachi:
  Oxford University Press.
– 1973, 'System is to blame for the 22 Wealthy Families', *The Times*
  (London), 22 March 1973.
Hazari, R. K., 1966, *The Corporate Private Sector*, Bombay: Asia
  Publishing House.
Helliwell, J. F. (ed.), 1976, *Aggregate Investment*, Penguin.
Hogan, Warren, P., 1968, 'Capacity Creation and Utilisation in Pakistan

Manufacturing Industry,' *Australian Economic Papers,* Vol. VII, No. 10, June 1968.

Holterman, S., 1973, 'Market Structure and Economic Performance in U.K. Manufacturing Industries', *Journal of Industrial Economics,* Vol, XXII, No. 2, December, 1973.

Hsing, Mo-Huan, 1971, *Taiwan – Industrialisation and Trade Policies,* London, Oxford University Press, 1971.

I.B.R.D. (International Bank for Reconstruction and Development), Bank Study Group, 1968, *Water and Power Resources for West Pakistan: A Study in Sectoral Planning,* prepared by a World Bank Study Group headed by Pieter Lieftnick, A. Robert Sadove. Baltimore: Johns Hopkins Press.

– 1970, *Industrialisation of Pakistan – The Record, The Problems and the Prospects.* Volume I, 'An Overall View', Volume II, 'Sector Reports', Volume III, 'Special Studies'. Report No. S.A.-11.a South Asia Department.

Ikram, Khalid, 1970, 'The Export Bonus Scheme and the Primary Commodities', *Punjab University Economist,* Vol. XIII, No. 2, December 1970.

Industrial Development Bank of Pakistan, *Annual Reports,* Karachi, various years.

Investment Corporation of Pakistan, *Annual Reports,* Karachi, various years.

– 1973, *I.C.P. Handbook of Analyses of Listed Stocks, 1971 and 1972,* Karachi.

I. P. & S. (Investment Promotion and Supplies Department), 1963, *Revised Industrial Investment Schedule,* Karachi: Government of Pakistan.

– 1966a, *Directory of Industrial Units Sanctioned During Second Five Year Plan Period (1960-65),* Karachi: Government of Pakistan.

– 1966b, *Evaluation of Performance of Private Industries Sector During Second Five Year Plan (July 1960–June 1965),* Karachi: Government of Pakistan.

– 1966c, *Comprehensive Industrial Investment Schedule for Third Five Year Plan (1965–70),* Karachi, Government of Pakistan.

– 1968, *Priority List of Industries of Comprehensive Industrial Investment Schedule (1965–1970),* Karachi: Government of Pakistan.

– 1972, *Directory of Industrial Establishments in Pakistan,* Vol. I to Vol. III, Karachi, Government of Pakistan.

Iqbal, Zafar, 1964, 'Concentration of Wealth and the Ownership Patterns of Private Manufacturing Industries in West Pakistan,' M. A. thesis (unpublished), Department of Public Administration, University of the Punjab, Lahore.

Islam, Nurul, 1965, *A Short Term Model for the Pakistan Economy,* Lahore, Oxford University Press.

– 1967a, 'Comparative Costs, Factor Proportions and Industrial Efficiency in Pakistan', *Pakistan Development Review,* Vol. VII, No. 2, Summer 1967.

– 1967b, *Imports of Pakistan: Growth and Structure,* Statistical Papers No. 3, Karachi: Pakistan Institute of Development Economics.

– 1969, 'Export Incentive and Effective Subsidy in Pakistan: An

Evaluation', *Bulletin of the Oxford University Institute of Economics and Statistics*, Vol. 33, No. 3, August 1971.

– 1972, 'Foreign Assistance and Economic Development: the Case of Pakistan', *Economic Journal*, Vol. 82, No. 325S, March 1972 (Supplement).

Jafri, S. J., 1969, *Woollen and Worsted Industry in West Pakistan*, Directorate of Industries and Commerce, Lahore: Government of West Pakistan.

Jorgenson, Dale W., 1971, 'Econometric Studies of Investment Behaviour: A Survey', *Journal of Economic Literature*, Vol. IX, No. 4, December 1971.

Jorgenson, Dale W. and Siebert, Calvin D., 1968, 'A Comparison of Alternative Theories of Corporate Investment Behaviour', *American Economic Review*, Vol. LVIII, No. 4, September 1968.

Kalecki, M., 1971, *Selected Essays on the Dynamics of the Capitalist Economy 1933–70*, Cambridge, Cambridge University Press.

Kemal, A. R., 1976, 'Consistent Time Series Data Relating to Pakistan's Large-Scale Manufacturing Industries', *Pakistan Development Review*, Vol. XV, No. 1, Spring 1976.

Khalilzadeh, S. J., 1974, 'Market Structure and Price–Cost Margin in the United Kingdom Manufacturing Industries', *Review of Economics and Statistics*, Vol. LVI, No. 1, February 1974.

Khan, Azizur Rahman, 1967, 'What Has Been Happening to Real Wages in Pakistan?' *Pakistan Development Review*, Vol. 7, No. 3, Autumn 1967.

– 1972, *The Economy of Bangladesh*, New York: St Martins Press.

Khandker, R. H., 1973, 'Distribution of Income and Wealth in Pakistan', *Pakistan Economic and Social Review*, Vol XI, No. 1, Spring 1973.

King, Blair B., 1966, 'Origin of the Managing Agency System', *Journal of Asian Studies*, Vol. XXVI, No. 1, November 1966.

King, Timothy, 1970, *Mexico: Industrialisation and Trade Policies since 1940*, London: Oxford University Press.

Klein, L. R., 1950, *Economic Fluctuations in the United States, 1921–41*, Cowles Commission for Research in Economics, Monograph No. 11, New York: John Wiley and Sons.

Koyck, L. M., 1954, *Distributed Lags and Investment Analysis*, Amsterdam: North Holland Publishing Company.

Krishnamurty, K., 1964, 'Private Investment Behaviour in India', *Arthaniti*, Vol. VII, No. 1, January 1964.

Kuh, Edwin, 1963, *Capital Stock Growth: A Micro-Econometric Approach*, Amsterdam: North Holland Publishing Company.

Kuznets, S., 1935, 'Relation between Capital Goods and Finished Products in the Business Cycle', in *Economic Essays in Honour of Wesley Clair Mitchell*, New York: Columbia University Press.

Lewis, Stephen R. Jr, 1969, *Economic Policy and Industrial Growth in Pakistan*, London, George Allen and Unwin Ltd.

– 1970a, *Pakistan: Industrialisation and Trade Policies*, London: Oxford University Press.

– 1970b, 'Agricultures Terms of Trade', *Pakistan Development Review*, Vol. X, No. 3, Autumn, 1970.

Lewis, Stephen R. Jr. and Guisinger, Stephen E., 1971, 'The Structure of Protection in Pakistan', in *The Structure of Protection in Developing Countries*, Bela Balassa (ed.), Baltimore, Johns Hopkins Press.

Lewis, Stephen R. Jr, and Hussain, S. M., 1966, 'Relative Price Changes and Industrialisation in Pakistan 1951–64', *Pakistan Development Review*, Vol. VI, No. 3, Autumn, 1966.

Little, I., Scitovsky, T., and Scott, M., 1970, *Industry and Trade in Some Developing Countries – A Comparative Study*, London: Oxford University Press.

MacEwan, Arthur, 1971, 'Contradictions in Capitalist Development: The Case of Pakistan', *Review of Radical and Political Economics*, Spring 1971.

Maddison, Angus, 1971, *Class Structure and Economic Growth: India and Pakistan, since the Moghuls*, London: Allen and Unwin Ltd.

Mann, H., and Meehan, J. W., 1969, 'Concentration and Profitability: An Examination of a Recent Study', *The Anti-Trust Bulletin*, Vol. 16, No. 1, Summer 1969.

Marris, R. D., 1964, *The Economic Theory of Managerial Capitalism*, London: Macmillan.

Marris, R. D., and Wood, Adrian (eds.), 1971, *The Corporate Economy*, London: Macmillan.

Mason, Edward S., 1966, *Economic Development in India and Pakistan*, Occasional Papers in International Affairs, No. 13, Harvard University: Center for International Affairs.

Meyer, J., and Kuh, E., 1959, *The Investment Decision: An Empirical Study*, Cambridge, Mass: Harvard University Press.

Ministry of Finance, 1971, *The Budget in Brief 1971/72*, Islamabad: Government of Pakistan.

– *Pakistan Economic Survey*, Karachi and Islamabad: Government of Pakistan (issued annually).

Minsky, Hyman P., 1970, 'Passage to Pakistan', *Transaction*, Vol. 7, No. 4, February 1970.

Naqvi, S. N. H., 1964, 'Import Licensing in Pakistan', *Pakistan Development Review*, Vol. IV, No. 1, Spring 1964.

– 1966, 'The Allocative Biases of Pakistan's Commercial Policy: 1953–1963,', *Pakistan Development Review*, Vol, VI, No. 4, Winter 1966.

Naseem, S. M., 1975, 'A Consistent Series of National Accounts for East and West Pakistan, 1949–50 to 1969–70', *Pakistan Development Review*, Vol. XIV, No. 1, Spring 1975.

National Investment (Unit) Trust, *Directors' Reports*, Karachi, various years.

Nations, Richard, 1975, 'The Economic Structure of Pakistan and Bangladesh', in Blackburn, R. (ed.), *Explosion in Sub-Continent*, Pelican.

Neild, R. R., 1963, *Pricing and Employment in the Trade Cycle*, Cambridge: Cambridge University Press.

Nordhaus, W., 1974, *The Falling Share of Profits*, Cowles Foundation Paper No. 408, Washington: The Brookings Institution.

Nordhaus, W. and Godley, W., 1972, 'Pricing in the Trade Cycle', *Economic Journal*, Vol. 82, No. 327, September 1972.

Nulty, Leslie, 1972, *The Green Revolution in West Pakistan: Implication of Technological Change*, New York: Praeger.

Nulty, Timothy E., 1972, 'Income Distribution and Savings in Pakistan: An Appraisal of Development Strategy', Ph.D. thesis (unpublished), Cambridge University.

Nulty, Timothy, and Nulty, Leslie, 1971, 'Pakistan: The Busy Bee Route to Development', *Transaction*, Vol. 8, No. 4, February 1971.

Observer, Dacca, English.

Ornstein, Stanley, I., 1975, 'Empirical Uses of the Price–Cost Margin', *The Journal of Industrial Economics*, Vol. XXIV, No. 2, December 1975.

Overseas Investors Chambers of Commerce and Industry, 1969, 'Memorandum of Industrialisation Policy of the Fourth Plan together with a Note on Foreign Investment', Karachi. mimeo.

Pakistan Times, Lahore and Rawalpindi, English daily.

Pal, Mati Lal, 1964, 'The Determinants of Domestic Price of Imports', *Pakistan Development Review*, Vol. IV, No. 4, Winter 1964.

– 1965, 'Domestic Prices of Imports in Pakistan, Extension of Empirical Findings', *Pakistan Development Review*, Vol. V, No. 4, Winter 1965.

Papanek, Gustav F., 1964, 'Industrial Production and Investment in Pakistan', *Pakistan Development Review*, Vol. IV, No. 3, Autumn 1964.

– 1967, *Pakistan's Development: Social Goals and Private Incentives*, Cambridge, Mass., Harvard University Press.

– 1971, 'Review of Lewis S.R. Economic Policy and Industrial Growth in Pakistan', *Journal of Asian Studies*, Vol. XXX, No, 2, Febuary 1971.

Papanek, Hanna, 1972, 'Pakistan's Businessmen', *Economic Development and Cultural Change*, Vol. 12, No. 2, October 1972.

Patnaik, Prabhat, 1973, 'Private Corporate Industrial Investment in India', 1947–1967', Ph.D. thesis (unpublished), Oxford University.

Penrose, E., 1959, *The Theory of the Growth of the Firm*, Oxford: Basil Blackwell.

P.I.C.I.C. (Pakistan Industrial Credit and Investment Corporation), *Annual Reports*, Karachi, various issues.

Planning Board, 1957, *First Five Year Plan, 1955–60*, Karachi: Government of Pakistan.

Planning Commission, 1960, *Second Five Year Plan, 1960–65*, Karachi: Government of Pakistan.

– 1965, *Third Five Year Plan 1965–70*, Islamabad, Government of Pakistan.

– 1966, *Final Evaluation of the Second Five Year Plan*, Karachi: Government of Pakistan.

– 1968, *Socio-Economic Objectives of the Fourth Five Year Plan (1970–75)*, Islamabad: Government of Pakistan.

– 1970a, *Reports of the Advisory Panels for the Fourth Five Year Plan 1970–75*, Vols. I and II, Islamabad: Government of Pakistan.

– 1970b, *Fourth Five Year Plan*, Islamabad: Government of Pakistan.
– 1971, *Evaluation of the Third Five Year Plan (1965–70)*, Islamabad, Government of Pakistan.
Planning Division, 1973, *Reports of the Working Group on Private Investment for the Annual Plan 1973/74*, Islamabad: Government of Pakistan.
Power, John H. and Sicat, Gerardo, P., 1971, *The Philippines Industrialisation and Trade Policies*, London: Oxford University Press.
Radhu, G. M., 1973, 'Trade Between East and West Pakistan at World Prices, 1960/61 to 1969/70', *Pakistan Development Review*, Vol. XII, No.2, Summer 1973.
Rahman, A., Md., 1968, *East and West Pakistan: A Problem in the Political Economy of Regional Planning*, Occasional Papers in International Affairs, No. 20, Harvard University Centre for International Affairs.
Rahman, M. A., 1963, *Partition, Integration, Economic Growth and Inter-Regional Trade*, Karachi: The Institute of Development Economics.
Robinson, Joan, 1970, *Economic Heresies – Some Old Fashioned Questions in Economic Theory*, London: Macmillan.
Safiullah., M., 1967, *Corporate Savings in Pakistan*, Bureau of Economic Research, Dacca: University of Dacca.
Sarkar, D., 1970, 'Investment Theories and Capital Formation', Review of Management, *Economic and Political Weekly*, Vol. V, No. 9, February 1970.
Sawhney, Pawan K., and Sawhney, Bansi L., 1973, 'Capacity-Utilisation, Concentration and Price–Cost Margins: Results of Indian Industries', *Journal of Industrial Economics*, Vol. XXI, No. 2, April 1973.
Schwartzman, D., 1959, 'The Effects of Monopoly on Price', *Journal of Political Economy*, Vol. LXVII, No. 4, August 1959.
Sengupta, Arjun, 1971, 'Regional Disparity and Economic Development in Pakistan. I. The Facts', *Economic and Political Weekly*, Vol. V, No. 4, 6 November 1971. 'II. Some Hypotheses to Explain the Growth of Disparity', Vol. VI, No. 46, 13 November 1971.
Shibli, A. R., 1972, *Baees Khwande* ('The Twenty Two Families'), Lahore: Peoples Publishing House. (In Urdu).
Singh, A., and Whittington, G., 1968, *Growth, Profitability and Valuation: A Study of United Kingdom Quoted Companies*, Cambridge University Press.
Sobhan, Rehman, 1965, 'Strategy for Industrialisation in Pakistan', in Anwar Iqbal Qureshi (ed.), *Third Five Year Plan, and Other Papers*, Rawalpindi: Pakistan Economic Association.
State Bank of Pakistan, *Balance Sheet Analysis of Joint Stock Companies Listed on the Karachi Stock Exchange*, various issues, Karachi: State Bank of Pakistan Printing Press.
– *Foreign Liabilities and Assets and Foreign Investments in Pakistan*, various issues, Karachi: State Bank of Pakistan Printing Press.
– 1972, *Banking Statistics of Pakistan, 1970/71*, Karachi: State Bank of Pakistan Printing Press.

Stern, J. J., and Falcon, W. P., 1970, *Growth and Development in Pakistan, 1955–1969,* Occasional Papers in International Affairs, No. 23, Harvard University: Center for International Affairs.

Syed, Aurangzeb, 1974, 'Private Foreign Investment in Pakistan', M. A. thesis (unpublished), Department of Administrative Sciences, University of the Punjab, Lahore.

Tareen, Ameen K. (ed.), 1970, *Directory of Pakistan Cotton Textile Industry,* Karachi.

Thomas, P. S., 1966, 'Import Licensing and Import Liberalization in Pakistan', *Pakistan Development Review,* Vol. XI, No. 4, Winter 1966.

Tinbergen, J., 1938, 'Statistical Evidence on the Acceleration Principle', *Economica,* Vol. V, No. 18, May 1938.

Tinbergen, J. and Polak, J. J., 1950, *The Dynamics of Business Cycles: A Study in Economic Fluctuations,* Chicago: Routledge and Kegan Paul Ltd.

Waterston, Albert, 1963, *Planning in Pakistan: Organization and Implementation,* Baltimore, Johns Hopkins Press.

West Pakistan Industrial Development Corporation, *Annual Reports,* Karachi, various years.

White, L. J., 1974a, *Industrial Concentration and Economic Power in Pakistan,* Princeton, Princeton University Press.

— 1974b, 'Pakistan's Industrial Families', *Journal of Development Studies,* Vol. 10, Nos. 3 and 4, April/July 1974.

Winston, Gordon C., 1970, 'Over invoicing and Distorted Industrial Growth under Artificial Exchange Rate', *Pakistan Development Review,* Vol. 10, No. 4, Winter 1970.

— 1971, 'Capital Utilisation in Economic Development', *Economic Journal,* Vol. 81, No. 321, March 1971.

INDEX

Abed, 102n
Abbas, S.A., 39n, 79n
accelerator, 28, 109, 110–12, 119–20
  empirical findings, 116–31, 158–65
Acids, Alkalies and Salt industry
  estimates of advertising expenditure,
    228
  estimates of capacity utilisation, 226
  estimates of capital–output ratios,
    224
  estimates of concentration ratio, 219
  estimates of exports, 227
  estimates of imports, 225
  estimates of price–cost margins,
    221, 222
Adamjee (Group), 41, 48, 49, 50, 51,
    102, 136n, 167n, 230, 231
  assets in 1970, 195, 196
  loans from P.I.C.I.C. & I.D.B.P.,
    201
  share in N.I.T. investments, 203
Adamjee Industries Ltd, 136n, 207,
    229
Adamjee Insurance Co., 49
Adamjee Jute Mill Ltd, 207
Adamjee Sugar Mill Ltd, 136n
advertising, 89, 104, 105
  relationship with price–cost mar-
    gins, 89, 103–5, 216
advertising expenditure estimates, 228
agriculture, 4, 5, 6, 176
  bad harvests, 174
  expansion in the sixties, 173
  growth rate, 15, 16
  prices, 80, 80n
  private investment, 192
  rural landed interests, 171
  share of G.N.P., 15
  terms of trade, 3, 3n
Agricultural and Chemicals Ltd, 134–
    5n
Ahmad Spinning Textile Mill, 149
Aid-to-Pakistan Consortium, 5, 33
A.K. Khan (Group), 49, 50
  assets in 1970, 196

loans from P.I.C.I.C. and I.D.B.P.,
    202
  share in N.I.T. investments, 203
Alamgir, Mohiuddin, 40n, 68, 76n,
    101, 206
Alfatah, 45
Almon Lag Scheme, 116n
Amalgamated Mines Ltd, 135n
Amins (Group), 230, 231
  assets in 1970, 195, 196
  loans from P.I.C.I.C. & I.D.B.P.,
    201
Amin Fabrics Ltd, 73n, 207
Amin Jute Mill Ltd, 207, 229
Amin Textiles Ltd, 207
Amirali H. Fancy, 41 (See also Fancy
    (Group))
Amjad, Rashid, 4n, 6, 9n, 12, 42n, 45,
    67n, 69n, 91n, 94n, 99, 169n
Andrus, J.R., 3n
Anoor Textiles Ltd, 149
Anti-Cartel Law Study Group
    Report, XV, 45, 99, 100, 102
Anwar, Abdul A., 76n
Anwar Industries, 149
Anwar Textiles Ltd, 149
Arag (Group), 48, 50, 231
  assets in 1970, 195
  loans from P.I.C.I.C. & I.D.B.P.,
    202
  share in N.I.T. investments, 203
Arag Industries Ltd, 208
Asbestos Cement Ltd, 115n, 207
Asian Development Bank, 57
Associated Industries Ltd, 208
Australasia Bank, 48
Ayub Khan, M., 7, 45n
Ayub government, 174, 179

Babri Textiles Ltd, 149
Bagchi, A. K., 10n, 115n
Bahawalpur Textiles Ltd, 207, 229
Bank of America, 30n
Baksh Group, 149
Baksh Textiles Ltd, 149